$

Davi

4

An Evangelical Theology of Missions

AN EVANGELICAL THEOLOGY

of

MISSIONS

by

HAROLD LINDSELL, PH.D.

ZONDERVAN PUBLISHING HOUSE

GRAND RAPIDS, MICHIGAN

PREFACE

We are living in a new age. The events of the past thirty years have conspired to change the thinking of men. Conclusions arrived at during these years which called into question and denied previously accepted Biblical doctrines are no longer felt to be valid. Ours is especially an age of transition.

In an age of transition there is always a sharp battle to determine which ideology or philosophy will dominate the new era. It is at this time that men who believe they have an eternally valid viewpoint must become vocal. It is of little consequence whether the views they make articulate to their age have been stated and restated before. It does not even become a necessity that they express these viewpoints better than their predecessors, although they ought to aspire to do this.

Whatever the viewpoint, the expression of it should attempt to appeal to faith, capture the intellect, and motivate to action. It must be expressed in language that is current for that age. It must seek after a definite response from men to its thesis.

What has been written in the pages to follow is not new. Perhaps in its synthesis, arrangement, and presentation it differs from other works. Its central ideas come, not from men, but from the Word of God. The purpose of the work is to present to our generation what the author believes to be eternally valid truth.

5

The ideas are revolutionary and they are as old as the Bible. They will become in reality revolutionary to men when they are embraced by men and put into effect in history.

More is at stake than is generally believed for we "wrestle not against flesh and blood but against principalities and powers . . ." It concerns the undying conflict between good and evil. It is a struggle in which men are lined up on either one side or the other. There are some men, however, whose loyalties superficially are with God but whose actions do not measure up to that loyalty. This book is aimed at God's children that in this critical hour of great opportunity they may see the picture, grasp the vision, and spend themselves (in death if need be) for the Person through Whom we have received eternal life and for Whom we fight the good fight until death's release shall come.

INTRODUCTION

Time has struck the mid-century point. Various mid-century inventories are being taken by religious, educational, social and political institutions. One of the most notable was the Massachusetts Institute of Technology mid-century convocation. There speakers like Winston S. Churchill took a backward look over the last fifty years. Speakers like Harold Stassen took the forward look, attempting to prognosticate the next fifty years. Scores of scientists faced the present problems in the light of the future.

It is certainly time that the church took a mid-century inventory of its missionary progress. Nearly two millennia ago the commission was committed to the church. Has it been fulfilled? What has the last century brought to us? What does the next century promise? Helpful indeed is it to have a young man of thorough academic training addressing himself to an analysis of the world in which missions operate, the ground of the missionary enterprise, the nature of the missionary evangel, the problems the missionary theology faces and the progress in terms of success which missions may expect.

It was only two centuries ago that the modern church was awakening to its missionary responsibility. Men like Philip Spencer and August Franke were able to inspire individuals to undertake missionary work, but the whole mood of the church was one of indifference if not hostility. The eighteenth century saw men like Bartholomew Ziegenbalg, Christian Frederick Swartz and Hans Egede, but for the most part the vision of missions was dormant. Only the Herrnhut community under Zinzendorf had really caught the vision. It was at the end of the century when William Carey kindled the imagination of the Baptists and became the first of that long train of modern missionaries, including Martin, Morrison, Judson and thousands of others.

To-day the tremendous advance of science has put at the disposal of the missionary cause the means of actually evangelizing the world. Speedy travel, almost instantaneous communication, blanket broadcasting, visual aids, technological progress are put at the disposal of missions and constitute a force with which to be reckoned.

Simultaneously, however, the impression of the shortness of the time to do the work has been generally made. It is widely recognized that the ideas of the Hebrew Christian tradition are the basis of Western culture. The Christian message has inculcated society with these in the form of the emphasis of the existence of eternal moral law, the responsibility of man to that law and the infinite value and dignity of man. The civilization which we call Western or sometimes Christian reflects these ideas. It is a society of laws rather than of rulers. It expresses its life in freedom of person, of speech, or worship, of action and of enterprise. It exhibits a morality based upon changeless law in which there is a difference between right and wrong, true and false and good and evil. Increasingly, however, the divorce of Western culture from Christian ideology and the reduction of its philosophy of secularistic naturalism is general. Great areas which formerly were included in Christian realms are now constituted mission fields, for example—Russia, Germany, large areas of Eastern Europe, to name only a few.

Commonly it is said that Western civilization is in a crisis. It is sad that the word crisis has been used so often that it has lost its meaning. It actually describes the condition of hovering between life and death. That crisis is revealed by the problem of population and food supply. Fairfield Osborn tells us that the world now has

2,400,000,000 people and is increasing at the rate of one per cent a year, so that at the end of the century there will be over 3,000,-000,000 people. At the same time, disease is being controlled in backward areas so that the production of foodstuffs must be very quickly increased or the world's population will be faced with starvation. One third of the world's population now is in precarious balance between subsistence and starvation. Large areas that once produced foodstuffs are now depleted of the resources and have to be rebuilt artificially. The Malthusian law is again operating and is demanding a solution other than war and pestilence, the former of which is staring the world in the face.

Then there is the problem of ideology and revolution. Competing with the philosophy of the West is philosophic naturalism and materialism expressed in Communism. Unfortunately, it has a strong ally in the naturalism indigent to America. Conditions in the mission fields are often contributive to the embrace of Communism by the population. Whenever such change takes place as has taken place in half of China, it is a menace to the continuance of Christian missions.

There is also the problem of politics and war. No longer do we have one world, but two worlds, with the lines dividing every area and continent. Competitions, conditions of cold war and threats of a hot war face the world. The nations of the world could not endure another World War and still continue free. The entire future of missions rests upon the protection taken against this hazard. Churchillian alarms are arousing the Western nations to their condition, but the problem remains.

Only one thing will reenforce the foundations of Western culture and that is Christianity. The great antidote to naturalism, secularism and rationalism is the Christian system of truth. This system of truth, in the past rejected by scientific and intellectual leaders must receive a new consideration if society is to be saved. The Christian view-point lifts man above the "sensory data" of the scientific method which is the basis of all naturalistic thought. The Christian view stands on revelation and it is this alone which can fortify the moral and spiritual convictions of society.

The world must again accept an absolute standard instead of its relativism. We must have norms of right and wrong so that the use of inventions and possessions is under the control of higher values than the law of expediency. National and personal interests must be subjected to the interpretive standards of right and wrong. Unless such a restraint is placed upon men, we will have very little stability in the future.

We have heard the dignity of the individual, the desirability of individual freedom reaffirmed, but one can only be equal and free with another before God. Without such a point of reference, the foundation of free nations, of free men, is destroyed. Only Christ can limit the destructive processes, the demonic influences and the dangers of civilization to-day.

The one great means of spreading this check to destruction is missions. Truth must be communicated by the Church and its members through every means at its disposal and with the greatest kind of sacrifice exhibited. The technique adopted by the great rival of Christianity to-day is a missionary technique. It employs authoritative scriptures, inspired prophets, dogmas, evangelistic methods, missionary propaganda, sacrifice, martyrdom and idealistic goals.

Thus it is time for Christians to go all out on the missionary enterprise or to recognize that the most precious things of their lives will be taken from them.

As we emerge into the second half of the twentieth century with its amazing changes in mechanics, medicine, mental attitudes and material, we ask whether doom or development awaits us. The only answer to that problem can be given by our use of Christian truth. Missions play the most important part in that undertaking.

HAROLD JOHN OCKENGA.

CONTENTS

An Evangelical Theology of Missions

Chapter 1

THE WORLD IN WHICH WE LIVE

EACH generation must find for itself a satisfactory answer to the question, "Why Missions?" In our generation this question is more pertinent than ever. Events of the last fifty years have produced a situation in which conflicting spiritual ideologies compete for control to determine the mission of the Church of Christ. Thoughtful men are increasingly aware of the spiritual drift away from the foundation of bygone days, and many see that having forsaken the old foundation the missionary cause is no longer a valid enterprise to them. This demands that we re-examine the whole enterprise and the base on which it rests. The adverse spiritual drift has been deadly for the cause of missions and this rightfully necessitates an effort to justify the missionary enterprise and to give it a Biblical orientation from which it lately has been separated.

In some ways the departure from the historic faith, which has so diluted missionary concern, has been beneficial to many people. The issues have been sharpened and the lines of battle clearly drawn. Thus for those who know the issues, a decision one way or the other is not difficult to make. If this be true, however, the bulk of the church people are ignorant of the vital factors in this struggle and are influenced in their actions by their leadership whether for good or for ill.

Many Christians still hold to the faith of our fathers and for them there has been no substantial shift so far as the bases of their faith are concerned. However, a more deadly foe has arisen to cut the nerve of missionary passion and to curtail the enterprise. This foe is the relevancy of faith to the day in which we live. Not having shifted theologically, these people are still adrift because they have been unable to make the change which changing times require. For them it is not a matter of re-examining the faith in its foundations, but of re-examining the application and relation of that faith to a new world. Knowing what they believe is far different from applying that knowledge and utilizing it according to the need of the hour. Unfortunately for them the will to action is not harnessed to the knowledge of what they ought to do and how it should be done. Stultification has resulted.

The crisis is the crisis of this generation. No choice is given to us whether we will accept or reject it. It is with us. We can choose, however, what we shall do with the crisis, and here lies the crux of the problem. We stand on the threshold of a new age and the attitudes and decisions of the Church of Jesus Christ have meaning, and will determine the future for generations of men yet unborn.

The crisis of which we speak has been developing over the period of half a century, but it would not be true to indicate that this period marks the limits within which the crisis has developed. The forces in operation for the last fifty years have become more obvious, but they have been working, seen and unseen, on the warp and woof of the total pattern for many more years. Examples of this may be found in the rise of the German school of higher criticism in the nineteenth century, in the theory of evolution with its consequent influence, and in what is called the watershed of the Victorian era in England.

The last fifty years are so important because the diverse forces have crystallized with results that are profoundly shocking. In the crucible of two world wars the prevailing optimism of the 1920s no longer dominates the thought patterns of the Christian world. Whatever optimism may have survived World War II has been dissipated by events since 1945.

It was in Europe where the impact of two world wars was felt the most that the significant and dramatic departure from the old optimism originated. Thus, Europe in ferment politically, socially, and economically has been Europe in transition theologically also. Barth and Brunner reveal strikingly the change in theological thinking from Europe of 1900. They represent churches and men whose experiences disenchanted them with the theology underlying early twentieth century optimism. In their efforts to find a reasonable basis of faith, and in the reconstruction they attempted, they pioneered a new theology for their European generation, a theology that resembled that of Luther and Calvin, but which still was a marked departure from what many hoped to find.

While Europe was slowly rising out of the chaos of the first World War, in America a spirit of confidence and hope marked the modern milieu. The social gospel more and more became the watchword for the major denominations. Frequently missionary leaders thought that through education, social uplift, and the worldwide application of the golden rule of Christ the whole world would be "Christianized." Beneath the crust of the social gospel concept and the educational approach were other premises that went hand in hand with the American post-war philosophy: acceptance of the theory of evolution, the assurance of the inevitability of progress, and the idea of the inherent goodness of man.

Until the depression began in 1929, at least, this boom philosophy of optimism which suited the American temperament so beautifully was blindly accepted and followed by multitudes who looked to their leadership for guidance. Many people easily accepted the social gospel as well as the modern idea that education would provide for the Christianization of the world. Few were aware of the premises hidden beneath the rosy exterior that proclaimed an abundant entrance into the promised land. If the lay people were ignorant of the basic premises, the same cannot be said for the leadership. They knew the premises. That the dominant philosophy represented a breakdown, theologically speaking, from the tenets of Luther, Calvin, and even Wesley, was not hidden either. Men like

Harry Emerson Fosdick publicly gloried in the fact that American theology had departed from the shibboleths of older days.

Humanly speaking, theological liberalism did all that could be done to break down and completely destroy vital views long held by Protestant Christianity. Supernaturalism, the true deity of Jesus Christ, and the inerrancy of the Scriptures were constantly subjected to attack and ridicule from the very pulpits which had been built by the preaching of these doctrines. No longer was it necessary to use fifth-column methods. The warfare was open, savage, and successful for the new way of life. Along with the destructive attacks on Bible truths commonly held by Christians over the centuries, other ideas in conflict with the Bible were introduced. The evolutionary hypothesis was one of them. The acceptance of this dogma, which required a special brand of faith since it lacked scientific proof, broke down previously held biblical concepts of special creation even as it destroyed belief in Bible inerrancy. Among the confused who bowed to the findings of the scientists and at the same time continued to believe in the Bible, theistic evolution was invented so as to obviate a choice between two apparently conflicting views. Inconsistency was less important than reconciliation which could enable men to satisfy both their religious beliefs and their subjection to science.

Side by side with evolution the idea of progress gained prominence. It happens to be inherent in the post-millennial framework, but it was in its newer context that it gained greater ground and became a commonly accepted dogma for the faithful. Its fairest flower and most potent verbal expression was in the phrase, "Every day in every way we are getting better and better." Again the prostitution of revelation and intellect resulted. It was claimed that the inevitability of progress was not to be thought inconsistent with the Biblical doctrine of progressive revelation. And so doubts were quelled, minds satisfied, and anxious fears allowed to subside.

In this period which saw the breakdown of belief in the Bible as the sole authority and the only real source of eternal truth the revival of the Pelegian teaching of the inherent goodness of man and his perfectibility represented a rank departure from orthodox theology. Here even the most wishful interpreters had to admit that the inherent goodness of man ran counter to the traditional view of total depravity or the inherent badness of man. The glory of the newer doctrine lay in its anthropocentric nature. Man was given a dignity he did not formerly possess, as well as a hope that he could become a perfect person. God became an adjunct whose nature and work were interpreted to fit the new scheme; few cared to test the new scheme to see whether it was in agreement with the revelation of God.

One other doctrine in agreement with the general trend of the times helped forward this movement. It was post-millennialism, at the heart of which was the teaching that the new age was to be ushered in naturally rather than supernaturally, and by the efforts of man (through the Holy Spirit to be sure) rather than by the divine intervention of the Lord Jesus Christ. To be sure, Christ will return in this eschatology, at the end of the millennium. It is unfair to say that post-millennial eschatology was of recent origin except as it was related to the new theology and philosophy of life. The post-millennial idea itself went back many centuries to Augustine and the Roman Catholic Church.[1] However, in its Roman Catholic context it made sense, providing one accepted their premises, because it was related to the Roman concept of the Church and its function. But none of the proponents of the new theology were prepared to accept the Roman Catholic conception of triumphalism with all of its implications. Curiously, then, two bodies of men standing in opposition to each other held to a post-millennial ideology, but in frameworks that were basically divergent.

Historically speaking, post-millennialism was reflected in political, economic, and social life, as well as in theological thought. It underlay external political, social, and economic phenomena. The Kellogg-Briand Peace Pact of 1928 in the political world demonstrated this optimistic post-millennial fervor. When it was signed, despite signs of warning in Europe, people felt and believed or wishfully wanted to believe that the era of universal peace had

---

[1] Although again there are striking differences between Augustinian post-millenarianism and modern Protestant post-millenarianism.

come. War as an instrument of destruction and as a tool of international policy was outlawed forever. And the emphasis on the word *forever,* in a day of relativism, of which we shall speak later, exposed the credulity and wishful thinking of those who truly believed that the political millennium had come. Obviously this idea rose out of the corollary thought that war was the root of all the trouble. Despite the shallowness of the diagnosis, vocal Biblical scholars who thought otherwise were drowned beneath the tumultuous shouts of the mob that had numbers, if not right, on its side.

Economically, in America the same belief found logical expression in the stock market rise of the twenties. On every side there was the same monotonous mad rush to buy and sell; always to buy for less and to sell for more. The economic millennium had come for many who saw only the continued rise of the stock market accompanied by a never-ending increase in profits. It was an era of "something for nothing" with no thought that as a nation sows it must reap. Somehow men thought that indefinite expansion and never-ending profits were part of the ideal economic system. To be sure, warnings were issued by astute observers, and men whose senses had not been dimmed by profit-taking envisioned a day when the mad spree would end. But American optimism prevailed and the economic band-wagon rolled merrily on its way to catastrophe. As yet no one was jumping from twentieth story Wall Street windows, but that day was soon to dawn.

Socially, the national scene reflected the same tendencies. Man was his own master who determined his own fate and destiny. Morals and ethics were relative and changed from age to age. The theory that one ought to taste, see, and experience for himself was popular. Gone, as some men thought, forever, were eternal and never-changing standards; gone was the Biblical conception of sin as a transgression against a holy God. In its place was substituted a homocentric theology of the psychologist who found sin to be a maladjustment within the individual. It was something to be regretted since it perverted personality, but it was something which could be treated like a medical doctor treats an organic illness.

Accompanying the loose morals and ethics of the age was the notion that you could do as you wished so long as you were not caught doing it. Lawlessness expressed in the violation of the Volstead Act and popularized by a flask in every hip pocket was a natural result. Disregard for traffic laws on the highways produced an annual toll of deaths that resembled a minor war. Newspapers were eagerly sought that ran serials of "The Bad Girl" whose chief "sin" was paying the price of fornication by having a baby out of wedlock. The wages of sin were portrayed in such a way as to encourage and condone it, the belief becoming common that we were now released from the shackles that had bound us and were free men indeed. The children of the land were encouraged in self-expression without inhibition. The sinners were those who exercised restraint, and the saints those who did what they pleased. It was true in the classrooms of America and in the homes also. Socially the modern milieu had a noisy, millennial-like air which captivated and charmed our nation, both among those who were not professing Christians as well as among those who were allied with churches. Secularism prevailed and the line of separation between the Church and the world was almost completely erased.

During this time voices in the wilderness tried to make themselves heard amid the din and clamor of the new approach. But these were not the voices of leaders who were being followed by the majority of the people. To such voices crying for a hearing the term "fundamentalist" was applied as against that of "modernist." The former represented biblical literalism and they included in their beliefs basic Bible doctrines which generally were a fair test of where a man stood. Those in the modernist camp, by implication at least, made the fundamentalists appear to be behind the times. They rested their case on the scientific and historical methodology which made the position of the Bible literalists a stumbling block and an offence to them.

So strong was the influence of the modernists that few defenses remained for the fundamentalist. As early as 1910 most of the denominational theological seminaries had been captured by the modernists. As a consequence, new seminaries were formed by the Bible literalists, but the development of these new institutions was to take time before their influence could be felt. In many instances the attack against the old faith was so powerful that whatever strongholds were left to the literalists became hideaways from the enemy rather than bases from which to launch a counter blow. For the greater part the modernists were able to ride roughshod over the prostrate bodies of their helpless "brethren."

Despite the internal American situation in the twenties the missionary program did not lack money or man-power. The place of irreparable loss was in the modernist theological convictions of many of the recruits who were sent to the fields of the world. Another place where serious damage was wrought was in the field of evangelism. The new emphasis on the social gospel called for more and more education and less and less direct evangelism. It called for more and more effort directed toward cultural uplift and the bringing of the good gifts of western civilization than the preaching of the cross with emphasis on the new birth. What it lacked in dynamic so far as the Holy Spirit was concerned it tried to make up in money, techniques, and specialized personnel.

Under the new concepts, missions were expected to flourish. It was part of the rosy optimism that prevailed in the political, social, and economic spheres of life. Just as the millennium was here or around the corner politically and otherwise, so it was anticipated that spiritually similar results would ensue. The whole world was expected to be Christianized.

Over against the optimism on the American scene, Europe was already experiencing adverse reactions. By 1928 the British had been in the grip of a depression for a decade and the leadership was seeking a way out of the problems which World War I had raised but had not settled. In Germany things were worse. Hard hit by reparations and by international trade and political barriers, the Germans were unable to meet their financial obligations. The internal economy was chaotic and various elements fought to dominate German internal affairs and life. France, too, was besieged by economic troubles that presaged dark days ahead. These

were warning signs abroad, but the United States either was unconscious of the implications or misread the signs.

It was just prior to the panic and collapse of the internal
economy of the United States that the Jerusalem missionary conference met in 1928. Ironically, this conference met in Jerusalem,
the city of peace, a few short months prior to the 1929 stock
market crash and just prior to the rise of Hitler that was to lead
to the second World War. Jerusalem marked a decisive turning
point in the history of missions in this century, for between the
time of that meeting and the present hour new forces have come
into play that have and are revolutionizing missionary thought,
theology, and world orientation. The importance of this and the
Madras conference of 1938 has been missed by many, due perhaps
to oversight, or to the failure of evangelicals to realize clearly that
their day of opportunity has dawned.

At Jerusalem the leadership of the churches discussed conditions, symptoms, hopes, and future possibilities. Absent from
these sessions were representatives of the faith and independent
mission boards who did not have organized denominations behind
them. Although there were evidences that some of the delegates
disagreed with the trend of the conference, nevertheless the weight
of the meetings tilted in favor of the social gospel. Christianity
was thought by some as differing from the ethnic faiths in degree
rather than in kind and many were wholly optimistic as to the future.

Rufus Jones probably expressed the majority viewpoint. He
decried the increasing secularization of the churches, and argued
that naturalism was inadequate even though both were normal products of the theology he embraced. His protest was a contradiction
in terms. When dealing with progress Jones denied that it was
inevitable in the sense that blind forces operated without reference
to men. But he indicated that he believed in progress dependent
"on the moral and spiritual cooperation of individuals and social
groups."

Linked to Christianity, this concept of progress still combined
within its womb all of the seeds of evolution and post-millenarianism. When it came to revelation, there was the same antipathy

toward the acceptance of the verbal inspiration and authority of the Bible as ever before. The problem, stated Jones, resolves itself around "the immensely important question of God's relation to us and the nature of His revelation of Himself through the ages." Here then was to be found the paradox of these sessions. Delegates were meeting, after nineteen hundred years of Christianity, to determine the basis of the faith! It was a confession that the churches were propagating a faith, the basis of which was uncertain in the minds of those primarily responsible for its propagation. The trumpet was giving forth an uncertain sound!

At the heart of the cry for reorientation lay the capitulation of Christianity to the theory of evolution in its theological aspect. What was true in the days of the Apostles was not necessarily true in 1928. Advances in thought had been made over the years, and our generation needed to reinterpret the faith for its generation. Here the thought was not that of relating the faith to that generation and demonstrating its relevancy. Indeed, it was quite the opposite. The problem was that of finding a faith to fit the generation, something which the generation could accept that would not violate the "findings" of modern science, etc. This was far removed from the task of relating an absolute faith to changing conditions. It carried in its bosom the deadly disease of relativity.

Mr. Jones claimed that historic Christianity is profoundly Platonic, and in its later development (again an indication of a belief in relativity rather than in the absolutism of the Word) in the days of Thomas Aquinas, this Scholastic "showed that there could be a fusion of Aristotelian thought with the basic conceptions of Christianity, and that the two together could meet the growing intellectual needs of the world." The conclusion was that in 1928 the need was for the "discovery of a similar use of the present-day intellectual conquests of thought for the enrichment and expansion of our Christian faith." And here again there was implied that conscious or unconscious acceptance of the idea of progress and relativism. The fusion of a watered-down revelation which was to be validated by human reason was the answer of the age, and the

Platonic-Aristotelian-Aquinas elements were foundational systems on which to build a superstructure for this generation.

The practical outworking of this philosophy with reference to missions lay in the attitude toward the non-Christian faiths. Voices were raised strongly asserting that there were men without Christ who were yet "in God." On every hand there was the eclectic notion that all men as brothers walk hand in hand seeking the truth wherever it may be found and under whatever label it may be bottled. The common Fatherhood of God in the non-biblical sense and the common brotherhood of man in a similar sense comprised the war cries of advance. The love of God could not permit non-Christian peoples without Christ to die and be doomed to a hell in which nobody believed. It made no difference what men professed so long as they were sincere and lived up to the light that they had. That such tenets cut the nerve of real missionary enterprise was not noted because the nerve had already been cut by the belief in the social gospel.

When the Jerusalem conference ended, the note of optimism was high. Christians were not yet disillusioned, and pragmatism, the final test for all things, had not been in operation long enough to demonstrate its utter failure. The hopes of the Jerusalem conference were dashed by the economic crisis in America in 1929. From that date until 1932 the picture was an ever-darkening one at home and abroad. The depression made an immediate impact on the missionary labors of the churches. Income for foreign work shrank at once. Instead of going forward it became clear that few agencies would be able to maintain what they had. Retrenchment became not only a slogan but a reality. On every side, mission work was cut to the bone, and often even the bone was removed. Radical surgery, which included the closing of stations and the return of personnel, highlighted the era. Many agencies and churches were in serious financial trouble due to over-extension without provision for such a financial setback. Those who held pessimistic views prior to 1929 were justified, although their predictions during the boom years had not won for them the acclaims of the optimistic.

This financial depression did something for missions in the providence of God that probably would not have been done if men had been left to themselves. Stringent financial conditions forced people to ask questions they had not asked before. People who were scratching to keep themselves alive were not eager to put money into enterprises that could not be justified. And missions along with other agencies that soaked up money had to be justified or forsaken. Under conditions which had prevailed in the early nineteenth century the results would have been discernible immediately. The theology of that day held that men without Christ are lost and on their way to hell. This was a sufficient answer. To rescue lost men from the nearing flames of eternal torment justified the expenditure of one's money. But the twentieth century differed radically from the preceding one. No longer did the theology of many square with earlier beliefs, and there had been no real opportunity to demonstrate how men would react to the new theology under the stress of financial collapse.

Whatever the conclusion was to be, there was a demand for a reappraisal of the missionary situation. Dissatisfied people wanted to find out more about an enterprise they had cheerfully supported when money was easy to obtain and which they now were being asked to support when every dollar counted. Any survey that would rethink missions would cost money. That money was supplied by Mr. Rockefeller, and the investigation was conducted, not by those whose primary interest was in missions, but by a laymen's group. The decision that the missionary task should not be investigated by those whose business it was normally was based on the sound theory that such investigators might be biased. Obviously, they would see matters according to their predispositions and would naturally tend to defend the labor of their own hands. However, this desire to avoid a biased report from the one point of view did not prevent the selection of people whose objectivity was questionable also. In escaping from the first dilemma the investigation ran full into the other.

The Laymen's Foreign Missions Inquiry committee included people from the major denominations from the United States.

Missing from the roster was one of the largest denominations in American life, the Southern Baptist Convention. At the head of the Commission was William Ernest Hocking, a philosopher from Harvard University. The Vice-Chairman was Frederick C. Woodward, Vice-President of the University of Chicago. The composition of the Commission spoke eloquently about what might be expected. Nevertheless, the most pessimistic observer was not prepared for what the Commision published in 1932 under the title *Rethinking Missions*. The Commission had done much work and had many suggestions to offer. Some of the material was helpful indeed. Little of the helpful material, however, made any impact on the churches. The main part of the report was so striking, and conclusions so devastating, that few went beyond that portion.

Rethinking Missions drew conclusions consistent with the humanism of the hour. Modern theology was fully represented in this report and no one could misunderstand the conclusion. The death sentence was imposed on missions, although the execution of the sentence was to be delayed, and still is subject to delay. For true believers, an alternative was hidden in the language of the death sentence. The sentence was legitimately passed on the missionary enterprise, providing one accepted the theology on which the indictment rested. But if the theology on which the indictment rested was wrong, then the missionary enterprise might still continue to stand. Its sentence of death was so radical that it produced a backwash of criticism. Men saw that the fruit of modern theology implied that there was no legitimate basis for missionary passion.

Certain conclusions of the Laymen's Inquiry stand out prominently in retrospect. First and foremost was the view that Christianity is not unique; that it is not the only avenue to God. In all religions God can be found. At the center of all religious creeds, whether Christian or not, there is a nucleus of religious truth. And in all individuals whatever their shortcomings, there is the "inalienable religious intuition of the human soul. The God of this intuition is the true God: to this extent universal religion has not to be established; it exists." Thus Christianity was seen as differing in degree rather than in kind. The uniqueness of the Christian faith was destroyed, or at least placed in the same category with the non-Christian faiths, although on a different level. This could not help but eliminate the sense of urgency to propagate the Christian faith. Since religious attainment was chiefly a difference in quantity rather than quality, little need exists to employ money, manpower and valuable time propagating that which will only make a slight quantitative difference. The plea was for a common search for truth together, recognizing the good and bad in each religion, including Christianity. Each supplements the other. Gone was the God of revelation who is self-disclosing; gone was the idea that without Christ the heathen are lost; gone were the reasons which made Paul the world's most daring missionary.

It was bad enough for the Inquiry to reduce Christianity to an ethnic basis in common harmony with the non-Christian religions, but what the committee left unsaid was at best as serious as what was said. No room was made for the Holy Spirit. Traditional Christianity always had held that the Holy Spirit is the third person of the Trinity whose office in relation to missions is that of executive director. He has charge of the enterprise both on the side of the churches and on the side of the heathen. He directs the enterprise, sends out missionaries, convicts of sin, and reveals Christ to the non-Christians. *Rethinking Missions,* however, indicated no consciousness that there is a Holy Spirit. The very absence of His person and work proved how far the departure from the faith once for all delivered to the saints had been.

The shock of this book rocked the whole missionary world. A few readers were enthusiastic; some were mildly interested; some were antagonist; the bulk of the people never read the book firsthand. But the work had values for the cause of missions. It made people who inclined toward missions either desert the cause entirely since they now felt missions had no apparent basis for existence, or it made them seek a way out through which missions could be retained in a theological framework that had significance.[2] No in-

---

[2] There are conflicting views as to the impact of *Rethinking Missions* on missionary giving. Following the publication of the Laymen's Commission there was a substantial decrease in giving to foreign missions. Some had felt that it simply reflected the second depression pit of 1932 and was due to economic reasons rather than *Rethinking Missions.* Still others believed that the book made little or no

telligent person could wish for the continuance of an enterprise just for the sake of enterprise. Henceforth, if missions were to continue, some adequate basis for that continuance would have to be found.

The cause of Christianity was further served by the work of the Laymen's Commission in that the death of the missionary enterprise was desirable if the enterprise was not really needed. Without an adequate basis, missions should endure a sickness unto death, for if the cause has no proper theological foundation it ought not exist. What is not right in principle will not be right in its outworking either. The real hope which came from the sickness of missions after the publication of the Hocking findings was the possibility of radical surgery by which the enterprise could be reoriented on a valid foundation. And if surgery could not accomplish this end it were better for missions to die than for missions to exist in bondage to modernism. The truism does not change, that non-Biblical missions are worse than no missions at all, for history shows that the admixture of truth and error is harder to overcome than error alone.

Rethinking Missions came almost midway between the Jerusalem Conference of 1928 and the Madras Conference in India in 1938. Between these years the political condition of the world was altered markedly. Instead of entering into the longed-for age of universal peace, the clouds of war hung thickly over Europe and the opening phases of the war begun. Old-fashioned commentators who held that wars begin when the first shot is fired might not have been convinced that war had begun on January first of the year 1938. Actually, in northern Europe it had not begun, but the Spanish Civil War with active intervention by Italy and Russia should have opened the eyes of the doubtful. Hitler's Germany was prepared for any

---

impact among the church members as a whole. It should be pointed out, however, that some denominations rushed into print in an effort to answer *Rethinking Missions*. Robert E. Speer, of the U.S.A. Presbyterian Church, wrote an article against the book, which article was reprinted in a small book. The Northern Baptists put out a book justifying foreign missions and "explaining away" much of *Rethinking Missions*. It is this writer's opinion that there was a correlation between the decreased giving and the report by the Commission. This opinion is based in part on the substantial increase in faith mission income and also because of the lack of evidence to substantiate the other view. This much we do know without controversion — that following the Laymen's Report there *was* a sharp drop in income, whatever the real reasons for the drop may have been.

contingency, and the contingency arrived in the fateful year in which the Madras Conference met. Before 1938 Hitler had cast the die and had made known his policies through his overt acts. He had already entered the Rhineland; by March, 1938, he had played his hand regarding Austria; and he was ready to move in on Czechoslovakia. England and France, unprepared militarily or politically and represented by the Chamberlain umbrella regime in England and the inept Daladier regime in France, betrayed Czechoslovakia when they capitulated to Hitler's demands. The shape of things to come was plain, even to the uninitiated. Long before 1938 competent historians close to the world drama predicted the inevitability of the coming war unless there were changes in the policies of the democracies. The lineup of the nations was specified and the midnight of western culture was prophesied unless a solution was found.

Against this background the Madras Conference met. The tone of the conference was in sharp contrast to that of 1928. At Madras significant questions were raised and answered differently than at Jerusalem. It is true that many did not like the new answers; it is true that a deep cleavage prevailed. The honeymoon of 1928 ripened into virtually a divorce in 1938. European missionary leaders spearheaded an attack on the social gospel. Suffering under the impact of the first war and what followed in Europe, and conscious of the Hitlerian threat, these leaders recognized that a new day had come in which the old answers, so beautifully framed in a spirit of optimism, no longer sufficed.

The attack at Madras centered around Hendrick Kraemer's book, *The Christian Message in a Non-Christian World*. Its impact at the conference and since then has been as great as that of *Rethinking Missions*. Of this book and its contents more shall be said later, but for purposes of orientation several observations ought to be made. Professor Kraemer declared that in the crisis of our age certain conclusions are now obvious. Relativism, the idea of inevitable progress, the essential goodness of man, and other prominent tenets are no longer valid. In place of the old, Kraemer substituted the divine revelation of God under the concept of what he called Biblical realism. This oft-recurring phrase was subject to misinterpretation both by modernists and conservatives. At the conference itself he was called upon to define what he meant by Biblical realism. Kraemer paid high tribute to both Karl Barth and Emil Brunner, without stating that he was in substantial disagreement with either of those continental theologians. It gave rise to the thought that while his main thesis was for a return to the divine revelation, perhaps this was the current neo-orthodoxy then rather than the orthodoxy that had been prominent among the evangelicals for decades. The volume itself did not make it clear whether Kraemer accepted the higher critical views of the Bible which had been instrumental in tearing down the belief in an inerrant Word of God. The self-disclosure or relevation of God appeared for Kraemer to be limited to the Incarnation, without a committal to the Bible as the verbally inspired Word of God, and without mistake historically, biologically, or otherwise.

The value of Kraemer's work for us does not necessarily lie in our agreement or disagreement with all of his views but it does lie in the point of departure. He sharply criticized the Jerusalem Conference of 1928 and he beautifully destroyed the current theologies underlying the conclusions of that conference. At the same time the effect of *Rethinking Missions* was nullified if the general thesis of his book was acceptable.

The Christian Message in a Non-Christian World pointed the way back to the fold for some who had wandered far away. It gave the lie to some who were still outside the fold and who neither appeared penitent nor wished to return. It also challenged those missionaries and agencies that had remained theologically true to the faith, but whose practices and methods did not always reflect the imperative that theology which is not followed in practice is almost as bad as theology that is wrong.

The book also threw light on questions that even fundamentalists needed to ponder. Not the least in this respect was the criticism leveled at some organizations and individuals who confused methods with aims and who majored on methods that were antiquated, believing that such methods were inviolable and not subject to change. It might be stated another way. In each changing age there is the problem of demonstrating the relevancy of the faith to the age. The faith does not change, but the demonstration of the relevancy ought to change because no two ages are alike. The essential message remains forever unchanged, but the approach by which the message is mediated may need revision. An apt illustration of this, easily understood, is radio and its use in spreading the gospel to all the world. Not having been in use during the apostolic period, it does not mean that this instrument ought not to be used today. Rather, the principles laid down in the early church period make it perfectly clear that this medium is acceptable.

The questions raised and the problems restated at Madras demanded that consideration be given to them by those whose faith has not changed with the years. What was begun at Madras needed to be continued and brought to full flower. The reason for this was plain in the year 1945. Since Madras the second World War had been fought and finished. But it was not won. A temporary lull in physical hostilities ensued. Basic issues were not resolved and more difficult decisions than have ever faced mankind in any previous age are being faced today. This is true since 1945 due to further and dramatic changes which have almost completely altered the whole missionary orientation or have reinforced some of the conclusions we have stated about the missionary situation with respect to events that occurred prior to 1945.

Since 1945 we have more than doubled the knowledge possessed by mankind and the accelerating rate of this knowledge increase staggers the imagination. Before the end of the twentieth century we will more than quadruple the amount of knowledge that we now possess. The population explosion threatens to engulf the planet and by A. D. 2000 it is anticipated there will be somewhere between six and a half and seven billion people. The transportation explosion and the communications explosion have altered the time and space circumstances of men everywhere. Via communications satelites we can know what is transpiring in almost any part of the world almost as soon as the events take place. By transportation changes we can now reach almost any part of the globe in less than 24 hours.

There are two other changes since 1945 that have altered the missionary picture. The first is the decline of the Judeo-Christian tradition in the educational processes in America, and the second is the theological dilution which has occurred not only in the educational world but also in the church itself. These changes have come about as a result of the compelling victory of the dialectic process which now grips the western world. The dialectic had its beginnings in the theology of Thomas Aquinas, who dealt with the question of grace and nature. By his exaltation of nature it became a predominant factor in the theological understanding at the expense of grace and led eventually to the rise of the philosophy of Hegel. He taught that for every thesis there is an antithesis and that the union of these opposites produces a synthesis. This synthesis he called a new thesis which eventually was opposed by another antithesis and by the union of these opposites a new synthesis occurred. The dialectic of Hegel was embraced by Karl Marx and was also furthered by Kierkegaard, the Christian existentialist. Today we have both Christian and atheistic existentialism and while there is some difference between them yet the carrying out of the dialectic has led to the virtual disappearance of the biblical foundation on which Judeo-Christian culture was founded. Existentialism today is the philosophy which has gripped the college campuses, is the foundation for the life-thought of the new left, and has heavily infiltrated the church of Jesus Christ. The existentialist who uses the Hegelian dialectic comes to the conclusion that life is absurd and meaningless. John Paul Sartre in his book *No Exit* enunciates the dilemma of the existentialist who is caught in the whirlpool of life and finds there is no way out. Everything is meaningless. The rise of the dialectic has therefore resulted in the disappearance of all absolutes.

As a result of the disappearance of absolutes there has come the new theology, the new evangelism, and the new morality. The new theology has no basic source for its theological knowledge. The immutability of God and of Scripture has been lost. The new evangelism has grown out of the new theology and it has destroyed the concept of heaven and hell as opposing and discontinuous states. Either all men are going nowhere or all men are headed for heaven in the new evangelism. As a consequence, the emphasis has ceased to be on the proclamation of the Gospel of Jesus Christ and in place thereof the new evangelism concerns itself almost exclusively with altering the structures of society in a political, economic and social sense. It is therefore not the evangelism of the New Testament. A new morality has also sprung up both from the new theology and from the new evangelism. Based on an undefined notion of love it is generally pragmatic and assumes that every decision has to be made situationally with no absolutes to undergird the ethical system.

Since 1945, even beyond the infiltration of an earlier age, the church has experienced new waves of anti-Christian viewpoints. It has been infiltrated by humanism which is homocentric. It has been infiltrated by liberalism which while it accepts the notion of a spiritual inheritance which is conveyed through Scripture has totally divorced itself from the true authority of the Word of God and does not regard the precepts and commandments as having any sense of the absolute which would constrain the consciences of men in our day. In addition syncretism has crept into the Christian church. Men everywhere are saying that there are many roads which lead to heaven and it makes no difference which road you pursue so long as you are engaged in the quest and are walking on the journey. This has been compounded increasingly by the rise of universalism in the church. In this view all men are conceived of as being in Jesus Christ now and assured of the gift of everlasting life. The fact that it has no credible support in Scripture does not keep its adherents from accepting this viewpoint even as their whole concept of missionary outreach is affected by it.

Since 1948 the World Council of Churches has come into being and is moving steadily in the direction of rapprochement with the Roman Catholic Church. The vision of G. Bromley Oxnam, one of the first presidents of the World Council of Churches, who predicted in 1948 that some day there would be one Protestant church and one Roman Catholic Church, is rapidly taking place.

He also predicted that these two giant churches would then merge into the one Holy Catholic Church that would cover the face of the globe. Meanwhile in the United States more and more churches are seeking to combine into one giant church with multiplied millions of members. (COCU).

In this hour of crisis we stand in a world of transition. It does not matter whether we are prepared for the transition or not. The parting of the ways is before us. We cannot stand still but must take one of the roads at a crossroads of history. In making the choice Christians are faced with many alternatives. And how they choose will make a difference. This opens the door in a unique fashion for Christians to have a witness in our generation and before Jesus Christ returns to earth.

The hour of choice is upon us in a unique manner and we Christians must present our way of life for consideration to the multitudes who must choose. The presentation must be made in such a way that will satisfy and fortify our spirits in the assurance that what we hold is adequate. It must also be a challenge to those who are in disagreement, that, with the challenge, they may accept what we offer as a solution.

We offer the eternal and unchanging Word of God. The problem surrounding this offer is not the fact that it is the Word of God which we bring. It is the manner of presentation and the attitude of the offerers. Oftentimes the bearers of the inerrant Word have not been sure of what they have offered. Not less frequently their only offer has been verbal inspiration without any development of the concept in a practical way. In other cases there has been a partial development of the Biblical view of the world, but it has been so confused with modern thought that the result has been the grafting of wrong modern ideas into the stock of Christian doctrine. The verbal-inspiration Christians have frequently found themselves clinging to their verbal inspiration with conclusions that are in contradiction to premises basic in revelation. An illustration of this tendency may be found in the field of overseas missions where conservative missionaries are sometimes guilty of confusing methods for aims, making methods an end in themselves, contrary to the clear teaching of the Word.

The presentation of the Christian view logically falls, in emphasis, on missions. The desire to convince one person that our view is right is missionary. And missions are the extension of this policy to the whole world instead of limiting it to one individual. In one sense we answer our question before we sift the evidence. To assume that Christianity is missions-centered and then to proceed with the demonstration of that assumption implies this. However, that assumption is also a conclusion based upon prior sifted evidence, the object being to present the conclusion and then the evidence on which the conclusion is based with the hope that good may come. This includes a presentation and clarification for our age of the historic view relevant to the modern setting. It is an attempt to show that we have a message for the day in which we live, a message with sound foundamental premises. This message has a positive content and it is the hope of man. To what extent we expect to be successful, and the measure of our success as postulated by our premises, will be analyzed in the course of this discussion. Over-optimism as well as an unfounded pessimism must be avoided.

In this approach certain questions should be kept in mind. The first is the question whether there is a Christian philosophy of missions. We must reckon with the problem whether this philosophy of missions, if there is one, is final. On what does such a philosophy rest? Is there any place for change in methods, approach, and thought patterns? Or does the finality of foundation make the superstructure just as absolute and undeviating?

If there is a philosophy of missions which is final, in what does it consist? What is its message? What are its objectives and what the hope of accomplishing these objectives in the light of modern conditions If we can find the Biblical answer to these fundamental problems there still remains the difficulty of making our philosophy relevant to the world in which we live.

To these ends the following chapters are devoted.

Chapter 2

A FINAL FOUNDATION—THE WORD OF GOD

C HRISTIAN missions are at the crossroads. In this thought there
is something hopeful for it implies that at this crossroads
there is the possibility of getting off the old road if we are
wrong and finding our way back to the right one. For some years
the missionary enterprise, by and large, has been traveling along *written in 1949*
one road (except for certain agencies and some missionaries who
have gone their own ways despite board policies), and this road,
as has been stated in the previous historical summary, has given
indication of being the wrong one. So much has the modern
world come to realize that the common pathway has been a
wrong one that voices are sharply articulate in expressing dis-
satisfaction with the present trend, and are asking for a change.

Some of the articulate voices now admit that the theories of
progress, man's inherent goodness, the hope of a Utopian dream
world, and salvation by education are not adequate. In place of
these they are offering substitutes upon which to rebuild their
shattered world. Their dilemma is whether men will respond to
their alluring philosophies when past history speaks so eloquently
of their previous blunders. The heart of man must have something, and unless truth becomes as eloquent and as persuasive once
again, there will be a repetition of the old hope and the final
crumbling to dust of that hope when the new philosophies fail.

The present crisis is not helped by the attitude of the visible Church today. In past centuries the Church proclaimed itself to be the bearer of an authoritative and absolutist message. It spoke with the assurance of "thus saith the Lord." But the Church of late has succumbed to the appealing tune being piped by its opponents, and in dancing to that tune in an effort to be termed "modern" it has lost its authoritative voice. To be sure some portions of the universal Church have not deviated from the authoritative position of former days, and this fact has resulted in divisions within the visible body of Christ.

The churches which comprise Christendom are not all united today in theology. The differences range from one extreme to another. One portion of the visible Church can be termed pure humanists, and the gamut can run from there to the other extreme which can be classified as the party of ultra-conservative reactionaries, where the theology, if not the actions, of the adherents places each one in himself as the only uncorrupted source of truth and believer in that truth. On the other hand the humanists have no enduring truth and make themselves and their own experiences the point of reference. In an hour when the world faces a crisis and is looking for alternatives it is tragic that the Church has no united voice with which it can offer a suitable alternative.

The religious horizon of the world, paradoxically enough, has been helped in past years by the theological divisions existent among Christians. The good fortune of our hour is that, as yet, there is no real theological unity. Were unity to come immediately it would probably be on the basis of views offered by those whose voices are loudest but whose theology is least acceptable. Thus division, for the moment, serves well the purposes of those who cling to the historic faith. When the time comes in which unity can be secured on a revelational basis, then division will be unfortunate.

If the lack of unity is fortunate at present since unity today would be founded on an inclusive and unbiblical basis, the further claim must be adduced that the very lack of unity now came about because there was a departure from a unity which previously existed. Granting that the churches of the Reformation disagreed considerably, the disagreement was almost exclusively over matters of secondary importance where it was not so disasterous. Differing over matters of polity, the table, and baptism, there was still a common framework of agreement about primary doctrines which gave to the world a united testimony for the faith. The crisis now springs out of disagreement about foundational truths, so that the corporate witness of the Church has been destroyed. This destruction of a corporate witness could not conceivably take place over issues of a secondary nature.

The primary question that divides Christendom today is that of the basis on which the faith rests. Unless there is agreement here, the outworking of the faith along other lines will suffer radically save in limited spheres where the unity will be accidental. The choice one makes regarding the basis of our faith determines the road to be travelled all the way. This may be illustrated when dealing with the aims of missions. Missionary aims must have a suitable foundation on which to rest. Then comes the question whether aims are to be determined by pragmatic tests. Are they to be derived from naturalism or relativism or what? Thus, aims are not actually the bedrock on which rests the missionary witness of the Church. The aims are derived from the bedrock itself and whatever the bedrock comprises, the missionary aims will reflect.

It is primarily over the foundation that the Church struggles today. The problem is not as broad as sometimes imagined by people who feel that there are many possibilities. The question of a foundation is nicely narrowed down to two choices. It is reason versus revelation.

When we speak of reason versus revelation, caution must be taken to avoid the conclusion that revelation then becomes antithetic to true reason which derives its force from revelation. There is a wide and inseparable gulf between reason and revelation, and the individual who begins with human reason will naturally and normally rule out revelation (as we shall understand revelation from our later discussions of this elemental doctrine of the faith) if for no other reason than that revelation is incompatible with this premise. Christians ought to recognize this truism with more appreciation than is ordinarily the case since it opens the door to a proper understanding of the so-called rational mind. So long as the Church stands divided between two opinions on the subject of the basis of our faith there is no hope for a united corporate witness.

A decade ago the possibilities for a united witness were greater than today because it appeared outwardly as though the forces of rationalism were due to triumph. It looked as though the battle for revelation was lost and along with the battle it appeared as though the war itself was lost. Recent historical trends prove that the earlier battle did not win the war, and more recent battles indicate that the issue is not settled by any manner of means in favor of reason as against revelation. The upsurge in positive apologetics, either completely in favor of the traditional view of revelation shows this, or what appears to be a tendency toward that in neo-orthodoxy leads some to believe that the day has arrived for the defenders of the supernatural revelation to recover the field. Here again a word of warning needs to be voiced with regard to obscuration. Oftentimes the opponents of revelation becloud the problem by the introduction of extraneous and peripheral argumentation that is only partially relevant or totally irrelevant to the case. The Christian cause has never been so . strong as when it has rested its case flatly on the revelational assumption. It has never been so weak as when it has tried to carry its program along consistently, having ignored or overlooked the premises on which these superstructural segments must rest. For a time the work of the Church may continue on the momentum generated from an earlier appreciation of the foundation, but when the foundation is lost sight of, the eventual outcome is the warping of the superstructure which no longer reflects the true foundation but the false one which has been substituted in place of the true.

The implication of the foregoing is plain. It is insufficient to have a knowledge of the foundation unless every aspect of the faith is aligned to agree with the foundation on which the superstructure rests. It is possible to have an intellectual perception of the foundation and at the same time employ methods, or even use a message, that is in contradiction to the basic premise on which the faith rests. Here even the most rabid conservative can be at fault. So, in addition to a true perception of the basis on which the faith rests, there must also be a proper relating of that to the remainder of the faith. Harmony and agreement in all of the parts is essential. The rationalist is wrong because he builds on a human premise. The conservative can be wrong if his superstructure, unwittingly, is in disagreement with the foundation. There are many Biblically centered Christians who are pre-millennial in their eschatology, but whose approach to missions is post-millennial and evolutionary without knowing that this is the case. And in our hour of crisis we need to be sure that what we do is in line with what we claim to believe.

In the present opportunity which the Church has to return to an absolutist position, we ought not forget that the battle will be won or lost on the question of the basis of the faith. Other matters may become sharp objects of contention, but the heart of the problem is joined over the issue of the place we begin. The acceptance of the Bible as the fully revealed Word of God, adequate and infallible in all of its component parts, is the battle ground. All else stands or falls as this doctrine stands or falls. Without a correct view here the eventual result is always a perversion, and the end always apostasy. It is difficult enough to make legitimate derivations form a correct premise as it is.

The world is vaguely conscious of its own need, and wishes to find something to meet that need. The split testimony of a discordant Church is not appealing to the world which intuitively misunderstands the divisions in a body claiming to be one. The Church itself does not militantly propagate an absolutist faith because it is sure in some quarters that it has no such faith, and in others because their works do not encourage the belief that the basis on which they operate is an absolute one. Those who have an absolutist faith have not been vocal in the right way any more than they have been able to demonstrate the relevancy of their faith to the world in which we live. Consequently, up to this hour, neither element within the Church has been able to triumph—the one because it had nothing with which to triumph and the other because it had failed to carry the day in spite of the assurance that it had the answer. Betwixt and between stood multitudes who were theologically untutored or simply bewildered, wishing perhaps for the right way, but never recognizing the way themselves. Thus they were forced to accept the kind of leadership expressing views which did not always represent them correctly. Untrained, they were not able to detect the difference, or else they were helpless against the rushing tide which swept away their feeble protests.

The Church was impotent in part due to the struggle within itself for the supremacy of one view, but the world was also responsible for the breakdown in the Church. The world had nothing to lose in the struggle except its unbelief. It did not lose that, and it did gain adherents to its views. It added numbers and vocal authority. The success of this group outside the Church cannot be overestimated (and frequently its most venerated members were the children of believers who had failed to inculcate in their intellectual offsprings the same beliefs they themselves held), and the damage they did to the Church was untold. The group outside the Church made its influence felt in the scientific world, and in its logical extension to other areas of life the result was a crisis.

In the field of biology the conflict between science and the Genesis account inevitably was reconciled by the acceptance of the scientific explanation. The psychologists developed a new view of sin which was bound to make the doctrine of transgression against a holy God ridiculous if their view was believed. Sociology explained civilization with its taboos and mores on an evolutionary hypothesis which invalidated the Bible and added to the confusion. Absolutes formerly held in morality, the social order, and in religion were not only disputed but denied in favor of a relativity.

Great inroads were made in the Church by the world so that instead of the Church changing the world, the world was changing the Church. The findings of science were frequently accepted by those who professed some kind of a belief in the Bible. Rather than be old-fashioned in a modern age, it became the practice to reconcile the Bible with the latest findings of science rather than to reconcile the findings of science in the light of the Bible. It was not long before those in the Church were raising their voices in favor of science against the Bible, eventuating in the denial of the Book they were supposed to be defending. The situation became so critical because the spirit of the world of science and unbelief gained entrance IN the Church. Outside the Church it had always been a threat and a potent danger. From within the citadel it was a fifth column movement opening the gates for the enemy to enter unchallenged. With many of the leading churchmen joining the movement, the cause of historic Christianity began to look black. And truly it was black!

The blackness of outlook for the Church was due to the fact that the one time impregnable fortress standing for an unchanging faith was itself in the process of change. In that process of change it lost its absoluteness except among small isolated elements whose voices were practically unheard and whose testimony was scorned by the wise and worldly. The moderns who had followed the beck and call of those outside the Church had done so still clinging to the notion that there was an absolute. For them the absolute became science and everything was measured by that yardstick. Later, to the dismay of the churchmen who left the basic theology of the Church, it was discovered that the world and science were not at all sure they had an unchanging standard.

About the only thing the world of science was certain in believing was that all things were relative. Science positively denied, in this view, holding to any absolutes since all things are subject to change and are in a state of flux. In time it dawned on the churchmen that they were wrong in thinking that science had absolutes in the sense that theology had absolutes. There was an absolute in science which created a fearful dilemma, but it was not an absolute that proved anything or which satisfied any inner longing. Science's absolute, whether in physics, psychology, or sociology, had to be the claim that all things are relative. The one thing that is not subject to change is the belief that all things ARE subject to change. This premise becomes their absolute. Those scientists who were relativists never did appreciate the philosophic dilemma their relativism forced them into, but that was because they were scientists and not philosophers!

Little or nothing of a spiritual or moral nature is contained within the premise that all things are relative. It destroys the one demand of the human heart which is to find something on which it can depend—something that is unchanging and not just the principle that all things change. Simply to have the belief that all things change, cannot satisfy the religious nature of man. It cannot satisfy man's nature because he instinctively seeks after religious certainty. To be told that all things are subject to change would exclude any true concept of a divine being that a man might have. Thus, the best that man can hope for by way of a supreme being is that he be unchangeable only to a certain extent. When carried out in practice, however, man did not accept a limited God in most cases. He merely assumed, and rightly so, if his premise of relativity was correct, that God was irrelevant to the world of today. Man would not have God in spite of his wish to have Him! Man was placed in the paradoxical position of wishing for that which he could but would not have. He had denied God a place in the world of today, while his heart continued to yearn after the certainty that only an absolute Being could bring.

The impact of two world wars has done much to bring man to grips once again with the problem of certainty which is the desire of his heart. We live in an age of insecurity and instability. Conditions politically, economically and socially are changing so fast that mortal man cannot keep abreast of the changes. Man wants something to which he can cling with a feeling of safety. He wishes for a refuge that will really be a refuge, not a device to make him believe something that is not true. Beautiful talk about the challenge that the new world offers, and swelling words about national growth to world maturity and a position of obligation and responsibility do not alter facts. Man is frightened; man is afraid of the future; man wants peace and quiet and a reasonable hope for the days ahead. The modern world can supply modern man with almost anything except this. It can produce motor cars, central heating, shorter working hours, new homes, and a thousand luxuries, but it cannot produce the spirit with which men can enjoy them. This is the reason why revelation is today the most important subject in theological thinking. Man wants to know that God is objective; that He is transcendentally and objectively real.

The day is past when man is satisfied with a subjective framework of reference. He has lost faith in himself and he craves some reality outside of himself which is objectively real and worthy of faith. That philosophy of religion which has been bald humanism concerned with individuals and their feelings, no longer suffices. Fewer people are interested in my experience based on a purely inner or subjective framework. They want objective values which can be experienced subjectively but which do not depend upon the subjective for permanent validity. They want help, but the help they desire must have worth and permanence. It must be found outside themselves.

God is the solution to our problem. He is the end of our quest, although it is wrong to speak as though man, by searching, can find God. God is only to be found as He reveals Himself, and that revelation does not come at the end of a road signifying our search for Him. It is an ever-present possibility and reality since He does not exist only at the end of the road. He is in the middle of the road and at the beginning as well. The eternal truth by which men must live is God, for He is the Truth. When we focus our attention on Him we have placed our eyes upon the Eternal. He is the Absolute on which all things rest, the unchanging Person behind all change, who Himself is unchanged. And this comes not by the search of man but by the revelation of God Himself. The real Absolute cannot be invented or measured, or discovered; it has to be revealed.

God is self-disclosing. The initiative is all on His part, and without His voluntary action there could be no knowledge of Him.

It is true that God has created man so that his heart yearns after the eternal. It is true that man gropes after God in automatic fashion because he has thus been made to do so. It is true that there is no rest for the heart of man until that rest is found in God. All of this seeking by man, however, does not imply that he can find God. Thus if we do know Him, it is because He reveals Himself to us. There is no other possibility. And in that revelation of Himself there is a unique finality and absoluteness that is a rock in the midst of shifting sand.

Some claim that God has revealed Himself in nature. This is true to a limited extent. Nature and all of its works manifest the power and might of its Creator. But nature does not reveal the Creator Himself, anymore than the watch reveals the man who made it. The self-disclosure of God does not and cannot come through the disclosure of His works, even in the case of man who stands at the top in order of these works. The disclosure must be by God Himself. And God decisively and finally and fully disclosed Himself in Jesus Christ, the Son of the Living God. The basic affirmation of this is that the Word was made flesh and dwelt among us and we beheld His glory. The glory we beheld is not the glory of a created being; it is not someone sent to represent God. It is God Himself who became flesh and dwelt among us. This, and this only, can be self-disclosure. For if Jesus is not God then He cannot perfectly reveal God, and He becomes for all purposes like the creation of nature which reflects the Creator but does not reveal Him. Jesus is the heart of the gospel. He is not just another historical figure who walked the earth, living and dying. He is the incarnate God in whom the Eternal God is once and forever revealed. The mystery of this incarnation we do not fully understand, but understanding it is not demanded of us. All we need to do is assent to that basic fact. Jesus did not bring a new concept of God; He did not more perfectly reflect Him than anyone before or after; Jesus actually is God and in Himself does not reflect the Eternal One, but He is the Eternal One.

There is no wider framework of reference than Jesus Christ. In His advent there is a completeness and a finality. This advent is totally destructive of any relativism and holds aloft the standard of the absolute and the unchanging. Were there any wider point of reference than Jesus Christ, then He would not be final or absolute. Then we would still have to come to grips with finality and the absolute. But since there is no other, the need of man could not be met in this hour. Naturally, the substantiation of this claim for Christ does not rest on the argument that if we did not have Christ, there would be no one to replace Him, so we take Him for the want of something better. That argument has a validity to a limited degree, but we refuse to rest our plea on the shaky ground that we resort to Jesus because there is none to replace Him, true as this is. We categorically and triumphantly and everlastingly proclaim that He IS final and absolute; that He IS the framework of reference in the light of which all else must be weighed and judged. This means that there is nothing by which to weigh the claims of Jesus Christ, for all things are weighed by Him Who is unchanging. So He who weighs all things cannot Himself be weighed unless His claim be relinquished.

In the disclosure of God in Jesus Christ, God did not then become what He is revealed to be. The incarnation simply shows God, in a period of time, as He is eternally, without change either by addition or subtraction. Thus Christ becomes our ultimate standard, the *a priori* for all things, who if He were not the *a priori* would Himself be subject to another *a priori,* the existence of which cannot be admitted and which must be dogmatically and categorically denied. Man must live or die by this supernatural revelation of God in Christ.

Jesus Christ has long since died, and has risen from the dead, and has ascended into heaven. How has the revelation of God come down to us who follow after? Here the origins of Christianity are irreducible. God revealed Himself in the Person of Jesus Christ and this revelation of God comes to us through the Word of God. Imperfect as my understanding and interpretation of the Word of God may be, it still remains for me the source from which I obtain my knowledge of the self-disclosure of the Eternal God. The Bible becomes for the Christian the absolute; the norm. It is not merely that this is a book which contains the revelation of God. This book IS the revelation of God, and the central, dominating figure is Jesus Christ. No one can fail to see that to question the written revelation is to make man the determiner of what the true revelation is. For if the Bible contains the Word of God, then man becomes the sole agent in making the selection of those parts which are true and those parts which are not. This is true, in spite of any doctrine of guidance by the Holy Spirit which men hold. Men who have been equally holy and equally sincere outwardly have claimed to be led of the Spirit of God to conclusions that are in disagreement as to the Bible. Some believe that the Bible IS the Word of God, and some believe that it contains the Word of God. The Spirit does not contradict Himself, so one side or the other must be wrong. To believe in a final and complete revelation pertaining to God in the Person of Christ will be to believe in a final and complete revelation of Him in the Word of God.

The Gospel of John is not truth as John saw it, but it is truth which he knew whether by revelation or through knowledge of the facts first-hand, in the writing of which he was preserved from error. If what John wrote is truth, then it is truth also to any man who reads it. If, on the other hand, it depends on how one looks at it, then it is not something absolute and unchanging, but is subjected to the decision of the one who does the looking. To say that the Gospel of John is truth as John saw it can mean nothing less than that it is John's conception of truth, and not an objective truth that is ever the same. Even if it were John's truth, to be truth it must be final. For if it is not final, and does change, then it is not truth but only what John THOUGHT to be truth. This form of sophistry by which the eternal validity of the Word is destroyed ought not deceive anyone into believing that it is John and not God who speaks. It is Biblical and more soul-satisfying to know that it is not truth as John saw it, but truth as John recorded it under the guidance and influence of the Spirit of the living God.

We can carry this problem of the exact revelation a step farther. In the case of Matthew and Luke, we have two men recording certain facts about the life of Jesus. They make the statement that

Jesus was born of a virgin who had never known a man. If we take the view that these Gospels comprise truth as the authors saw it, then we must either assume that what they thought to be truth in connection with the virgin birth was not truth and thus was error which they thought to be truth, or else we must admit that what they wrote in connection with the birth of Jesus is true. In the latter case we have a confirmation of the virgin birth of Christ, which, if it is truth, is not a conception foisted on these men, but a real fact. We know, however, that the acceptance or rejection of the virgin birth of Christ does not in itself constitute a premise. Always the decision follows naturally and logically upon a prior premise. The prior premise is whether one believes in the supernatural or not. If the supernatural is denied then indeed the virgin birth is ridiculous, and logically the claim can arise that Matthew and Luke are recording something (not truth, for if it is truth then it cannot be wrong) which they thought to be true, but about which they were actually fooled. In spite of all of their good intentions, they passed on to us a story that has no foundation in fact. No one, however, who reads Matthew and Luke, can deny that at least they give every evidence that they believe they are telling the truth.

It is precisely at this point that the true believer must be dogmatic without apology. As has already been stated, we hold that God is self-disclosing and that the revelation of Himself is objectively treated and stated in the Bible. This Book is not the simple tale of wandering peoples of all ages giving us a record of their thoughts and actions and religious hopes, aspirations, and progressive developments. It is definitely not a record of people who are groping after something that is intangible, a something to which they never attained since there is no absolute to be attained. The Bible is a record of God's thoughts and acts in relation to mankind. It is God's and not man's. And the standard of reference is God's standard of reference and not man's standard of reference. The truth of the Word of God is not altered even slightly by the reaction of a man to its contents. It stands objectively true without apology and man can either accept it or reject it as it is. The battle over the acceptance of this supernatural revelation is not to be decided in the reason of man, nor is it to be decided in higher criticism, whether it be a historico-grammatical or a form criticism. It must be decided in the soul of man through the work-power of the Spirit of God.

In the struggle over the Word of God it is not possible for man to decide for himself what is to be accepted and what is to be refused. It is a question of "either-or." You take it or leave it, but you do not break down its contents on a basis of personal selectivity. Furthermore, it does not matter whether you like it in what it says. That is immaterial since most people run into facts which they do not like but which they cannot change. The thief who is caught does not like his capture; the man who has the sentence of death in his physical body because of cancer does not like the fact but he cannot change it. The natural man will not like much of the Scriptures and in his condition this is understandable. But his dislike of what the Scriptures say does not change their authority nor alter the truths which they enunciate. The Word of God must be taken whether it is liked or not.

In my acceptance of the Word of God as my standard of reference, it follows that all of my opinions and decisions come from that revelation. Whatever I conclude must be WITHIN the framework of that book. It becomes for me my authoritative guide subject to no other criterion of truth; in principle, subject to nothing save the Person who gave it, God Himself in the person of the Holy Spirit. At best, my understanding of the revelation will be incomplete and in some cases fragmentary. Finite limitations make this reasonable along with the knowledge that the infinite cannot be reduced to terms which can be fully explicable to the finite. Great minds have attempted to climb the heights and descend to the depths of the meanings of the Word of God and have only been able to hew out a few blocks of marble from an inexhaustible quarry. Some, in sincerity, have even misunderstood obscure portions of the Word of God, obscure not because God is obscure but because there were some things which God did not choose to make clear. And in misunderstanding, man has evidenced his finiteness in relation to the infinity of the Eternal God. However, and this is the point which needs to be stressed again and again, the Bible is perfectly clear in every essential point about which there is any need for discussion. No man approaching the Bible to discover what the Bible says can leave it without having found enough of the truth in it to satisfy the needs of the human heart. It is only when an approach is made which rejects what the writers of the Bible say that error and trouble become the order of the day. This is a prejudiced view to be sure; it is a dogmatic view, too; it is the Christian view historically; and it is the view which the plain reading of Scripture will substantiate to anyone who is doubtful.

There are people today who say that they believe in the revelation presented in the Word, and yet they claim that we need innovators who will offer us further interpretations of the great truths which the Bible presents. Barth and Brunner have been hailed by them as great emancipators who have ploughed new furrows for this generation. The representatives of this school were at Madras in 1938 and they pointedly named Brunner and Barth as representing their point of view.

The newness or freshness of approach in the writings of these two men springs, not out of anything that is really new, but out of the fact that what they say constitutes a radical departure from the humanism and relativity of the average theological mind of our day. Barth and Brunner represent a movement away from the theology of modernism, a movement back toward orthodoxy since they do not represent orthodoxy in its traditional sense. It is true that these men speak of a self-disclosing God and of an objective revelation as against the vicious pantheism and pragmatism and naturalism of their contemporaries, but they also clearly distinguish between their views of revelation and those of the historical school which believes in a supernaturally inspired Word that is verbally inerrant and which higher criticism cannot alter.

One cannot escape the suspicion that Barth and Brunner hold ideas concerning the dramatic meeting of God and man in experience which have subjective references making man the center of a theology as well as the center of an experience from which he emerges a new creature. As against these men, we must declare that we believe in changing applications of truth, but the truth itself remains unchanged. In spite of them, we must hold the belief that the Bible is eternally valid in its truth, and that the truth does not change with the passing years. This objective truth must ever be the standard by which all other theories and ideas are tested.

Religious certainty becomes a living reality for the person who accepts the Bible as the final and complete objective revelation of God, recognizing that Jesus Christ is supremely and completely and finally revealed in the Word. This means that every area of the Christian life must be made subject to this revelation and that all decisions must be made in the light of it. Quite apparently, though, our quest is not ended when we accept the revelation, for there remains the undertaking of uncovering its teachings and its applications.

Some earnest souls claim a real desire to believe the Bible but they are continually faced with the problem of giving intellectual assent to some of the contents of the Bible which seem to be in error with science or some other apparently substantiated fact. And again, the Christian is faced with many difficult portions of the Word and even with some things, few though they be, which give the appearance of being contradictory. We can claim honestly that most discrepancies are easily cleared up when investigated, but we must also admit honestly that there are others which stubbornly refuse to be answered in the light of the knowledge which we have at present. Still others, on the surface, have the appearance of being actual discrepancies with regard to differences in numbers and the like. It is in these areas that the acid test of faith must be faced by the believer. His reaction here will reflect his true belief in the Word of God. The problems of the old and new testaments are the proving grounds which clearly demonstrate whether the premise a man is supposed to hold is being held. Rightly, a man will interpret other data in the light of his premise; he will not interpret his premise in the light of the data.

The law of gravity is not disproved nor is its law broken because objects heavier than air float through the skies. Superficially, one might disclaim the validity of the law of gravity because some objects do fly through space, and in an equally superficial manner one can claim to disbelieve the Bible because isolated portions (disregarding the weighty majority of which this is not true) APPEAR to be in disagreement with each other. Wherever it can be done without violence, the Christian finds a happy solution to Biblical problems. Where it seemingly cannot be done at present the true believer does not then arrive at a position which contradicts the premise with which he began—namely, that the Bible is truly the inerrant Word of God. To deny his original premise is to lose religious certainty and return to a relativity which is the very conclusion the true believer must avoid. A question of choice consequently means that the Christian would normally prefer the inerrant Word. It is not to be thought, however, that the Christian position rests upon the idea that we stupidly accept verbal inspiration in the face of known and demonstrated facts to the contrary. The Christian simply rests his case with the admission that he does not know everything and that if all of the facts were known the Bible would be substantiated. He realizes that archeological research gives him presumptive ground to rest on, for its discoveries have consistently verified his view of inerrancy and have demonstrated that supposed historical and scientific errors were not really errors and that the Bible was right. Of course, the most conclusive argument of all is that the Holy Spirit witnesses to our spirits that the Bible is the Word of God.

Speaking from a scientific point of view it can be claimed that true science does not disagree with the Bible. Science does not even answer the same questions that Christianity answers nor ought real science to pretend that it can. The question of origins will never be determined by science, for science has to do with observations which can be made through the study of available data. For science, then, to deal with the problem of creation *ex nihilo* is entirely outside its realm. That belongs to the field of religion and not to science. Science may offer all of the theories it wishes as to the so-called evolution of man, but it must be silent (yet it is not and thus becomes unscientific) as to the origins of man. Not to be silent, and to attempt an explanation as science does in various ways, makes science far more radical than Christianity with all of its claims, and far less reasonable except to the natural mind that has not been moved by the Holy Spirit of God to belief.

No, the Christian believes that his position is sound and acceptable even when the isolated sections of the Word of God that are difficult do not submit themselves to a ready and simple answer. The Christian generally has reason to believe in many cases that so-called errors are errors in transmission via manuscripts. In other cases he simply admits that he refuses to believe there is an error even when the particular point in question has the appearance of being substantiated by some data, for faith tells him that further data will inevitably and most certainly demonstrate the accuracy and authority of the Word. Faith withholds judgment in cases of doubt with the steady, unwavering assurance that additional can do no harm to the Word of God which liveth and abideth forever and does not change.

The Christian does not fear, but welcomes investigation, for he knows that the Bible cannot be harmed by that. The experiences of the years reveal that foolish men have thrown out many portions of the Word which other men have restored through archeological or other investigations. The only fear the Christian has, and this is rightly a fear, is that the natural man will take the results of scientific findings and interpret them according to his own preconceived notions, weaving a pattern and developing a conclusion which, although theoretically based upon the results of investigation, are actually results that the natural man wished for all along.

The Christian himself is always subject to the same bondage of finiteness when he interprets the Word. It is possible for the commentator to find in the Word support for foolish and silly interpretations which are grounded in imagination rather than in the Word. This explains why we have such diverse theological views even among those who believe in the inerrent Word but who develop Calvinistic or Arminian interpretations of the Word. Such differences are to be looked upon, however, in a light entirely different from that of the people who deny the validity of the Word. In the one case it is a difference WITHIN the framework and in the other it is a denial of the framework. A variety of pattern can be woven in the same framework as, for example, in the numberless varieties of Christian experiences, all of which are within the pattern, as against those experiences which are completely outside the motif and pattern.

In spite of objections from without and differences within, the Christian stands whole-heartedly on the objective revelation of God in the Person of His Son through the Word which we call the Bible. There is a danger in this view. That danger is to so objectify the Word of God that no room is left for the experiential. Here we need a word of caution. By experience we do not prove the validity of the Word. It is valid whether experienced by an individual or not. But by experience we come to a knowledge of the truth of the Word.

The experience of an individual is valid only if that experience is in accordance with the revelation. An objective revelation without a personal experience does not mean for an individual salvation from a Biblical viewpoint. The objective revelation for the Christian becomes real subjectively in experience and in accordance with the Word. Experience can never be alien to the Word nor in defiance and contradiction of the Word. They jibe. The test cannot be one by which the revelation is tried via our experience. The test always and ever must be one where the experience of the individual is tried by the Word. And if that experience accords with the revelation, then it is a valid and true experience and worthy of giving the individual the name of Christian. If it does not stand the searching scrutiny of the Word, no matter how beautiful the experience, nor how moving the emotion, it is false and spurious. One might go further and say that such an experience is of the devil himself and not of God. No matter how educated the man; no matter how lofty his concept; no matter how philosophic and scholarly he may be; the

God of men whose experiences are inconsistent with the Word is not the God and Father of our Lord Jesus Christ.

The reason why a subjective experience is needed for a man to become a Christian is plain. Revelation as we find it is accessible to all men who wish to read the record. But by its very nature it is in a spiritual sense totally inaccessible to anyone except under certain conditions. To read and to study the Word of God does not guarantee that it shall be comprehended. Comprehension comes not from reading alone but from faith, for faith is the avenue through which the Word of God brings meaning to the individual soul. The reading of revelation is there for all. The understanding of revelation comes from God Himself. The natural man will not and cannot make spiritual sense out of the Word. The hearts of natural men turn against the idea of a God who can be found only by self-disclosure and revolt against this radical truth. All salvation outside the Word of God, though, is self-redemption and centers in man's own effort to redeem himself. That is why men reject the Biblically revealed truth that God and God alone can work redemption. Why God works this way is essentially immaterial in the face of the truth that He does work this way. This, no doubt, is the offence of the cross and the stumbling block which keeps men from God. To admit His thesis that salvation is His own work and must originate with Him is to deny self and the competency of man. Thus it is that man must have an experience, for apart from that experience which comes from God there can be no spiritual apperception of the objective facts of redemption such as the work of Christ on the cross and His eternal deity. It is the denial of these divinely revealed and divinely witnessed to truths in the Word and in the heart of man which show the natural man to be what he is—unregenerate and outside of Christ regardless of any argument specifying some type of a religious experience. The only valid experience is that one which brings the natural man to the acceptance of divinely revealed truth as mediated through the Word of God, the Bible.

Faith is necessary to salvation and is related to the self-disclosure of God Himself. Immediately there exists a tension between faith and reason as the latter term is usually employed. We must deny that the natural man with all of the reason he is able to gather together in any effort or series of efforts can find God through reason, or that he can use reason as a standard of reference for faith. In the end, the truth of the Christian faith does not and cannot, by its nature, rest in reason or in any rational argument. For rational argument has to do with philosophy and the things of philosophy differ as radically from the things of religion as mathematics differs from a physical science. This does not mean that the unregenerate man is stripped of any kind or form of reason and that he has become a totally irrational creature. Rather it implies that reason just is not the conveyor of spiritual truth *per se*. In other areas of life there are analogies which explain what we mean here. In the physical sciences or in mathematics, faith is not necessary to apprehend their truths, but whatever is necessary must be brought to bear before they can be understood. Thus the feebleminded man usually cannot bring enough mentality to bear to comprehend much, if any, of chemistry. And the natural man cannot bring reason to bear in the apprehension of Christ in God, for apprehension demands that faith be brought to bear. This does not mean that man ceases to be a reasonable creature when he approaches God, or that salvation is contrary to true reason. It simply means that the approach is not made via reason but via faith. "He that cometh unto God must believe that He is."

Faith implies that reason has been ground to the dust since reason is the very thing that keeps men from God. The essence of faith is to take God at His word and to make Him the center of everything and His Word the ultimate authority in every area. The acceptance of the revelation of God through faith, which brings salvation and regeneration, does something else too. The acceptance of Christianity carries with it adherence to a certain view of life; to the Biblical view of the world, sin, man, salvation, and whatever else the Bible speaks about. The contract of the Christian with the Bible is an ever expanding and enlarging con-

tact, of which we shall say more in a moment. But we stop here
to make definite mention of the work of the Holy Spirit in
connection with apprehension of truth, and in regeneration.

In speaking of the Word of God we said that it was supernaturally revealed by God through the Holy Spirit to men who
wrote what God wanted written and who were preserved from
error as they wrote. We then proceeded to state that for the
understanding of this revelation which is hidden from the natural
man, faith is necessary. Now it remains to specify clearly that the
sole agent of faith is the Holy Spirit of God. In experience the
Holy Spirit bears witness with our spirits that we are the sons
of God. It is the Spirit who quickeneth and who giveth life.
The mind and heart of the natural man, which is darkened by sin
and which is alienated from God and a foreigner to the things
of God, must be changed. This work of change through regeneration is done by the Holy Spirit. His work is to make the things
of Christ plain to the hearts of men and He also witnesses in the
hearts of men to the accuracy and authority of the Word of God.
No man can call Jesus God except by the Spirit and no man can
believe in the Bible except as the Spirit prompts. This does not
mean that the free agency of man is destroyed with reference to
choice in salvation. It does mean that without the Spirit's work
no man can make any choice for God because of original sin.
Unless one holds to a supra-lapsarian view or an infra-lapsarian
view, this free choice of man, although a problem and a paradox
in the divine order of events, is nonetheless regarded as part of
the divine order. Its part can be recognized without being fully
understood for if it is truly a paradox it is not likely to be understood. Biblically this view is susceptible to less difficulty than the
supra and infra-lapsarian views and our interest here is not so much
a rational presentation as it is a biblical presentation.

The Biblical doctrine of the Holy Spirit is perfectly consistent
with the total picture. We have a self-disclosing revelation in the
Word we call the Bible and in the Word which is Jesus Christ.
It is completed by the spiritual disclosing of these objective

truths through the inward work of the Holy Spirit in the lives and hearts of men. The witness of the Holy Spirit in the Word of God objectively and the witness of the Holy Spirit subjectively in experience are complimentary. They go together, and are not found alone in the Christian. The experiential witness of the Spirit subjectively is always accompanied by a witness to the truth of the Bible objectively. And if a man believes the Word of God to be that actually, then he will find in it all that he needs to know about the person and the work of the third personality in the Trinity.

The Spirit of God does more than simply regenerate a man. He also enlightens the intellect and understanding so that the Word of God becomes plain. It is true that there are many portions of the Word which are objectively plain but which are not believed by non-Christians. No man, even with the natural mind, can deny that Matthew and Luke teach that Christ, the historical man, was born of a virgin and that Joseph was not His father by generation. Acceptance of this dogma comes normally and logically from the work of the Spirit in regeneration. But beyond those elements of the faith which are expressed so clearly that even the natural mind must admit that they are there although refusing to accept them, the regenerate man needs the aid of the Holy Spirit for purposes of further understanding and interpretation of that Word. Always there is the temptation, even for the regenerate man, to bend the Scriptures and make them subservient to rational and coherent thinking. In this sense it becomes true that any system of theology cannot exhaust the Scriptures, and in some cases the desire for a thoroughly rational presentation of the doctrines of the Bible leads to a disregard of Biblical theology which may contain apparent inconsistencies and paradoxes. Pure logic, for example, well supports the view of a limited atonement, but biblical theology alters this by the presentation of strong scriptural evidence contrary to a limited atonement which is outwardly more consonent with reason. The Bible has a rationality and a coherence of its own and is frequently distorted when men try to read into it their own viewpoints.

The Bible is not a textbook in systematic theology and in no place does it present a complete world view or an ordered system of theology as such. It does have, nevertheless, a theology and a world-view. Not being a textbook does not mean that the Bible cannot be interpreted and explained in a systematic manner or that the Bible is not systematic. It is just that the Book was not meant to be a text in theology nor is its arrangement intended to convey this impression. Perhaps the Apostle Paul stands out in his writings as the one who presents more theology in a systematic arrangement than any other writer, and yet it is clear that his writings are not a systematic arrangement as we think of it today. All of the Bible is a radical presentation of eternal truth to man with the demand that he conform immediately and obediently to its commandments. Man is expected to make an immediate decision in the light of what the Scriptures contain. And in this radical departure the Bible does not become irrational but supra-rational.

The inspiration of the Bible has given people much trouble. Some say that all views on inspiration are, after all, only theories, the Bible not making a definite claim itself. It is true that the Bible does not "theorize" about inspiration and it is true that the theological dogma on inspiration which the Church has accepted down the years does not appear in the Bible itself. But it is wrong to think that the Bible does not have a view on inspiration. The whole book is plain in teaching the concept which we label theologically as verbal inspiration. Throughout, the Bible is written to convey the impression that it is God who is speaking. Again and again we find the recurring phrase, "thus saith the Lord". It does not formulate a systematic statement of inspiration, but it does take it for granted that it is God's Word to man with God doing the speaking. The same truth operates for other doctrines. The Bible does not use the theological formulation called "substitutionary atonement." This is the man-made formulation of what is expressed in the Bible, but the fact that it is a man-made formulation does not invalidate it since it expresses in theological language what is found to be true in the Word. To formulate a statement of the atonement, such as the "moral influence" one which is contrary to the Word itself is to invent a "theory" of the atonement and is to make a serious error. But to formulate a statement of the atonement which agrees with the Bible is to do no damage, but has often been a help to the Church of Christ. The doctrines of plenary inspiration and vicarious atonement may be man-made statements, but they express the dynamic realism of the Word of God.

The Baptists have been guilty of subverting true Christianity in their resistance to creeds, albeit their original thought was good. They have always claimed non-adherence to any creed with a kind of pride that has sinful implications. Again and again Baptists have claimed that they accept only the New Testament, and this, despite the formulation of more "statements" of faith than any other peoples! Plainly creeds exist for a legitimate purpose and express specific beliefs. It is this specificity that many object to because a creed is often a measuring rod to determine orthodoxy. Since a creed expresses something that one holds to be true we find once again the futility of trying to escape having creeds. The man who claims that he has no creed is already guilty of establishing a creed. For the dogma that you will have, no creed IS a creed! We must be done with this nonsense by which infidels try to hide their unbelief. If the Bible has any meaning, that meaning is to be found in the expression of dogmas having immeasurable value to man in his relationship to God.

It is increasingly important for the Christian to be unfailingly plain in his contention that the revelation of God in Christ is, for us today, to be found in the written Word of God. The Bible is what we have today. Since Jesus ascended into heaven, the believer has to depend upon the Bible for his grasp of the person of Christ, under the guidance of the Holy Spirit. Apprehension is linked indissolubly to the Word as well as the Spirit, for it is the Spirit who witnesses to the truth of the Word. God speaks to us through the Bible as the Spirit enlightens our understanding in its perception. The Bible is the source and the ground of our faith. Remove it or destroy its validity and the total Christian position falls to the ground.

The absolutist position of the Christian when thinking about missions is that we have a sound and solid foundation on which that enterprise rests. That foundation is the Word of God. Any missionary enterprise and all aspects of such an enterprise must be conducted along lines which are consonant with the revelation of the Word. The message must be directly derived from the Word; the methods must be in full accord with the Word; the aims of missions must jibe with the Word; and the theology of missions with regard to its view of man and the world or any other doctrine must be able to meet the same test. The unalterable test is agreement with that written Word either directly or by reason of any logical and reasonable derivation therefrom. The Word is the only adequate standard of reference, the measuring rod by which all tests are to be made. In itself it is not subject to an antecedent or subsequent test. It is the basic *a priori* assumption from which all other decisions are derived. Its understanding comes through faith as the Holy Spirit works in the hearts of men.

In connection with the spread of the gospel and the carrying of that gospel to the ends of the earth, the only satisfactory ultimate on which our case is rested is the Word of God. We begin and end with that Word. It is the rock which stands amid sinking sands; a rock that cannot be shaken. It is the pivotal point around which we build our entire enterprise. We assume responsibility for this grand *a priori* belief and realize that if it is all wrong then the missionary enterprise falls with it since it will not be grounded on ultimate and final truth. It destroys, once for all, all relativity and in place thereof substitutes an absolute which we hold to be true. In a changing world when men are seeking for religious certainty, and in an age when the other ideas and concepts have failed to supply the answer that satisfies, Christians need to make it plain that we have an answer that is satisfactory, one that is adequate for the hour and its needs. Our philosophy of missions, then, whatever that philosophy shall be, must fit into the framework of the revelation which we take as the point of origin and the center of reference. This philosophy which will be developed now will have a finality and will be absolute to the extent that it is grounded on the finality of our revelation. It actually begins with the revelation and then goes on to those principles and doctrines which are contained and expressed in the Bible.

Chapter 3

A FINAL THEOLOGY—THE GOSPEL

A LL THINGS must have some foundation on which to rest. The foundation may be erroneous or the derivations from the original premise may be wrong. But there must be a foundation. Such a foundation may be a pure materialism; it may be relativity; it may be pragmatism; it may be idealism; it may be utter nonsense and complete foolishness. In the nature of things, however, there needs to be something on which all other things are based.

So it is with Christian missions. There is a foundation on which the enterprise rests. This has been the conclusion reached in the last chapter, although some people within the visible Church will not accept this conclusion as stated. It is fair to any opponent to point out that the conclusion we have reached concerning the foundation on which a true Christian missionary enterprise rests is a conclusion which has the backing of history. The premise is no new one; it is old and tried. This premise was the faith of our fathers which has run like a golden strand through the otherwise black cords of secular and religious history. The conclusion, in many ways, brings us back to a Reformation position, and even to an apostolic position to which the Word itself bears witness that what we claim is true.

Whatever others may claim to be the foundation on which

the true missionary enterprise rests, this much is plain: we believe that the only true foundation for the missionary enterprise is the final and complete revelation of God in the Book we call the Bible, which is inerrant in all of its statements. The Bible is not simply a presentation of truth, it is very truth itself in every regard. This Book was written by different men under the inspiration of the Holy Spirit of God who preserved them from any error, the same Spirit getting written what He wanted written without addition or subtraction. This Book is the final authority which decides all other questions, and without which there could be no philosophy of missions worthy of such a name. It is not that the Bible makes possible a philosophy of missions, which is to be derived from something in this Book as such. It is simply that the Bible in itself IS the philosophy of missions in its full embodiment. And as the revelation itself is final, so then can we determine from it what the final theology of missions is, remembering always that such a theology is not independent of the revelation, but comes out of the revelation, or may be logically derived from the revelation without doing violence to any aspect of the revelation.

The need for a restatement of a final theology of missions is absolutely imperative. There are a multitude of reasons to support this contention. One of them is that conservative Christianity has not been sufficiently vocal in our age. Another is that we must have the application of this theology to every age in the language and thought of that age. The theology will not change for it is final, but its relevancy to each age must be demonstrated and defended. Another equally good reason is that there are theological differences of a not inconsequential nature among conservatives themselves. These differences are not ones that affect theology with reference to the nature and work of the members of the Trinity, or with reference to the doctrine of salvation. They are differences, nevertheless, which do have practical consequences in the furtherance of the missionary enterprise. A good illustration of this would be that school of thought that is anti-missionary, believing that God will save the heathen apart from human means. For a missionary theology, this concept, obviously unscriptural, is destructive of the whole fabric of such an enterprise as we conceive of it. So it becomes doubly important to state the theology of missions in such a way as to remove any doubts as to what action Christians ought to take in spreading the gospel. Another pertinent reason is that some fine Christians are planning to serve as missionaries or are actually serving as missionaries without being properly oriented to the total picture. To "feel" called to serve is wonderful, but hardly enough. To serve because of a belief that the heathen are lost without Christ is excellent, but that too is not all of the picture. Christian ministers, missionaries, and other workers need to be informed concerning this enterprise in its totality so that by an intelligent grasp of the overall picture there may be a renewed consecration to the task. To do something is important, but it is equally important to know WHAT you are doing and WHY you are doing it. It is because of this serious lack that missionary endeavor has fallen on hard times.

Whatever theology we shall find that is final will be so only because it rests on a final revelation. Such a theology must find its roots in that revelation apart from any other mitigating factor. The theology of the Bible may not be in agreement with the likes and dislikes of certain individuals. That is immaterial. Indeed some truths taught in the Bible may not be to the liking of many Christians. This does not change either the truth of the theology or the need of the true Christian to be guided by that theology. Further, the theology of the Bible may not be completely understood by the Christian, raising the question whether we ought to be guided by that which we do not properly understand. Again this has no bearing on the truth itself. Whether I understand it is not of great importance relative to its acceptance by myself. I must believe it whether or not I understand it, even when there appear to be naturalistic reasons why I ought not to accept it as it is presented. A missionary theology is not a matter of what I think or believe, and I am not come to propagate my own ideas.

People are not truly interested in speculation and theory. They are concerned about final truth. The real Christian is simply the agent who passes on what is revealed to him in the Word and which he believes to be, by the work of the Holy Spirit, truth. Within the Word itself there is a proper sphere of activity for every Christian to use methods and means to come to the full knowledge and understanding of the Word of God. This is legitimate and desirable so long as it is properly confined to the limitations prescribed for it by God Himself. There are limitations beyond which man is forbidden to go, just as Adam was not totally unconditioned in his Eden environment and was forbidden to go beyond the limits set for him by God.

Before we can enter into a discussion of a final theology for missions, one point of supreme importance arises. This is the problem of obscuration, theologically speaking, that has come in the long history of the Christian Church. Christianity, the historical development, and the Christian revelation have often been thought of as synonymous. When this is the case, confusion is inevitable. The Christian faith as a historic religion has to be separated from the Christian revelation. To identify loosely the one with the other can never produce straight thinking. The Roman Catholic Church constantly alludes to this erroneous conception and on it bases her claim to be the church universal. In making this claim the Roman Catholic Church perverts the revelation of God, for that Church has departed from the revelation in many important doctrines. To cover this infidelity to the Word, the Roman Church makes the interpretation of the Bible by the Church the center of reference. The measuring rod is not the Word of God but the interpretation of that Word as seen in its perversion by its self-styled vicar of Christ, the pope. Tradition and the Church, which are historical in development, become vital to Roman Catholic theology. The natural and logical consequence is that they measure all others by their standards, which standards themselves cannot remain intact when measured in the light of the Bible itself. The revelation stands apart from historical Christianity, and cannot be interpreted in the light of historical Christianity. Christianity in its historical development must be tested by, and stand or fall in the light of, the revelation. So our theology here stands apart from the history of the Christian Church, although we employ and use that history in a helpful way to demonstrate the rise of error and to point out results springing out of error.

In practical missionary work this obscuration we speak of has been felt keenly. The historical Church has not always remained true to the theology of the Bible, and with a change in theology there usually comes a change in missionary motive. When the conception of hell changes, or when hell is denied, or when attention is drawn away from the punitive justice of God in everlasting punishment and torment, the motive of missions changes and obscuration results. The original Protestant motive for missions, for example, was dominated largely by such a belief in a real hell. Another instance of the same attitude is found among those who feel that sincere and earnest seekers after truth in other religions are not to be damned by God. And usually this view holds that salvation is not so much the avoidance of eternal punishment as it is saving men from lesser goods for the supreme good, whatever that hazy and sentimental phrase may mean.

So it is because the average Christian, including vocational Christian workers, seems to be wholly at sea about the Christian faith and what it entails relative to missions that we state the final theology for missions. This statement is not meant to be complete nor can it be a detailed exposition of the doctrines mentioned, but it ought to provide a skeleton on which an interested reader can build for himself a more complete theology through the Bible or some reputable book in the field of Biblical or systematic theology. In our treatment it seems better to state first the positive side of a final theology applicable to missions, and later discuss the negative side, dealing with assumptions that are non-Christian or anti-Christian.

At the heart of the gospel, and central in the teaching of the Bible, is the sinful nature of man. The other doctrines of the faith turn about this cardinal doctrine. If there were no sin there would be no need for the incarnation; without sin there is no need for reconciliation and atonement; without sin there is no need to restore man to something that he has not lost. In short the whole Bible is predicated on the sinful condition of man in relation to his creator.

Man is for some reason separated and needs to be brought back into his former relationship.

In dealing with man, the Bible does not mince words. It states how man became alienated from God through Adam the first man and through whose transgression sin passed to all the race. Consequently all men are born inherently sinful and have sin imputed against them. Everywhere in scripture is the reality faced that man is in a state of hostility toward God as He really is. Everywhere is the teaching to be discerned that men know there is a God, that they seek His face, that they build altars to Him, but they still do not know Him. And this Biblical fact is fully supported in history for all who wish to observe it.

At the center of man's alienation lies the desire to enthrone himself in his own heart; to be like God. Man wishes to be an autonomous creature, not subserviant to anyone above him, the master of his own fate and the captain of his own soul. It is the deification of man and the dethronement of God from His rightful place in the hearts and lives of men. It is not to be thought that sin is maladjustment to environment, or that it is some tendency which may or may not lead man away from God. It is a corruption which has worked death, and man is not going to die spiritually. He is already dead. It is this sinful rebellion of the creature against the creator that is the fundamental fact upon which Christianity is built. Man in his ego, with his everlasting "I", has asserted himself against God and His holy will; he has freed himself from its bondage as he thought, only to enter a bondage that is not imaginary but real. The deepest sin which can be committed is the sin of making one's own gods, or worshipping the false and the untrue gods of that creation while at the same time making a pretense (for that is what it is) of seeking the true God.

In its essential nature sin must involve two personalities. It must involve the one who sins and the one against whom the transgression is committed. This is particularly true when a man sins against his neighbor except that a third personality is then involved because a sin against a neighbor is also a sin against God. In no case then can less than two personalities be represented when sin is committed. The very word sin bespeaks the existence of a standard by which it is possible to know what is a sin and what is not a sin. Nevertheless it is always a transgression against a holy God whose nature and laws are unchangeable.

We must be done with the notion that makes sin relative and tries to pretend that what is sin for one generation is not necessarily sin for another generation. Thus when the social modes change, the thing which had been sin previously is no longer sin. We must further be done with the absurd lie that sin is simply hidden or secret guilt that has a psychotic origin and which can be cured by psychology or psychoanalysis.

Sin is sin in every age and for each generation. Adultery is sin regardless of the civilization or the age in which we live. An act is not socially wrong because of the bad results which may accrue to society because of it (although this is important, and national sins like adultery do make themselves felt in the fabric of society in the long run) but it is wrong because it violates a law of God's nature which is unchanging in its demands and applications. This thesis can be enlarged to include as illustrations many other acts on which society frowns such as theft, murder and lying. All of these are wrong socially, but not because social custom has found it expedient to make them wrong. They are wrong whether society condemns them or not, because they violate God's eternal law and any violation will prove to be bad for the social structure of society over a period of time. The recognition of this is a good testimony to the truth of Scripture which teaches that the wages of sin is death in an eternal as well as in a temporal sense. In the temporal sense in the social structure of the nations, general society eventually pays the price for the violation of God's moral laws, for violation leads to the decay of civilization and then the fall and decline of that civilization. In this sense civilizations or society feel the impact and effect of sin, although individuals are primarily held responsible.

Sins which work against individuals and society are bad enough. Worse than these is the basic sin where the individual refuses to recognize and acknowledge his creator. All other sins in the light of this first sin can be understood although not forgiven. It is when men are away from God that all other sins become a possibility.

Because of the first man's choice, all men since that sin have been born alienated from God. Men do not have in them just the tendency to sin when they are born. They are born dead, spiritually speaking, and in a state of alienation from God before they see the light of day. This condition is overtly signified in the sinning of all men openly and actually during the course of their lives. And it makes no difference what the color of a man's skin or the background which he has when he enters the world. Each individual, whether born into the home of a pagan or even a Christian, is born with the taint of sin on him and unless renewed by the grace of God is subjected to the penalty for sin which is eternal death.

Of man's actual condition of depravity in relation to God there is a wide difference of opinion. Some fine Christians have revolted against the supposed teaching of what is called total depravity. Total depravity does not mean, nor can the scripture be stretched to make it mean, that all men are without any shred of morality or ethics, but are totally and completely and fully vile. Total depravity does mean that with reference to spiritual matters in connection with man's relation to God, he is totally void of, and without, life and is unable to make a choice in favor of God apart from divine grace. It does not mean that all sinners are *ipso facto* murderers overtly; nor that they are adulterers overtly. It does mean that their minds are clouded and darkened by sin and that they stand condemned in relation to our holy God. Whatever degree of morality or ethics a sinner may have springs from the common grace of God for the benefit of mankind generally.

In conjunction with the alienation of man from God (and this doctrine is an ultimate and final one that is not subject to change. It is in the order of things in the history of man until the end of the world and, so long as men are born into this world which also lies under the curse, an effect of sin) Christian theology cannot overlook the consequences of that alienation. For the individual the immediate consequence of sin is separation from God, ending in an eternal separation at the final judgment. This separation is not simply that the sinner is not permitted to come into God's presence, awful as that thought is to the regenerate heart. It also means that there is a positive and definite punishment meted out to the sinner who refuses the grace of God. This punishment is hell, a place which is of eternal duration when thinking of time, where suffering and sorrow and pain reigns supreme. The scriptures give us a partial picture and prefiguration of this awful place which description in itself makes the thought of it horrible to the Christian conscience and heart. It is here that the average non-Christian and even the Christian pauses to reconsider his theology. The idea of a literal hell and multitudes living in that condition forever is revolting. It is revolting to the non-Christian mind for the truth of hell means the condemnation of the individual and the assurance that he will spend eternity there and in that condition. It is thus to the advantage of the non-Christian to deny hell and create for himself a God who would not permit the existence of such a place. All of the fantastic imaginings of the natural man's distorted mind will not, however, alter the real existence of a literal hell which is mentioned and majored on by Jesus Himself. Man's mind cannot change truth nor destroy the witness of God's revelation.

Hell is revolting to the Christian mind for no Christian can delight in the spectre of people suffering eternally. This revolt is not against the doctrine as such, nor is it against the holy God whose creation it is. The Christian realizes that those who go to hell are there because they deserve to be there, and that the holiness and the righteousness of Almighty God is vindicated. The revolt in the Christian mind lies in the thought that men have to go there at all, recognizing that God has made it possible for men to be redeemed and to escape hell. It is precisely this aspect of hell with reference to the Christian mind that has stimulated missionary enterprise. American foreign missions rising out of the Haystack Prayer Meeting in Massachusetts was based largely upon the belief that men without Christ are doomed to an eternal hell which was so revolting to Christian conscience that these men had to go in order that the heathen might have an opportunity to come under the hearing of the gospel with the possibility of salvation. There is no satisfaction to be derived from the thought that men go to hell so far as the Christian is concerned, except as that satisfaction is known in relation to the unutterable holiness of Almighty God.

For the true Christian there can be no pious cant about hell. It is a present reality and an awful possibility for those who die without Christ. Here we must pause to note that hell in all of its awfulness has been too strong for many Christians, who falsely add a paragraph to their theology for which there is no substance in the word of God. They like to believe that only those who reject Jesus Christ will go to hell. This opens the door to possible salvation for the heathen who has never heard of the Lord Jesus, and incidentally provides an escape for the Christian who does not wish to be held responsible for his failure to take that gospel to the heathen. The conflict over the status of the heathen raged for years as did the problem of second probation. It was decided frequently in favor of the natural man's wishes and contrary to the Word of God. We cannot be equivocal about the condition of the heathen when we are dealing with a theology that is founded on a revelation that is final. The period of probation for man consists in that period during which he lives in the physical body. Beyond this life there is no probation and no possibility of a second chance. There is no foundation in Scripture for such a doctrine and the weak-kneed, watered down Christianity that often advances this idea is not the vital, dynamic, realistic Christianity of the Bible. Further, a final theology that is final does not provide for salvation for men who have never heard of Jesus Christ. The heathen who die in their sins without having heard are lost and lost forever. Hell becomes their portion as well as for those who have heard and who have rejected. Differences in punishment exist, but hell is the portion nonetheless. Concerning that argument often used to the effect that those who have not heard through the agency of man have been granted a special revelation from God, we shall offer a refutation later.

The thought of hell is sobering and no Christian can take a vicious delight in the idea. It is not expressed in these pages with such a thought in mind. Hell has got to be linked always with the obligation and the responsibility of the Christian to do something about it so that men will have an opportunity to hear of Christ before the time of their probation is over. As we shall have occasion to state again, hell becomes a powerful force which constrains us to labor in the Father's business; to do something lest I bear a measure of responsibility for those who die because of my personal failure in response to God's demands and commands.

Man's lostness with the assurance of judgment and hell is organically related to redemption. It is the certainty that man is lost, and it is future adjudgment which makes redemption necessary from man's point of view. It is either redemption or it is judgment. Judgment as used here implies the doctrine of future accountability that makes morality and ethics reasonable. Otherwise they become mere expedients, and such an expediency which grounds ethics and morality on universals apart from God and judgment is untrue and unrealistic. Indeed, redemption arises out of the need for it. If there is no violation, there is no need for redemption; unless there is sin, redemption becomes ridiculous, and the revelation of God is a bizarre and untrue document.

The undeniable existence of sin, to which even the moderns are returning, albeit not always all the way, makes the Incarnation intelligible. We are not here worried about the mystery of why God acts as He does. His actions are grounded on His attributes which cannot be violated, else He would not remain God. Thus the problem of why God should reclaim lost men is not one we can answer. Biblically we are told that God so loved the world, and yet there is here the imponderable mystery why He should continue to love those who are in a state of rebellion against Him and who have nothing in themselves to commend them to God or to His saving grace. We do not need to know the full answer here, and even without the full answer the revealed truth remains that God did choose to do something in regard to the lost creation. Redemption is a part of the divine plan.

At the heart of redemption stands the Incarnation. Here we see in time and in human history the Word becoming flesh and dwelling among us. It is an unthinkable act of divine revelation that enters into our lives in a given moment of history. It is incomprehensible for mortal mind, but deep as is its mystery, it has saving value for man. God revealed Himself in the person of His only begotten Son, and in this revelation of Himself it is plain that empirical man and the empirical world are realities of infinite worth to God. They are of such concern to Him that He surrenders Himself in Christ to the shame and suffering and death of the cross. The Incarnation finds its deepest meaning in the cross of Calvary, which, while it is an act of divine revelation, is an act of divine judgment on sin. God reveals His loving heart at the cross and also His unchanging hatred of sin. It is also at the cross that man shows his blindness to God's revelation because the natural man tries to escape from the knowledge that divine grace in Christ means divine judgment on man.

The significance of the Incarnation is lost on those who cannot accept the true deity of Christ. It is possible to deny Christ's deity only when the Word of God itself is disregarded. This deity of Jesus is not to be thought of in terms of likeness or similarity, nor can the teaching of the Bible be construed to mean that Jesus Christ is simply the manifestation in human form of the unitary God, the modal monarchian conception which was current early in the history of the Church. The Bible states that God became flesh and dwelt among us. Thus Jesus is Himself God, the second person of the Trinity in whom there is a distinct personality apart from the Father and from the Holy Spirit, yet of one essence with them. One cannot speak euphemistically that God did not need to become flesh truly in order to provide salvation, and that the idea that Jesus is God in the flesh is unnecessary. A Biblical theology for missions is derived from the absolute foundation on which we build our whole philosophy of missions. And whether it is to our liking or not, the doctrine does not change. Neither is it of consequence whether man thinks that God ought not to have done it that way. Just as it is essential for a missionary theology to be certain about the sinfulness and lostness of man, so it is imperative that the Christian mission be certain that Jesus is God.

The virgin birth of Christ requires a word, although it appears to many that the central truth about the birth of Jesus lies in the truth that God became flesh (one person in two natures), rather than in the manner by which He became flesh. Nobody who accepts the Bible as the foundation that is final can repudiate the virgin birth. We do not need to argue here whether the virgin birth was a necessary means for the entrance of Jesus into the world of humanity. That settles no question and is purely a philosophical problem for unbelievers to argue. To be sure the virgin birth presents a miracle and can be discussed and argued under that category or it may be questioned as it was by the Roman Catholic Church as to how Jesus could be sinless when born of a woman who was sinful herself. The Roman Church resolved the issue by attributing to Mary an innate sinlessness of which the Bible makes no mention. The Bible, on the other hand, and in the face of such arguments, is realistic. It simply states that Jesus was born of a virgin who had not known a man. We either accept it or reject it, and what we do with it is a good index of our attitude toward the Word of God. It is most often an excellent test by which to discover whether a man is in agreement or disagreement with the revelation.

Thus far we have mankind lost and undone, alienated from God, Whose existence and personality we see taken for granted in the Word. God reveals Himself in the person of Jesus Christ. The Incarnation is an essential part of the structure of reality as is the Sonship and Godhead relation of Jesus, the Trinity, and the fall. In this essential structure is included the redeemership of Jesus. To proclaim His Incarnation is insufficient. He came for a purpose, an object that has eternal validity and which is rooted and grounded in the nature of the Godhead. In the redeemership of Jesus there are three important elements which fit into the missionary theology that is final. These include justification by faith, reconciliation, and atonement.

The atonement in its primary reference has to do with God Himself. Its purpose was to render satisfaction to the holy God whose righteousness had to be vindicated before the sinner could come back to his God. It meant that the sinner could be reconciled to God by the payment of the penalty for sin as found in the death of Christ as a substitute for the sinner. Christ's death is not that of a martyr, nor is it a heroic death, nor is it death as an example to man. It is a Messianic act; an act of satisfaction in which the righteousness of God is vindicated. The penalty for sin is paid and a basis is established by which fallen man can return to God. Paul speaks of God as being just and the justifier. Justice in accordance with the nature of God demanded that the payment for sin be met, and Christ, in meeting the penalty at the same time, made it possible for God to justify those who could never justify themselves. This doctrine is expressive of that deep and abiding truth that God alone is the One who can restore the broken relation with man. His is the divine initiative which no one else can contribute, for man himself is unable to make good his rebellion. Consistent with the self-disclosing nature of the revelation, we have here the self-sacrifice without which there could be no possible restoration of fellowship between God and man. It is the basis on which such a restoration becomes any kind of a hope.

The extent of the atonement has been a problem to many, and especially to those interested in missions. For the missionary-minded, this problem connects itself with the idea that if the atonement in extent is limited, Christ dying solely for the elect, then the heathen will be saved if elected, and lost if not elected, regardless of all other considerations and factors. This is not true, however, since God not only ordains ends but the means by which the ends are accomplished. The preaching of the gospel is the means by which men come to a saving knowledge of Christ. In spite of this perfectly good answer to some who hold to a limited atonement, it appears plain that from the view of Biblical theology the Bible teaches that Christ died for all man potentially. I Timothy 2:4, "Who will have all men to be saved, and to come unto the knowledge of the truth," and I John 2:2, "And he is a propitiation for our sins: and not for our's only, but also for the sins of the whole world," are passages very difficult to combat. But in this aspect of the atonement, one cannot find in either view sufficient evidence which will radically alter the philosophy of missions we are here developing. The responsibility and obligation of the Christian Church in either case, as we shall see later, does not hinge on, nor is it vitally affected by, this difference of view as to the extent of the atonement. The gospel must be preached, whichever view you embrace.

Reconciliation, which may have a twofold reference, is grounded in the atonement. By virtue of the atonement, that is the death penalty of the Lord Jesus, God is reconciled so far as the penalty for sin is involved. We need to be careful, nevertheless, to state that the payment for sin does not mean that all men are *ipso facto* freed from the guilt and the penalty of sin. This freedom from the penalty of sin has a further dependence on the relation of man to God subsequent to the work of Christ. Reconciliation is the bringing together of man with his God on the ground of, and the intrinsic merits of, the atonement, made prior to the reconciliation. Thus the Scriptures speak, "when we were enemies we were reconciled to God by the death of His Son." The death of His Son is the antecedent to reconciliation. Man can be reconciled to God, but only through Jesus Christ. In all of it God takes the initiative; and the solution, radical as it is to the natural mind, produces an equally radical certainty in the mind and heart of the Christian. It is that radical certainty which only the regenerate heart can know that "neither death nor life, nor angels, nor principalities, nor powers, nor things present, nor things to come, nor height, nor depth, nor any other creature, shall be able to separate us from the love of God, which is in Christ Jesus our Lord."

The act which brings man and God together is justification which is by faith. It is purely an objective act wherein God imputes the righteousness of His Son to sinful man who acknowledges his sin and recognizes that if he is to be justified at all it must be by God on a basis that is purely gratuitous. Justification by faith be-

longs to the core of our faith since it again stresses what we have
been previously insisting upon—namely that God is the One who
initiates and carries out this redemption. The impossible becomes the
possible and in the realm of reality is accomplished by the sovereign
creative act of salvation in Jesus Christ. Immediately we are conscious that man is not a child of God naturally and normally by
birth in this world. To be a child of God is a gift of grace and
not a birthright. Jesus Himself always stressed that for men to
become children of God it was necessary that their sins be forgiven,
and Jesus constantly reiterated His authority to forgive sins, which
was His important function, far exceeding that of performing
miracles of healing and the like. As soon as we see that no one
is born into this world as a child of God, a vicious doctrine, so
current today, is eliminated. I refer to the fatherhood of God concept in which it is generally held that God is the Father of all
men, implicitly denying that men are evil and have been separated
from God by sin. The corollary idea of the brotherhood of man
is also shown to be unbiblical. If the word Father is used in the
sense that God is the creator of all men, then He is still Father
even to those who are outside the kingdom. But the Biblical
meaning of the Fatherhood of God symbolizes a unique relationship
that comes to those who have been born into the family of God,
and who have been justified by Him through the merits and
atoning work of Jesus Christ.

Essential to a missionary theology, and a doctrine that is unalterable, is that of the changed life. Justification is objective and
takes place outside man himself. But when a man is justified he
is also regenerated which means that he has an experimental knowledge of God's grace in his own heart. So Christian faith opens the
way to a new life of a different order. This life is not a different
one in degree from the old life, but it is different in kind. It
is a life-giving death and constitutes, from the human aspect, one
of the greatest mysteries and miracles perceptible to the human
heart and mind. The new life is the way of the cross; it is the
giving up of self-assertion and self-regard; it is the way of conflict
with the world, the way of martyrdom and ruin. But the way of

the cross is, in addition, the way to a life of victory, of a new creation in Christ. It is the way to a life of faith, hope, and love. This new life reflects absolute trust in God and in His acts and promises. It is the way of obedience. The new life is the touchstone of Christian faith. The Apostle James was especially conscious of this aspect of Christian doctrine. He placed postregenerative works in the spotlight and taught that any faith that was void of fruit was not a true faith. To claim that one has been justified without having a life that matched the claim was, to him, unadulterated evil. Works do not justify and there is no atoning value for sin in them, but works do reflect and testify to the actuality of justification in the human heart.

An experimental knowledge of salvation alone can be a dangerous thing, for it includes emotional aspects. We ought never judge our state of heart by our feelings since feelings are subject to change. Feelings and emotions can never be an adequate test of salvation. The final test ever is the Word of God by which feelings and emotions are tested for their validity. So if a man discovers that his experience is in accordance with the revelation he has no need to fear. If, however, his experience cannot stand the test of scripture he had better be sure that his salvation is founded more securely than on the experience he had. So as we look at it from the opposite side we can say that if a man, instead of taking heed to the subjective part of salvation, places his entire faith in a purely objective salvation without a co-operative subjective experience, he is likely to become involved in a difficulty. The objective act of justification without the changed life is an impossibility. In short, justification by faith is ever accompanied by a transforming subjective experience in which the outcome is a changed life. As an apple tree brings forth apples so will the new-born person bring forth fruits of righteousness, the normal and natural expectation of a transfigured life. This has been repeatedly demonstrated in real missionary work, and the glory of one's labor finds its fairest flower in the lives of pagans which have been transformed by the gospel so as to leave no doubt in any mind that the grace of God has been operating. Especially is this true in those lands where there is the greatest spiritual darkness and where the change from darkness to light appears far greater outwardly.

If Jesus is the only way and if coming to Him involves a personal experience of regeneration, then every missionary is a proselyter instinctively. This view of the missionary as one who proselytes is not always popular. The Moderns rather think that this represents an invasion of the sacredness of personality. They feel that any effort to alter the views of others religiously is in violation of inviolable right. Too often the opposition is eager to alter the views of the heathen in every other conceivable way. Why they should stop here is an unanswerable question. And on what grounds it is to be felt that religiously man has an inviolable nature or personality, when all other portions of life are treated relatively is an enigma. Their own arguments in favor of relativity should answer this question. For unless the sacredness of personality is grounded in an immutable law (which it is not) then it, too, is logically subject to change and invasion. However noble may be the wish to respect other religious outlooks of people, there is no substance to the argument that we ought not proselyte. Needless to say, if Christianity were to lose this characteristic, it would be shorn of its vitality and power. The presupposition of the gospel is the necessity for the conversion of everyone, including the finest and the best (naturally speaking) among men. So God does not choose to respect personality in the way that detractors of our proselyting think it desirable so that He may redeem personality instead.

We have been dealing with the work of Christ but have not mentioned the resurrection. A final missionary theology which stops at the tomb of Christ is never a dynamic faith. To speak of the atoning merit of Christ's death is required, but a Christ still subject to death is not a redeemer. "Black Friday" would be blacker still if it were not for Easter morning. In His bodily resurrection, we have a witness of His triumph over the forces of evil and of death. It signifies the truth that full atonement has been made and gives final proof to the effectiveness and completeness of His mediatorial work. A cross without a resurrection is a contradiction.

It is self-evident that because He lives we shall live also. This bodily resurrection is proclaimed boldly and dogmatically in the revelation. Once again we pause to note that the Bible is intensely real in its presentation of this truth. There is no argument involving problems whether His body was stolen, whether He had not actually died, or whether His post-calvary appearances were hallucinations. All of the Biblical truth of the resurrection can be compressed in a few words. "He is not here. He is risen." For any mind that will approach the revelation properly there is no difficulty. The natural mind ought also to find here enough external evidence which, when judged as all other evidence is judged, will satisfy the most demanding skeptic. As in the case of the Incarnation, the sinfulness of man, and the redemption in Christ, the resurrection is a final truth of the Word and necessary to our missionary theology. If the missionary cannot honestly preach Christ risen he cannot honestly preach Christ crucified in its Biblical context either. They go hand in hand.

So far, the theology we have advanced is comprised in what we speak of as the gospel. As that term is defined in Paul's Epistle to the Corinthian Church it seems, on the surface, to be limited to the death, burial and resurrection of the Lord Jesus. Actually the gospel, to be the gospel is not so sharply delimited. It has more to it than that. Understood and implied in the gospel is the sinfulness and lost condition of mankind. Upon this basis the gospel is able to answer the need of the human heart. If there were no need, the gospel would be superfluous. Another implied and understood part of the gospel is the nature of the person and work of Christ Jesus. It is of utmost importance that we know something about this Jesus Christ who died, was buried, and rose again the third day. We must know Him as the living God, able to save, which is the good news of the gospel as revealed through His death, burial, and resurrection. Now any gospel which does not include what we have here stated would hardly be an adequate gospel. It certainly would not be the gospel of revelation. Any gospel which is preached that does not have for its content these essential doctrines of the faith, is not the revelational gospel. It is customary for some missionaries to go to the heathen with a nebulous theory of the gospel and under the guise of preaching the gospel do everything except that for which they purportedly come. To be the gospel there must be content and message, and only by the content and message will it be recognized as the gospel. We ought not to think of the gospel as being a doctrine, but as representing a group of doctrines which, when brought together, comprise the gospel. As never before, the Church of Christ must be crystal clear in its notion of what the gospel is. That notion, to be clear, must be derived from the revelation, the basis on which we can construct a final theology.

High-minded people with sincerity of intention often mistake their personal notion of what the gospel is as being the Biblical view of the gospel. Current missionary operations in large areas of the world have been subverted because of this. One does not wish to impugn those who leave country and home for a foreign shore, much less accuse them of being hypocritical, yet the observation must be made that missionary work based upon other than the revelational gospel is hypocritical and unethical if not downright dishonest. To claim to be a messenger with a message, when the essence of the message has been altered to suit personal inclinations and points of view, is a highly questionable procedure. To speak of the gospel when the advocate does not mean by that what the word has always meant is surely less than honest. No one can question the right and privilege of an individual to go any place to serve mankind, but one can question such an individual's right to mis-state and misapply, or even use the term gospel when that is not what he means. It is detrimental to true missions and unfair to real Christianity for men to assume the garb and religion of the Christian when something else is to be propagated.

Strenuous objections must be raised against the misapplication of the gospel in that tragic phrase "social gospel" which covers a pure paganism. Anything that is truly the gospel will normally have social implications. Every missionary realizes this. Medical missions, educational missions, agricultural, and other allied forms of endeavor take cognizance of this undeniable fact. All true missionaries are interested in the social application of the gospel, as well as the political, and economic implications of the same gospel. It is wrong to qualify the gospel by the addition of an adjective whether it is the word "social," or "economic gospel," or "political gospel". In practice the social gospel has covered a pagan philanthropy which is well intentioned in its desire to raise the cultural level of various peoples. But to confuse that with the gospel of Jesus Christ and to assume that there is a vital relation to the Word of God in this endeavor is the worst form of chicanery. Truthfully the social gospel is "another gospel" and as such falls under the awful anathema of God's curse as expressed by the Apostle Paul. However well intentioned this social gospel effort may be, it still falls under God's curse just as the good intentioned sinner and the highly intellectual unbeliever fall under the same curse. No one will despise the efforts of those who wish to help the people socially providing that desire is properly linked with the primary goal of missions and the preaching of the gospel which is the redemption of sinners from the guilt, penalty, and power of sin.

Sometimes true Christians fall into a pit unconsciously, too. There is always the danger that the true gospel will be subverted by other things which in themselves may be important but not primary. Any medical man can easily cease to be a missionary and quickly become only a medical doctor. Any teacher can quickly and easily cease to be a missionary and become just a teacher. Any missionary administrator can easily cease to be a missionary and operate solely as an administrator. Whatever the particular line of endeavor, whether it be medical, educational, linguistic, or otherwise, it must be geared to the primary function of the missionary, which is the proclamation of the good news that Jesus saves. Truly the vastness of the missionary task demands that we have differences in secondary functions relative to efficiency and the like in carrying out the task. Someone must administer, someone teach, someone do medical work, someone keep watch at the home base. The capacity is immaterial providing the individual is heart and soul immersed in the accomplishment of the primary task, and also striving himself to have a part in that primary task wherever possible. Thus the teacher who finds no opportunity to win souls is misdirected, and the physician who treats the body without finding opportunity to treat the worse malady of sin is also misdirected. The aim of missions is the redemption of men and any failure along this line means that a renewed sense of direction is required else we too shall be guilty of abusing the gospel as revealed by God.

As never before there is a need for a return to the gospel of revelation and for a heightened concept of that gospel in the plan of God. As the cross was central in the life and teachings of Jesus, just so must the gospel, which is the preaching of that cross in its total fullness, be central in our theology, our thinking, our planning, and our execution of the missionary enterprise. For it is the gospel as we find it in revelation which is the power of God unto salvation, and only this particular gospel has any saving power. The end of the gospel is always the return of lost and erring man to the fold from which he has strayed. Faith is the means of receiving what the gospel has to offer, but the object of faith is Jesus Christ. This much is clear, that Christianity from beginning to end is Christocentric. Always it is God who takes the initiative, in providing redemption, in His self-disclosure through the eye of faith in reconciliation, and as the object of faith itself. So the gospel is Christ the originator, Christ the ground on which the reconciliation rests, and Christ the object of faith. The gospel is clear in its view that we are to have faith IN Christ. We do not regard Jesus as the superb example of what faith is like, nor do we require a faith like Jesus had. Either of these modern innovations remove Christ as the object of faith and bring ruin to the gospel of grace. It is faith IN Christ that is central in the gospel for men to be saved. It is that same faith IN Christ which is so important as we live after we are saved.

Regardless of the high conception we may have of the gospel of Christ, a missionary theology that is final and sufficient ought not stop at that point. It must go on and deal with other pertinent dogmas, the lack of which, or the failure to recognize them, does immeasurable harm to a Christian philosophy of missions. Among the dogmas which must be accorded treatment are the following: the nature and function of the Church, the eschatological picture with reference to missions, the work of the Holy Spirit in missions, and the part and place of the individual Christian to the whole enterprise. Before we approach these issues, there are certain negatives of a missionary theology that fit into our pattern better at this point. We have been stating the positive missionary theology that is final, the acceptance of which automatically rules out other assumptions that are contradictory to this theology. A few major assumptions or problems which press for an answer we will now touch on, in the light of developments so far.

Chapter 4

A FINAL THEOLOGY—THE INADEQUACY OF THE NON-CHRISTIAN RELIGIONS

U P TO THIS point in the philosophy of the Christian mission the treatment has been limited to the Christian faith. The soteriological aspect of the Christian faith has been developed in regard to the condition of man and the altering of that condition in the redemption provided for man from above—not by man but by God who discloses Himself in His revelation. No Christian philosophy of missions can be written that limits itself to this. It is not because the Christian philosophy of missions is inadequate or that it does not meet the need of men. Rather, an extension of the treatment to include the non-Christian religions is required for a reason of utmost significance. That reason is that Christianity meets every other religion face to face, and in the meeting, the problem of the non-Christian faith relative to the Christian revelation always arises.

Christianity does not live in a vacuum. In its essence it has a quality which demands of it that it come into contact with all other religions in a fight to the death. Christianity must triumph or perish. Since we have already concluded that Christianity must triumph because it is a supernatural faith rooted and grounded in the absolute as disclosed in the person of Almighty God, it follows that in the ultimate triumph of the Christian faith, all other religions must succumb. The implications of this ideology must be made crystal clear to every true believer. To be clear, it involves a study of the relation of the non-Christian religions to Christianity, and it also strikes at the heart of one of our greatest problems today—that of demonstrating the relevancy of our faith to the actual world in which we live, a world that is firmly bound in the grip and tentacles of non-Christian systems of thought and life.

Just as soon as we bring in other religions for consideration we are tied up to a study of comparative religions. And it is here that present day departures from the faith have wrought such destruction in the Christian mind. The study of comparative religion has been exploited by those who do not see in Christianity anything uniquely different from other religions. Their basic assumption has been that all religions are more or less on the same level, the differences between competing religions being one of degree rather than kind. Each religion is treated as a variant springing from the same stem. Each is assumed to be similar or the same in its essence. No doubt the best expression of this theory comes from Professor Hocking of Harvard. He holds that at the core of all creeds and expressions of religious faith there is a nucleus of religious truth. In spite of all human additions, superstitions, and innovations, "there is this germ, the inalienable religious intuition of the human soul. The God of this intuition is the true God: to this extent universal religion has not to be established, it exists." Assuming this to be true it is obvious that there is little if any fundamental difference between religions, including the Christian faith. This view is the extreme view which represents naturalism carried to its logical end.

The view of men like Hocking has serious consequences for a philosophy of missions. Apart from any consideration as to whether this view is scriptural (which it is definitely not) there are certain conclusions which stand out when considering foreign missionary work. Plainly, if all religions are generically the same, it follows that all of them disclose the same God, and despite their differences in approach to that God it is possible in all of them to reach God and have fellowship with Him, although along variant lines and under different conditions. The nerve of missions is automatically cut and the imperative is gone for spending precious lives, time, and money to do what other vehicles are already doing, although somewhat less perfectly. If, for example, Hinduism is a satisfactory religious vehicle which leads to God, there is little reason for Christianity to step in and demand a radical departure from Hinduism to Christianity, a departure which brings with it a break, sharp and distinct, from all previous relationships. This is recognized by the holders of this view who believe that we ought to combine the most worthy elements in all religions and together, hand in hand, walk down the pathway to eternal glory, there being one pathway which all men tread toward the Kingdom of God. Hocking himself raises the question whether there is any justification for Christian missions to continue in such a case. Surely if his premise is correct, anyone can enthusiastically agree that missions are superfluous and ought to be discontinued since thely serve no purpose that can be justified sufficiently in the light of the total cost.

The people who hold to the concept we have just mentioned constitute a small but influential group. Some of them, including Hocking, are widely recognized for their scholarship and the high positions they hold in the counsels of the various church groups. The very fact that Professor Hocking was appointed the chairman, and in his name rendered the report for the Laymen's Committee is proof of his importance. That the report shocked many is quite another matter, for the only people who were shocked were those who assumed that all was well with the missionary enterprise and that it had been functioning on bases held as absolute over a long period of time. The advocates of Hocking's view are not always as outspoken as the Professor, and the damage they do is even greater because it is more subtle and is propagated in a manner less likely to be detected. The importance of the Hocking report has supreme value to the true Christian for it unveils and admits that all religions are more or less equal, and eliminates the generic uniqueness of the Christian faith. This conclusion is so valuable for it makes a re-examination of our premises necessary, and once more forces missionary agencies to justify the sending of men and women to the non-Christian regions of the world. We now MUST know whether the non-Christian religions are adequately too, or whether they are totally inadequate as our early missionary endeavors assumed.

In addition to those who see little or no difference between religions, the Christian included, there are many others who take a middle road in connection with comparative religions. They state that Christianity has in it a peculiar quality which distinguishes it from, or differentiates it from other religions. But they also find that these other religions have in them strands of good. These strands of good they find to be similar to strands of truth found in the Christian faith. Over against this middle of the road group stands the third group which is on the other side of the issue from the Hocking group. The position of the third group has been called extreme as has the position of the Hocking group. It has for its conclusion the belief that the non-Christian religions are evil and that God has not revealed Himself to or through the ideal representatives of these religions even to a limited degree.

The disagreements as to the relationship of the non-Christian faiths to Christianity in the last two great world missionary gatherings was not hidden from general view. In the Jerusalem Conference of 1928, Professor Heim of Germany called attention to the differences and laid bare the results of accepting a view similar to the one Hocking was to announce a few years later. Professor Heim stated that if no distinction was made between Christianity and the non-Christian faiths a serious question had to be faced. That question was whether mission work has not reached its end, and in place thereof something else needed to be substituted. He felt that missionary work had reached a crossroads in its forward progress. One road was to state that all religions are simply expressions of the same mystic feelings, with the choice of religion an immaterial matter. The fruit of this belief, of course, was the end of missions as such. The second road was a rapid increase in mission work, sending the best men with the message, underlying this work, there being the belief that there is something false in the non-Christian religions. At this conference there were many middle-of-the-roaders who tried to please the radicals representing the two most divergent views. Their solution was to evolve a synthesis by making Christianity a faith which had gone along the same road that the others were traveling, but which had gone further than the others. In other words, in the evolution of religion, Christianity stood just a bit higher in the ascending scale. This solution did not really appeal to the intelligent minds present, for none of them could see that to bring men a little further along the way they were already traveling was worth the effort in manpower, suffering, and money. Those who rejected the attempted synthesis pointed out that before one could suppose a synthesis possible one had to assume that all religions were on the same road. Those who believe in the Biblical revelation were not prone to admit that Christianity walks the same road with the non-Christian faiths. In fact they were violently to oppose any such contention then, and now, believing that Christianity walks alone while all other religions are on a different road.

At the Madras Conference in 1938 the problem arose again. The voice of Kraemer was heard in defense of the view that non-Christian religions are totally inadequate. He stated that the confusion arose because there was no standard of reference by which to judge the religions. This was true for those who let relativity hold the day against those who favored an absolutist view. Kraemer himself militated against the relativist view and called for a return to a revelationally centered standard of reference in which the uniqueness of Christianity is admitted. He held that the human mind and heart are so constituted that they must have a stable point of reference and that they cannot exist without a belief in indestructible truth and certitude. It was W. Horton[1] who, in conflict with Kraemer's view, produced the ultimate in his philosophy of the adequacy of the non-Christian religions:

> I met a Buddhist priest whom to this day I persist in regarding as my brother in Christ . . . If I belong in any sense to the body of Christ, then he does, too. It would be blasphemy against the Holy Spirit, the Wind of

[1] Horton, *The Author of the Faith,* (New York: International Missionary Council, 1939) p. 138.

God that bloweth where it listeth, for me to deny my
Buddhist brother his place in that Body. When I ventured to say as much to a group of Christians in Kobe
the next day, I was sternly reminded that "there is none
other Name under heaven given among men whereby
we must be saved"; but I thought to myself that I would
rather have the Spirit without the Name, than the Name
without the Spirit.

On this quotation only one comment is necessary. If Horton's
basic assumption is correct then his conclusion with reference to the
Buddhist priest is also correct. Fortunately for the cause of missions, Horton is not correct and he represents, numerically, the
smallest school of thought, although elements of this view have
filtered into the thinking of many who try to synthesize the views
of Horton with the views of the Bible.

Other views were presented at Madras. Some were in agreement
with Horton and Hocking and some in agreement with Kraemer. Many were not sure what they believed. The fact that this
conference included in its numbers those who were supposed to be
the leading representatives actively engaged in the pressing of the
missionary claims of the Bible on the world was somewhat startling.
Normally one would have expected from the leadership a unanimity of opinion on the question of the adequacy or inadequacy of the
non-Christian religions. After all, the answer to this primary question
determines the fate of the missionary enterprise. Dr. A. G. Hogg[2]
in expressing disagreement with those who think the non-Christian
religions inadequate had this to say:

> For my own part I am persuaded that it is radically
> wrong for the missionary to approach men of other
> faiths under a conviction—no matter how sincerely
> humble that conviction may be—that he and his fellow-
> believers are witnesses to a Divine revelation, while
> other religions are exclusively the product of a human
> "religious consciousness."

[2] Hogg, *Op.Cit.*, p. 97.

So the situation stands in its recent historical perspective. This much is clear. There are widely differing viewpoints on the subject. The differences arise because the premises on which the conclusions are based do not agree. Unless there is some unanimity on the original premise there can be no final agreement in conclusion on the subject of the adequacy or inadequacy of the non-Christian religions. Each age must decide for itself whether the premises on which previous ages have built are acceptable to the present age. Each generation faces anew the decision of accepting the philosophy on which their predecessors operated or of finding a more adequate philosophy for themselves in connection with the missionary enterprise. Always we need to remember, however, that there are people who accept conclusions that are in conflict with the basic ideology they claim to hold. They do not happen to know it. Then there are always those who accept both an ideology and the conclusions of someone else for varying reasons best known to each individual and sometimes unknown even to the individual himself who makes the decision.

Having glanced at the differences in the missionary camps, it is now time for us to clarify the Christian view of the non-Christian religions having in mind certain conclusions we have already drawn. The first conclusion we have drawn is that Christianity represents a unique religion that is absolute or final. By it all other religions and also human pretensions must be judged. It is for the true Christian the norm by which all other things in life are determined to be valid or invalid. This is as much the case for the non-Christian religions as for the prevalent philosophies of the Christian world. Christianity is final in its revelation, the Bible. This second conclusion automatically closes the Christian in to the specific revelation, an objective touchstone by which other religions must be judged. Further than this, the specific theology of the revelation has a definite and final content, and the theology of the non-Christian religions must be judged by the content and finality of the message we have. Specifically every religion must, in order to be a valid religion from a Christian point of view, harmonize with the Christian religion on the doctrines of God, man, and salvation.

Whenever Christianity meets any other religion in such a test, no harmony can be discovered. The Bible itself presupposes the fact that no other religion is adequate and stamps them all as foreign to the true revelation and thus man-made substitutes no matter how elevated the ethics nor how high the concept of the divine being behind the religion.

In the main, the living religions of the world do have similarities. It is these similarities which bring some to conclude that there is a common core to all religion whether Christian or non-Christian. The doctrine of man in non-Christian religions is one dogma in which most religions have a somewhat common meeting ground. Superficially these religions seem to have something in common with Christianity here too. The superficial similarity is the fact that most religions recognize either implicitly or explicitly that there is something wrong with man. They are conscious that there is such a thing as sin. But to recognize that man is sick and ailing does not constitute an organic likeness between religions. The test of likeness comes when the decision is made as to what the disease actually is. In the physical world, sickness can readily be detected in men outwardly but that is far removed from actually knowing what the disease is. Then again two men can have their organic illnesses diagnosed as being the same when in reality they are utterly different. Resemblance is one thing, actuality another. The use of the word sin does result in a resemblance. But a closer inspection of the meaning of the word as it is used in both Christian and non-Christian religions reveals that the word does not mean the same thing at all. Several examples will demonstrate this.

In Hinduism there is no real sin. Philosophic ignorance or the violation of caste rules are defects. The resulting penalty is successive reincarnation until the law of Karma (a cosmic power of justice which is purely impersonal) has been satisfied. There is no personal God against whom transgression is committed, no righteous being whose holiness is violated. In Buddhism, sin is not against a divine Being. It consists in selfishness, the cure for which is the suppression of desire. In Jainism, the other religion which sprang out of Hinduism, as did Buddhism, the same thing is true. Here sin is explained as being located primarily in the body, and by asceticism one can get rid of this sin. In no one of these three religions does sin, when defined, even closely approximate the Christian view.

Confucianism is not thought of as being truly a religion, yet it is claimed by millions of people in China today. Its view of sin is as far removed from the Biblical view as it can be. Here the assumption is that human nature has a fundamental divine goodness. Man is not born evil but good. Thus if man is born good, sin ceases to have significance. Confucius was vague about deity, and he proclaimed no doctrine in which any conception of sin was related to deity in the form of transgression against that deity. So any resemblance to the Christian doctrine of sin did not exist.

Shintoism, too, has a doctrine of sin far removed from the Biblical viewpoint. Here sin or defilement or disease or guilt are contagious evils. They are physically transmissable and physically removable. Sin with them is essentially a matter of the defilement of the flesh and has nothing to do with the spirit of man or with the problem of transgression against a personal God. In fact, Shintoism does not have a unitary Being in the scriptural sense but it is a hopeless polytheism which is being shattered into many segments right now.

Anthropologically speaking, the religions just mentioned are respectable when measured against animism. In animism there is the belief that numerous evil spirits exist who are bent on the destruction of the individual. These spirits ruin crops, bring sickness, cause floods, and commit a thousand other evil tricks. However, I do not believe that many of the most hopeful protagonists of the adequacy of the non-Christian religions would hold a brief for this form of religion. There is no sense of sin as transgression against a personal God. There are only good and evil spirits who must be propitiated by sacrifices.

This much is clear from what we have said concerning sin in some of these religions, and which will be clear to anyone wishing to investigate all the others: the sin of the non-Christian religions is not the same as sin in Christianity. The name may be the same but the meaning is not the same.

When the relation of man in connection with sin is studied, it is not just a question whether the Christian view of sin is more advanced that the others, or whether it implies that Christianity is a bit ahead on the same road. The question which arises is whether, in defining sin, Christianity and the non-Christian religions can be thought of as being on the same road. Unequivocally the revelation-ist must insist that the concept of sin is not a difference in degree, but a difference in kind and that there is no sameness of Christianity with other religions. There is a common sense of something lacking in these other religions, but there is also a real difference as to what it actually is that is lacking. The non-Christian religions' diagnosis that something is wrong is correct. But what it is they do not actually know. Only Christianity has the answer here. Thus an external similarity becomes a striking dis-similarity. Sin, out of its context in other religions, may have the sound of the Christian doctrine of sin, but in its own context no one can be fooled except those who refuse to measure sin in other religions by the standard of reference we have in the Christian faith. By this standard no one can claim that they are even remotely the same.

A deeper question than the definition of sin faces us in the non-Christian religions. The concept of God in these religions is tied up with the doctrine of man. One has good reason to suspect that the doctrine of sin in relation to man more often than not depends on the nature and being of the deity worshipped. If the god of the religion is a perversion, then it follows that the doctrine of sin will also be a perversion. However we have here dealt with the doctrine of sin in some of the religions before dealing with their ideas of God to show that even apart from their views of God, their views of sin are wrong.

Already we have stated that the Christian position relative to God is that He discloses Himself, and has done so in His revelation, the Bible. We know that the non-Christian religions profess to have "revelations" from God also. They frequently claim that the books around which their religions center are inspired and have come from "heaven." This poses a problem for the Christian since something obviously must be done about their "holy" or "sacred" books. It is easy enough for us simply to deny that they have any books which are truly from our God and let it rest there. In this modern age such a decision is open to question, especially when we have reasons for making such a denial which are valid when the basic assumption of the Christian position is accepted. We claim to have a final and complete revelation from God. It should be easy enough to measure any of the other "sacred" books against the standard of reference. If they can match up to this standard then we must admit there are other revelations equal to, or at least comparable to, ours. If they do not meet the standards set up in our revelation then it becomes evident that the other books are not really revelations from God despite any claims to be such.

In the long run it must be conceded that any religion finds its true meaning in the God at the center of the religion. The essence of all religion, in fact, turns on the question of the Being at the heart of the religion. The Christian has a self-disclosing, holy, righteous, personal God whose attributes are clearly defined in the Word. As in the case of sin we meet the same difficulty in that similar names are used for beings who are utterly different in essence. All religions do have deity in their structures, but we soon discover that what is meant by deity is not the same in any of them when judged in the light of the Christian revelation. In no case can it be concluded that any of the non-Christian faiths remotely approach the Christian faith in the conception of God. It must be reiterated again and again that the Christian knows God and Who He is simply because God has graciously disclosed Himself. It is not due to the activity of man that God is known in Christianity but simply the activity of God Himself who initiates and carries through the revealing of Himself. From this, one can rest assured that God can never reveal Himself to some other peoples in a manner or form contradictory to the Christian revelation. Thus if He reveals Himself to be a personal God in the Christian faith He cannot reveal Himself to be impersonal in another. But having revealed Himself as we believe, finally and completely, in the Christian faith, we have an objective test by which we can examine other faiths.

Hinduism's God in no way resembles the Christian God. Hinduism's supreme being is the impersonal Brahma. "It" is a philosophical absolute. It is unhampered either ethically or metaphysically. In this scheme man is an emanation of the impersonal essence. He is a temporary manifestation, and the end of physical existence is the wish to be reabsorbed into that impersonal essence. Man, so to speak, is a fragment of the supreme essence.

Jainism, which sprang out of Hinduism is equally obnoxious in its view of God. The religion began with a denial of any supreme being in the world at all. The founder, Mahavira, objected to the polytheism of Hinduism and did not wish his followers to pray to, or talk about, any deity. So here the lack of a supreme personal deity, in spite of the worship which is given to the founder flagrantly contradicts Christianity.

Buddhism is no better. A personal God is denied. Morality is thought of as apart from a divine Being. At best one can claim for original Buddhism an agnosticism, although it is not unfair to state that it was even worse than that. It was originally atheistic. In the light of the Scriptures it falls to the ground, failing to indicate that it has any common meeting ground with the Christian faith.

Confucianism exhibits the same tendency we have already noted in the other religions just mentioned. They have man-made concepts of the ultimate, different in kind from that of the Christian. It is true that Confucius did mention the supreme being once, using the personal name for that being. Confucius himself, however, tried to depersonalize the faith. Among the common people, polytheism was prevalent indeed. The forces of nature, plus mythical Chinese figures of early days constitute his concept of God. It lacks, generically, the kind of God found at the center of the Christiain faith, and constitutes a polytheism in reality if not philosophically. This, despite the claims of some that Confucius and Lao-tze are children of God as are Christians, and are in heaven.

In Shintoism there is no unifying force or being in the universe Cosmically speaking, there is no unity. They have a vague and uncertain polytheism which is based upon a series of unbelievable myths that have no logical or other coherence. Their worship comprises a polytheism that is fantastic, with no single deity worthy of worship as an ethical or even a moral ideal. It, like the others, does not fall short of the God of revelation. For to fall short means that there is a logical basis of comparison, when they are totally unlike, with nothing in common by which a true comparison can be made.

Were we to trace each of the nine living religions existent today, not including Christianity and Judaism, the same result would be as apparent in the remaining ones as it is in the ones we have traced. The so-called revelations of the other religions are not revelations at all, but poorly constructed contradictory efforts of man-made origin which bear out the contention of the Christian revelation that God can be known only when He discloses Himself, and that He has disclosed Himself ONLY in the revelation we have in Jesus Christ, objectively found in the Bible. This is special revelation, though, and does leave us the problem of deciding whether there is natural revelation, what it is, and how far it extends. This we shall discuss shortly.

So far in this treatment of non-Christian religions, we have the two points of primary reference under discussion. The one concerns man and the fact that all religions find something wrong with man. The second is that we have some concept of a force or being outside man, but in a relation to man in such a way that man wishes to get right with this force of being. Already it is perfectly apparent that Christianity and the non-Christian religions do not agree in principle on the sin question with reference to man and they do not agree on the question of deity. It still remains for us, nevertheless, to see how the non-Christian religions stand over against the Christian faith with reference to salvation. If it be true that in this area also the non-Christian religions do not meet, there is then no need to explore other areas which, although important, do not touch on basic problems. If the doctrines of salvation cannot meet the test of the Christian doctrine, remembering the truism that God does not reveal Himself in a contradictory fashion, nor are His methods in any way contradictory at any time, then we can rest our case with the assurance that the non-Christian religions are inadequate.

In Hinduism salvation may be obtained in one of three general ways. The intellectual way of knowledge, the emotional way of devotion to a particular god, or through works as prescribed in the ceremonial law. In Jainism, self-renunciation which is purely a matter of works in conformity to a principle is the basis of salvation. It must be denominated as a narrow self-saving scheme of salvation. Buddhism, too, has self-renunciation at the bottom of its soteriology. It is really the suppression of desires as against the asceticism of the body in Jainism, but it is also a man-centered scheme of salvation. Confucianism is a matter of social relationship that centers around the idea of doing good. The Silver Rule of Confucianism is a negation of the Golden Rule of the Christian faith. "Do not unto others what you would not have them do unto you." Objective critics of the Confucian faith acknowledge that its salvation is excessively self-centered and operates in a homocentric framework. In Shintoism, works of righteousness as centered in forms, ceremonies, and sacrifices make for whatever salvation the faith has to offer.

There are certain generalities which can be offered in criticism of the methods of salvation in the non-Christian religions. Negatively none of them is in agreement with the Christian revelation. None of them is based upon anything resembling the Gospel truth that "God was in Christ reconciling the world unto Himself." And nowhere are there any series of concepts like those revealed in Christianity under such terms as incarnation, atonement, reconciliation, justification, and sanctification. To be sure in isolated instances there are what seem to be resemblances outwardly but which are never more than superficial resemblances. For instance, in some religions there are stories of a virgin birth, in some there are stories of miracles, and in others there are ideas that appear outwardly like the incarnation. Most of the similarities have to do with other than the soteriological aspect of the religions. In examining any outward resemblances it must always be remembered that no single strand of a religion may be properly removed from its relation to the other strands which go to make up the religion. To speak of the doctrine of salvation in a way which isolates it from the doctrine of sin, God, and the like, is an impossibility. So we can say that while the idea of salvation in the non-Christian religions is unlike the Christian revelation, this idea cannot be divorced from the rest of the religion or examined and understood apart from the whole religion.

In further expansion of the negative argument against the doctrine of salvation in the non-Christian religions, is the obvious, and yet most important fact that none of these religions have in the pattern of salvation the Person of Jesus Christ. In no case is Christ the object of their supposed "revelations." Nowhere is He the object of saving faith, and in no religion is His sacrifice the ground on which the soteriology is built. No matter what good elements one might wishfully find in any religion; no matter how close these religions approach that of the Christian faith (which they do not); no matter how high and exalted may be their ethics, morality, and the lives of their founders—in other words, no matter what good may be introduced in favor of these religions, the absence of the central and necessary Person of Jesus Christ stamps them as false and spurious. They become man-made, homocentric inventions, naturalistic creations of human ingenuity. But they lack in each case (and more than this) God made known in the Person of His son, the Lord Jesus.

Further it must be said that the best which has been produced in any non-Christian religion is so far removed from the worst in Christianity as reflected in the people who practice the faith, as to warrant again the assertion that Christianity differs in kind rather than in degree from all other religions. Along this line it can be stated with honesty that among the non-Christian peoples there may be found men and women of complete and genuine sincerity; there are many earnest and honest seekers after the thing they call truth; there are those who try to live lives of purity as they know the meaning of that term. These instances are exceedingly rare, however, and generally conditions are quite the opposite. In either case, however, the fact of the matter does not change that in spite of anything done, thought, or said, without the Christ of the Biblical revelation, the non-Christians have no hope for salvation. So far as special revelation has anything to say, the non-Christian religions have nothing in common with Christianity and do not even answer the same questions. In the light of special revelation, all other religions are unbelief. They are attempts at self-justification, self-sanctification and self-redemption.

So far we have resolved the question satisfactorily in comparing or contrasting the non-Christian religions with the Christian revelation. No one can say that the non-Christian faiths constitute special revelation. But the question of whether there is such a thing as natural revelation arises. It also raises the question whether natural revelation, assuming there is such a concept, is sufficient for salvation. Can those who have never heard of Christ, and who cannot benefit from the revelation as we know it, be saved? And if they can be saved on what basis is their salvation granted? In other words, is there anything in the non-Christian religions which will give enough light so as to make salvation possible? Are there elements of truth contained in these religions or are there values of a saving nature?

There are many people who firmly believe that the revelation of God in Christ is the true revelation but they find it difficult to believe that there are those people who, because, they have no such revelation, are lost forever. It appears as though the justice of God is impugned if some men had no possibility of knowing God simply because they did not have the true revelation. Thus a general or natural revelation eliminates this problem and permits the heathen an opportunity even though they do not have the gospel, or if they have died without having heard of Jesus. For a proper missionary philosophy, this question and its implication ought not be overlooked. Whichever way it is answered, it will definitely alter the missionary outlook, and humanly speaking, much of what we do in missions will be determined by the view we hold with reference to general or natural revelation and its bearing on the salvation of the heathen.

Philosophically there is a fine distinction between natural or general and special revelation. If salvation is possible through natural theology, the gospel becomes only a higher or the highest development, of which natural theology is but a lower form. They are not organically different, but are different levels of the same seed, save that one is further developed than the other. The Christian faith would have to be spoken of as a fulfillment of this lower form of natural theology, and fulfillment means bringing to a state of perfection what is approximated in something lower. This is an evolving concept of the Christian faith and is abhorrent to the scriptures. This cannot be.

General revelation, to be a vehicle of salvation, must insist that God is revealed sufficiently so as to restore the broken relationship with man. This can be in general revelation through the works of God's creation (nature), or it can be through man's conscience, or it can come through the quest of man for beauty and goodness. If God has so revealed Himself in special revelation on top of this general revelation, then again it is in fulfillment of what has already begun and what has in it enough to get man back to God, making special revelation only a higher form of the same basic thing. But the essence of special revelation is the truth that God is not revealed unto salvation in general revelation and this constitutes the necessity for special revelation. Whatever there may be in general revelation, and whatever testimony it may bear as to the Divine Creator behind the universe, this much is perfectly evident: general revelation is totally insufficient as a vehicle for salvation in answer to the problem of man's broken relationship with God. There is no fulfillment which can be used in relating the non-Christian religions to Christianity; fulfillment simply is not applicable to the revelation of God in relation to the non-Christian religions.

Since general revelation is not sufficient it does not make a particle of difference whether we think it just or unjust. The creature accommodates himself to the revelation of His Creator and does not impugn Him who worketh all things after the counsel of His own will. Where it does make a difference is in the responsibility which comes to the saved of God when they know that without the revealed gospel of Christ men are lost. This side of the conclusion awaits further development in another connection, however. It is imperative that we never lose sight of the truth that general revelation so far as salvation is concerned is as inadequate as are the non-Christian religions that are supposed to reflect this revelation. The only way in which general revelation can become effective is when it is made intelligible in the light of special revelation.

Admitting that the non-Christian religions are specimens in which there are transient elements of a general revelation, and remaining firm in our conviction that they are not vehicles bringing true salvation, we must still confess that in all of these religions there are elements of truth. Whatever truth there was originally has been distorted and is out of focus so that it is no longer fully truth. This can be demonstrated in innumerable ways. Theft is wrong in certain non-Christian religions, and although this sin is centered in a different orientation relevant to the supreme Being, it still remains true that the overt act of stealing is truly wrong in many societies. This is an element of truth regardless of the religion that adheres to it. In Hinduism the immanence of the divine in the world is stressed. And the Christian believes in the immanence of God. However, the Hindu immanence is a pantheism which the Christion revelation can never accept nor allow to exist. Yet the idea of immanence, perverted as it is in Hinduism, has an element of truth in it. In Jainism the ideal of the liberation of the spirit is an aim accomplished by the subjugation of the flesh. Subjugation of the flesh is necessary and represents a truth in the Christian faith. Again the difference lies in the orientation. In Jainism this doctrine encourages self-renunciation to subjugate the flesh, but it is a means of salvation. The Christian faith encourages subjugation of the flesh but in no way makes it necessary to salvation.

Buddhism claims that selfishness is the root of evil. The Christian must agree that selfishness is evil but again the orientation of selfishness in the Buddhist pattern does not mean that the root of evil lies in transgression against a holy and just God. So again there is a real distortion of the truth that selfishness is evil. Even at that these are only strands and ought never be pulled apart from the cord which constitutes the whole. As individual strands they always look better than they actually are in the total picture. The main trouble comes when religions are broken into fragments to study specific doctrines comparatively. The true scholar soon sees that it is impossible to do it this way and preserve the integrity of the religion. The atonement of Christ apart from an understanding of the nature of God, the alienation of man and the Person of the offering is an impossibility and a travesty. So is the same thing true when done for non-Christian religions.

There are in the non-Christian religions apparent similarities to Christianity. There are apparent points of contact. There are apparent elements of truth contained within the total picture of the faiths. But on careful examination all of these similarities become dissimilarities, all of the points of contact do not prove themselves to be what they are called. All religious life, not including the Christian faith, no matter how high or how low it seems to be, lies under the condemnation and judgment of Almighty God, if for no other reason than that the best in any of them is always misdirected and thus wrong. Those who speak of "values" in non-Christian religions and who try to exalt this aspect of the picture do serious and lasting harm to Christianity, to missions, and to the non-Christians too. The value of the so-called "values" must seriously be questioned, and generally the insistence upon them comes from those who are hesitant to commit themselves to the absolute and final revelation which we have in Christ. For those who are misled they need to be reoriented in the revelational framework and in so doing lose the false sympathy that so often forces them to try to find good in pagan religions.

We ought not remain unconscious that the indictment against the inadequacy of the non-Christian religions is extremely serious. It is indeed radical and produces conclusions in other areas equally radical. One way in which the radical indictment touches modern theology is in the area of the fatherhood of God and the brotherhood of man. We cannot expose this misconception too often nor can we deny it too specifically. We must be clear in stating that the denial of the adequacy of the non-Christian religions and the denial that there are completely true elements of eternal truth in these religions does great violence to the fatherhood of God idea. We stress gain that God is the Father of all men ONLY in the limited sense that He created all things. The scriptural use of the term Father when referring to God's relation to mankind is that in which the relationship between God and man has been righted in and through the merits of Jesus Christ. In no other way and at no other time is it Biblical to speak of God as Father. God is distinctly NOT the Father of the non-Christians, as He is the Father of those who put their trust in Jesus Christ as Saviour. We are not to think of this as constituting a valid reason for a Christian to boast or to feel exclusive. It can and ought to be said by the Christian in the spirit of deepest humility, for the grace of God to the Christian is not of works lest any man should boast.

The brotherhood of man springs out of the fatherhood of God concept and it is wrong too. There can be no universal brotherhood so long as there are sinners and saints. Indeed it is difficult enough to have a real brotherhood among saints let alone extending the idea unscripturally to include all men without regard to their relation to God. Then too, real Christians need no incentive like this to hold them to brotherhood. If they truly practice what the revelation teaches they will become brothers to all men in outlook and in desire. It is to the non-Christian that brotherhood is never a reality because of sin and never can be a reality apart from the saving grace of God in Christ. True brotherhood springs out of salvation. This we ought never forget in our philosophy of missions because if we really wish for a universal brotherhood we can be assured that the only way in which it will be attained is via the universal preaching and acceptance of the gospel. Inasmuch as the gospel will never be accepted by all men everywhere, we can still rest assured that as much brotherhood as shall be attained will still come through the gospel of grace and not through any man-made ideas or ideologies.

In our treatment of the non-Christian religions we have dealt with them as religions. We have stated that they are inadequate in their conceptions and unable to lead to true salvation. This has been an abstract way of handling the problem because we are dealing with three-quarters of the world of men and each of them as an individual has worth to his Creator. Does the denial of the adequacy of the religion leave the individual without any hope? This is the important question, now, for we must have a definite and interested concern for the individual, and how we answer this will alter our basic philosophy of missions. Answer it we must, however, in order to formulate a full philosophy of missions.

Again we go to the source of our final theology and here we discover that there is absolutely nothing in the revelation which states or infers that there is any hope for those who die without having heard of Christ. Positively the Scriptures assert that there is no other name under heaven whereby men must be saved. There is the direct teaching that the body of Christ, the Church, comprises only those who have been born again through acceptance of the work and the merit of Christ. Without Christ there is absolutely no hope for men. It is an impossibility for any man to be saved without Him. But there is one weakness in this assertion which must be covered lest any escape from the dilemma be held tenable. It is one thing to state that no man can be saved without Christ. It is another thing to relate this proposition to the world of men and say that there is no hope for men unless they hear of Christ through other Christians and their efforts. Many people give lip assent to the proposition that without Christ no man can be saved. But in an effort to tear down the essential fabric of this structure they refuse to state that we can be sure that there are not supernatural revelations granted to the lost who have never had an opportunity to come under the hearing of the gospel through the world of men. Here an important divergence appears and we need an answer.

The view that a man who has never heard of Christ from other men can still be a child of God manifests itself in two forms. The one form is that in which the advocates of the position claim that a man can be hid in God when he has not yet learned Christ. At the Madras Conference of 1938 this view was expressed by Principal Hogg:

> If God be willing and able to hide "in the secret of His tabernacle" some—perhaps many—who have not yet "learned Christ", this graciousness of God toward men, like all His graciousness, is morally conceivable only because of the Name that is above every name. . . . How can one (a missionary) presume to make an evangelistic approach to a man regarding whom one ashamedly wonders whether, without Christ, he is not leading a life more "hid in God" than one's own? . . . And if, within non-Christian faiths, such fine levels of spiritual life can be reached, why should Christian effort be directed toward getting men to change their religion instead of to make progress within the religion they already profess?

Principal Hogg was not at all conscious that this view introduces a difficulty into one's theology. He stated himself that "any Christian who accepts the affirmative answer (that such a condition is possible) has on his hands the problem of discovering how to reconcile it with the scriptural conviction: 'neither is there salvation in any other'." In spite of the trouble he faced in reconciling the view that men can be "hid in God" without being "hid in Christ", Hogg gave as his principal reason his own personal experience. He believed it because he had met and talked and lived with men to whom Christ was not "absolute Lord and only Saviour" and yet who "manifestly were no strangers to the life 'hid in God'." Principal Hogg's view is based on his experience and not on the

Scriptures. He sees the contradiction which his experience works as his experience is balanced against the statements of the divine revelation. He does not clarify the picture for us by stating just how it is possible for a Hindu, who is typical in his beliefs as a Hindu, to be a recipient of the grace of God. The implication is that natural theology is enough and opens the way for such redemption apart from Jesus Christ. To him it is repugnant to deny that such people as he met and talked with are lost and outside the kingdom. To the Biblical revelationist it is equally repugnant to believe that they are in the kingdom. Hogg would be convinced on the basis of his pragmatic test; the Biblical believer would be convinced because the Scriptures so teach they are lost without regard to the subjective reference or pragmatic test. And again we see that the conclusion reached depends on whether one limits himself to the revelation or employs the use of human reason.

The second form of rationalization that opens the door of the kingdom to the non-Christian denies the adequacy of natural revelation, but at the same time refuses to believe that the Scriptures teach that God has not then worked on the minds and hearts of men OUTSIDE the sphere of the Christian revelation. Kraemer held this view at Madras and stated that he believed there are men who "have been, and may be now, acceptable men of faith, who live under the sway of non-Christian religions, products, however, not of these non-Christian religions, but of the mysterious workings of God's Spirit." He further validated this thesis by exclaiming: "God forbid that we mortal men should be so irreverent as to dispose of how and where the Sovereign God of Grace and love has to act." Truly this displays magnificently the faith of those who will not limit the working power of the Holy Spirit who operates how, when, and where He pleases. But we shall see in a moment that there may be an answer which destroys the Kraemer thesis.

The same idea that Kraemer had was expressed by a Chinese representative at Madras who claimed that Confucius, Mencius, and Moti no doubt had been influenced and affected by God in a supernatural manner. He inquired, "Who can deny that these sages have not been truly inspired by the Spirit of our God, the God of the Lord Jesus Christ? Who can judge that the Almighty has not appeared to them in His holy loving essence and that they have not been among the pure in heart of whom Jesus speaks?" One might well ask the commentator the opposite question: "How can you be sure that God has appeared to them in His holy and loving essence?" In answer to Kraemer and all others who try to explain away human problems by suggesting that we ought not deny God the right and the power of acting how and when He pleases we can say two things. First of all we can state plainly that there is nothing in the Scriptures which makes this assumption tenable. If it were at all possible there is nothing expressly stated or which can be derived from implication to suggest the possibility. Secondly, we can go further and state that by implication the revelation of God makes it appear unreasonable to assume that He works apart from the revelation we find in Christ. On a question such as this which is so important to the philosophy of missions it is hardly credible to believe that God would be silent if it is true that He works in the way men like Kraemer claim. No one is willing to deny that God can work when and how He pleases. But to make this a basis for God to do things which are in apparent contradiction to His nature and character is unbiblical and irrational. There is no foundation for such a view except as it springs from a sympathetic heart that is wishful in hoping that the heathen do have an opportunity for salvation apart from their religions which are inadequate.

It would be simple if we could claim the mysterious working of the Spirit of God bringing salvation to some men apart from the Christian revelation. But whereas it resolves one problem, it introduces still others that do not clarify the problem and only add to the trouble. Basically the idea that God may work outside the Christian revelation in salvation springs from the thought that God ought not let the heathen outside of Christ die without some kind of an opportunity. Even where the working of God is claimed apart from Christianity, there still remains the problem of the justice of God to let some in on this mysterious working and not let in others who are lost unless they have the chance too. This would be just as queer a form of justice as the other form which adherents for the mysterious working power of God do not like. The answer to the problem is not improvisation to escape from difficulties. We need simply to admit that God IS just in whatever He does. In all cases His justice is operative despite any appearance to the contrary. Being finite we do not know nor do we understand many of the elements which go into the total picture to make it just and right. Faith here includes the belief in the justice of God in every case without trying to invent escape mechanisms for areas or places where we do not happen to see the light. Too frequently it is to be suspected that the Church of Christ uses escape mechanisms such as those above, and the erroneous idea of a second chance for the heathen in an effort to relieve the Church of its obligation and responsibility. The idea is "what we fail to do God in mercy goes ahead and does in spite of us." And this cuts the nerve of missions by making the Church not so necessary as the Scriptures indicate in the carrying out of the purpose and the plan of God for this world.

Denying the idea, then, that God reveals Himself apart from the gospel as mediated through the Church, it does make the situation with reference to the heathen look very bad. The blackness of the picture, on the other hand, ought to break the heart of the Church and bring the Church to its knees in an honest and sincere effort to remedy the condition that there are so many men without Christ and thus without hope in this world or in eternity. However, the most orthodox Christian has a hope in the midst of the black picture and does find that God works for the heathen in specific cases where they are truly seeking for light even when they do not know what the true light is. But the way God operates is consistent with the revelation and in full accord with the method of working which God employs in our age. Missionaries do tell of people who have been contacted with the gospel who have been saved by that contact. In conversation it develops that these heathen have longed for truth and have sought for truth. But

truth has not come to them through a supernatural revelation but
through the sending of missionaries with the gospel. The contact
has been normal and natural and in the God ordained and divinely
appointed way. Instead of God granting the unregenerate heart
some supernatural revelation, God has brought them under the
hearing of the Gospel of Christ and they have been saved.

The New Testament bears witness to this divinely appointed
way in which the gospel spreads. The Ethiopian Eunuch was a
seeker after the truth. Curiously enough he had documents which
gave him truth but he understood not the truth. Further explanation was necessary. But God did not reveal the truth to him in
the mysterious working of His Spirit. He sent him one who knew
the truth and through the mediation of God's servant the Eunuch
found Christ and attained eternal life. Here we also have laid down
a valid principle illustrating the way in which God really does work.
By the moving power of His Holy Spirit, instead of enlightening
the Eunuch without the aid of a Christian, God moved the
Christian to go to the place where the Christian could and did
accomplish the divine plan of God in the life of the Eunuch.
In no case, of course, is it to be assumed that salvation was found
by purely human means totally apart from the Holy Spirit of
God who is the agent of salvation. But it does mean that the
Holy Spirit worked through the means divinely appointed of God
for the purpose of bringing salvation to men. There are three
constituent elements in salvation: the Word of God which comes
via the Christian Church, the Holy Spirit of God who reveals
Christ through the Word, and faith which reflects the attitude of
the sinner to the message which has come through men, enlivened
by the Spirit, and which the man must accept to be saved. The
view that God will find a means of reaching the sinner, who is
really sincere, with the gospel can be the hope of the Christian,
but he cannot accept nor believe that there is salvation apart from
Christ or that God works without any self-imposed limitations in
a free manner so as to make it possible and actual that men are
saved outside the means spoken of in the Scriptures.

Dr. A. T. Pierson expressed a Biblical truth which answers the problems which men have concerning the salvation of heathen by supernatural means. He stated that God never does supernaturally what He can do naturally. And God can, by normal and natural means, accomplish the salvation of any man without straining the Bible to accommodate a doctrine of the sort Kraemer advocates.

In concluding our discussion of the non-Christian religions we cannot help but insist that the following propositions are valid ones regarding the heathen. First, every non-Christian religion is inadequate and does not provide a real or sufficient revelation of God. Secondly, there are no real values in the non-Christian religions. Any of the so-called values have been distorted and pushed out of focus by sin although there may have been true elements known to the religion in its initial form. Similarities are thus not really similarities. Third, if a man is not in Christ he cannot be in God either. For no man knoweth the Father save the Son and he to whom the Son shall reveal Him. And lastly, God does not reveal Himself redemptively through other means than those presently indicated in the Word of God: i.e. through His children's missionary activity to a lost world.

Chapter 5

A FINAL THEOLOGY—THE NATURE AND FUNCTION OF THE CHURCH

I N THE development of a philosophy of missions there is a progression which arranges itself more or less logically. So far the basis on which the faith rests has been discussed; then the final theology which is a derivative of this has been uncovered; then the uniqueness of this faith and this theology was treated to indicate the soteriological (to say the least) inadequacy of all other religions. Now our subject unfolds itself before us and forces a consideration of the Church.

Before the Church can be discussed properly, the definition of the word needs treatment, and our idea of the Church should be so clear that no error can creep into our thinking about it. For our purposes, therefore, the Church can be dealt with in two general areas. First we must know what the nature of the Church is. Knowing this we can then sketch the function of the Church. In the first case we will find out what the Church actually is; in the second case we will discover what the Church is supposed to do. In both cases there is a widespread need to eliminate common misconceptions currently held with regard to the nature and the function of the Church.

Negatively there is one concept that must be destroyed before any other in dealing with the Church. This concept is that the Church is a human organization, begun by human beings, and

114

continued by human beings. It is the idea that the Church is a human institution which is anthropocentric in nature. Many people believe that the Church is a human institution today. Many others profess to believe that it is a divine institution but they live and act as though this were not so. This can be said so dogmatically since the original premise one accepts as to whether the Church is of human or divine origin will determine human action. And here, even among rabid adherents of the views already proposed in this work, are many whose actions belie their outward protests that they believe the Church to be a divine institution. This misconception arises from that pernicious relativism, and lack of clear thinking, that has confused even believers for several decades.

The distinction we make about the Church is one which is a matter of life and death. It is almost as important as one's views of the person and work of Christ for it is part of the warp and woof of the revelation. In sequence it follows after other doctrines which are prerequisite to it, but this in wise takes away its tremendous importance. This distinction is not one of theory, having little bearing on practical Christianity. It is vitally significant because the view we take determines the future course of action with reference to the missionary enterprise as a whole.

Instead of being anthropocentric in nature the Church is theocentric in nature. It is a divinely created and God-willed organization or organism. Immediately we distinguish between the visible and the invisible Church. The invisible Church comprises all believers everywhere without reference to sect or other differences. In it are those who have been redeemed by Jesus Christ. This group of people collectively is called the bride of Christ. It is spoken of as His body. It is called His Church. The visible Church or Churches are the concrete embodiment of the divine institution. In this sense the Church is much like the individual Christian. Each Christian is in the world and yet not of the world. The Church is in the world and is yet not of the world. But it exists in the world for the benefit of the world.

A Church or ecclesia as it is called in the New Testament is a communion and fellowship of people who are united in a common faith, having common worship, and a common love. This common faith, common worship, and common love revolves around the Head of the Church which is Jesus Christ. The people who comprise the Church are bound together because of the work of Christ and remain together because of loyalty and love to Him. And the Church is governed and operated and controlled by the Holy Spirit of God. The people making up this fellowship are called in the New Testament "saints" and "priests" and "sons of God."[1]

At the head of a true Church is the Lord Jesus Christ. He is its King and Lord. His authority and powers transcend all other authority or loyalty. This institution is unique because each member of the Church (at least theoretically) is under a solemn obligation to follow the divine leader of the institution. Since Christ is the Head of the Church it is impossible for the Church to be finally or completely beaten or destroyed. At different stages in the history of man certain philosophies have appeared to dominate the lives of the people. No matter what the philosophy or the force, the divine-human community which is called by the name of Church shall not, nor can it, be destroyed for it is God's. It is indestructible. The Church does not have life within itself. It is not an organism which is self-sustaining. The Church lives and feeds and continues through the working power of the Holy Spirit. This is a gift of divine grace and every gift in the Church is worked by the Holy Spirit. Thus does the human institution which is the concrete embodiment of the divine universal Church have a theacentric nature. Every human provision is made for its establishment and every gift is granted for its sustenance and

---

[1]Let it be understood that the author, when referring to the Church, takes the Baptist view that the Church means the local Church; that this was the divinely created body of which there can be any number throughout the whole world. The Presbyterian Church, on the other hand, includes many local churches, all of which are part of a single Church. As the term is employed in this volume, the desire is that it shall cover all of the Evangelical bodies of the world (some of which may be spotted with heresy) without arguing the question which view of "Church," Presbyterian, Baptist, etc., is correct. Any comments to the Church, then, can be construed to include any Baptist Church, and the Presbyterian Church, and the Methodist Church etc; in fact, the whole visible body of Christendom professing Christ as Saviour and Lord.

continuance. More than this, however, every grace is added so that the Church can fulfill its divine function.

A careful distinction must be made here in order not to confuse the nature of the Church as do the Roman Catholics. They confuse the divine invisible Church with the divine visible Church. Further, they make the visible Church the recipient of divine grace and the sole dispenser of that grace through the sacraments. Soteriologically they find salvation WITHIN their Church, and those outside their Church are without hope. Thus arises the expression that "he who does not have the Church for his mother does not have God for his father." Actually there can be no salvation within the Church. Neither the Church nor the sacraments, despite what Roman Catholics proclaim, can bring eternal life. It is this confusion that has produced other inventions and distortions of the Scriptures to bulwark the idea of the Church. Episcopal ordination involving apostolic succession enters into the picture. Since baptism is a saving sacrament derived from the Church that sacrament must be administered by properly qualified agents of the Church. Remove the priesthood in any episcopal setup and the Church has disappeared. Eventually the Roman Catholic Church held that without the presence of a bishop there was no church. Immediately we see that the divine purpose is contravened and the Church has become anthropocentric rather than remaining theocentric. We must ever insist that the Church exists and continues to exist and will ever exist apart from any select group through whose hands continually from the apostolic days must pass in unbroken succession the power and validity of the Church. We say this because the revelation of God in connection with the Church makes this plain, and also because history bears out this contention and fails to demonstrate the claimed unbroken succession through the ages.

In standing against those who claim the episcopal succession there is no possible compromise. They cannot recognize that a Church exists without there being present one of the episcopally ordained, nor can they admit the validity of actions taken by those who claim to be ministers of the gospel but who are without that episcopal ordination. Thus, to those who hold to episcopal ordination very few of the protestant Churches today are to be considered true Churches. They are not to them, nor can they be, true Churches unless they surrender the one thing they hold to be the mark of a true Church. The Roman Catholic Church has never relinquished its claim to be the only true Church, nor has it ever reversed its view that every other Church is a false Church. The invisible Church, then, is not to be confused with the visible Church as though they are one and the same as the Roman Catholics pretend. They are different.

The difference between the visible and the invisible Churches requires further elaboration. In the visible Church which has human aspects, there may be included many people who are not a part of the invisible Church. It is perfectly evident that there are pseudo-Christians who are organically united with the outward corporate body of the redeemed, but who have never been united organically with the inward spiritual body of the invisible Church. Such an outward Church connection with the Kingdom of God is transitory and is broken off at death; there never was a true spiritual connection to begin with. Further, one can say that it is perfectly possible for a person to be a member of the invisible Church without having identified himself with the outward concrete form of the visible fellowship. The thief on the cross who found eternal life at the death of Jesus is an example of one such case. In other cases where there are men who are a part of the invisible Church for many years while not maintaining any relation to the visible Church, we must conclude that they are living in ignorance of the divine command or in disobedience thereto in not coming together in some fellowship. It is the divine will that men relate themselves one to another in fellowship.

A visible Church does not constitute a building any more than it constitutes a priest. To be a Church, Christ must be at the head and associated with Him two or three must be gathered together. Thus a Church is not an impersonal, quiescent, dead invention, but a living organism involving men and women who are in a saving relation to the Lord Jesus Christ. If this New

Testament conception of the Church is carried out logically and seriously, gone would be many of the problems and difficulties which beset us today. A dogmatic ecclesiasticism with its resultant idiosyncrasies would evaporate into nothing. The human side of the Church would tend to disappear and in its place would be the dynamic theocentric cast which ought to dominate completely and effectively the Church of Christ.

The Roman Catholic Church has not been alone in its misconception of the Church. In Europe, added confusion came from the identification of Church and State. The State Church concept did much to injure the true faith because Christianity under the State was bound to be perverted. The early Church knew something about a State religion, in which every citizen of the State was also a member of the State cult. The Church fought a life and death struggle against this—and won. When Christianity completed its conquest of the Roman Empire it became the leading religion and before long it was the state religion, people who were citizens of the state being considered members of the Church. Down the centuries there was no religious freedom and even after the Reformation the State-Church view continued.

The union of Church and State has no support in the Scriptures. Religious freedom which the Bible does support nullifies the possibility of a union between Church and State. The Bible clearly indicates that the Church differs from any earthly organization as to its origin, its continuance, and its function. Any interaction with human organizations is detrimental to the New Testament idea of the Church.

Again and again we hear men speak of a Christian civilization and a Christian society. At times we hear the same thought expressed in terms of the existence of a Christian state. This thought is erroneous in connection with true Christianity and must be destroyed. There is no such thing as a Christian society within national boundaries, nor can we speak of a Christian civilization with reference to individual states. No state can ever be Christian. It is not the expectation of the Church to accomplish this end and the warning against it is clear. The possibility of a Christian state or a Christian world in the future arises from the unscriptural post-millennial view which likes to believe that in history through the efforts of men there will be introduced a world-wide Utopian age of universal peace and righteousness.

To create a Christian state or society whether nationally or internationally would come over a period of time and be a process. As a process it would support the evolutionary concept of history. The view that envisions this, pictures each religion borrowing one from the other, and bit by bit Christianity will be assimilated by these religions without calling it Christianity. One might say that this is a process of osmosis in which Christian modes of worship, hymns, preaching, aspects of the Christian conception of God, ethical notions, and the honoring of Christ may be taken over. This evolutionary view which assumes inevitable upward progress (with perhaps temporary setbacks) happens to violate several principles laid down in the revelation which we have taken as the basis for a missionary philosophy. First, the Scriptures do not warrant any assumption that there has been any organic or sociological evolution. Secondly, we know quite definitely that the Bible does not permit the view that Christianity can take hold on peoples through a process. It is not to be assimilated and one does not become a Christian progressively. To become a Christian either by upbringing or through some progressive process does violence to the biblical doctrines of instantaneous regeneration and also to the fact that the new birth is from above and begins and ends with divine grace through the gracious operation of God's Holy Spirit. Man is an instrument through which God works to reveal Himself, but regeneration is not a matter of absorbing certain ideas. Rather it involves a transformation in which the dead becomes alive, and where one passes from spiritual death unto spiritual life. And the destruction of the view that individuals can ever become Christian through such a process also destroys the idea that a state can ever be totally Christian or that the world can ever be totally Christian.

Another objection to the idea that there is some form of organic relation of Christianity to states in the sense that we can speak of a Christian state or nation is the obvious truism that the Church is at odds with the state and cannot make peace with the state. The state always represents the world and the Church is constantly witnessing against the world, although curiously the Church belongs to the world, physically speaking. It witnesses against the world because the world is dominated by the forces of evil and the world is the object of divine wrath. That the world is the object of divine wrath is not a popular doctrine but it is a Biblical one; that the Church cannot be connected with a world that is the object of divine wrath is easily seen. The Church in time waits for its deliverance in the consummation, and meanwhile witnesses against the nations and seeks to serve them by pointing them to Christ. Thus the Church in the world lives in a state of tension or crisis that logically ought to extend itself to the life of each individual Christian. The difference here between the Church and the state or between the Church and society is the foundation on which each is built. The world is empirical, imperfect, finite, and sinful. The Church is rooted and grounded in a divine order of life. There is no common meeting ground without the sacrifice of basic principle. When the Church sacrifices its basic principle of a life that is divine and supernatural in origin it dies. The state never has and never will forsake its sin and cleave to the divine. There is, therefore, an impasse.

Neither the world nor individual states will ever be distinctively Christian. This does not mean, however, that Christianity will not reach out and influence and affect life everywhere. While Christianity does not aim to dominate and control the economic, political and social life of all peoples, it does produce effects on peoples and nations. An example of this would be the prohibition by the English of child widow burning in India. English consciences, stimulated by the influence of years of Christian impact, could not stand by and see this crime against humanity go on even though done in the name of religion. But to identify the fruits of Christianity, socially, economically, or politically, with Christianity is to fail miserably. To suppose that the accumulation of such rules would ever make India Christian or that national conduct similar to that of Christian people would make for a Christian India does not follow. The elimination of this pagan practice is a fruit of Christianity but it is not Christianity. The time will never come when society or the world is peculiarly Christian.

Going beyond the idea of the Church and its relation to the state with the problem whether there can be a Christian state, we advance to the problem of the Church and society in a broad sense. There are many who see that there is a distinction between state and Church which can never be broken down, making it impossible for the full realization of Christianity *en toto* over the world. But these same people are thinking in terms of ecumenical Christianity as never before. To consider the nature and function of the Church without taking cognizance of the tremendous movement designed to unify protestant Christendom would be to fail to meet this challenge. To fail to meet and to deal with ecumenicity is wrong when we are developing a philosophy of the Christian mission.

At the heart of the ecumenical movement is the desire to unite all protestant forces into some form of a federation. It is to bring together in a more cohesive manner the divided and divisive elements which go to make up the Christian world outside of the Roman Catholic sphere. On the radical periphery of the scene are men like Professor Hocking of Harvard. He sees the hope of the world to be in a world faith. Against the attainment of a world faith are the differences between peoples. Hocking would break down the assumption that there is an only way to God and he would abandon this doctrine forever. His ecumenical faith could then easily contain most anything, with foundations broad enough to cover all kinds of faiths and religions. To Hocking this world faith would open the door to the Hindu, Mohammedan, and all others.

The view represented by Hocking is not the general ecumenical view, however. In general the moderate view holds for unity within the Protestant and Eastern Orthodox Churches, doing away with those elements which produced disunity to begin with. Questions of baptisms, forms of Church government, and the like are included. Even in this case there are matters of great moment extending beyond the differences which originally tended to separate and divide protestant Christendom. For example, in Luther's day the issues which separated him from men like Zwingli and Calvin did not include issues which work against ecumenicity today. Calvin and Luther were agreed as was Zwingli on the foundational truths of the faith. This is not so today. Today the ecumenical movement is trying to unite Christendom by removing barriers like questions of baptism, the table, etc. But the movement is also trying to bring into some form of organic harmony people whose faiths are founded on differing premises. The movement is trying to bring into one fellowship those whose views on the authority of the scriptures, the person and the work of Christ, the resurrection, and the like are utterly divergent and irreconcilable. The constant cry is for unity without uniformity. The truth of the matter is that there cannot be any semblance of unity without much more conformity than there is at present. Ecumenicity is doomed to failure.

Ecumenicity must fail for several reasons. It must fail because there are large segments of the protestant world who see that unity can be attained only by sacrifice of principle. The modernist in this picture does not stand to lose anything because he makes no sacrifice. If he is a true liberal (which most of them are not) he is willing to confess that the conservative view is one way of looking at things. And if this satisfies a man the liberal permits that man to hold the view, although he may doubt the intelligence of the man who does. Since the modernist clings to a relativist position he rather sympathizes with the men who have not yet reached his stage of intellectual development. But there is room in his setup for the brother who is behind. In time the modernist feels he will be able to shake the conservative one out of his stupidity. So long as the conservative will play along with the modernist and permit him control, there is little argument. But let a conservative minority rise up in arms and the forces of hell will be unleashed to crush the protestant. But it is not the modernist who prevents the success of the ecumenical movement. It is the "stupid" conservative whose vision is limited and whose view is narrow. And the vision will be limited and the view narrow so long as the conservative retains his basic premises. Among the premises which the conservative holds is the one which refuses to admit that a modernist is a Christian by Biblical definition. By this definition the modernist who denies the authority of the Word, the true deity (not the weasel words) of Jesus, and His vicarious atonement, is not in the kingdom. And if these modernists are not in the kingdom the conservative finds adequate scriptural injunction to avoid fellowship save as he seeks to convert them. To join in an ecumenical movement designed to produce one Church, at least theoretically if not actually organically, means the sacrifice of principle for the conservative, the sacrifice of which destroys his distinctive position. For the conservative to unite, while at the same time believing that principle is not sacrificed, is foolish. The basic foundation of the conservative is not sufficiently broad to include men like Hocking or even more moderate ecumenicists who are nonetheless modernists.

In relationship to the nature of the Church the conservative finds that the ecumenical movement fails again. According to the conservative the Church is comprised of people who are "saints" and "priests"; those who have experienced regeneration through the new birth. By its nature there ought not be in the Church any unsaved. Yet it is evident that there are unsaved within the visible Church. This is not unexpected (although there are provisions for weeding them out in every fellowship), nor does it become the essential hindrance in the ecumenical problem. Conservatives could find good reason to consider ecumenicity if and when those who are known to be modernists were ejected from the Churches and a basis for unity found in a creed that was orthodox. This will not be done and further there is a wide gulf between conservative and modernist about the definition of the nature of the Church. The conservative links the union of the individual with the Church to Biblical doctrines like the new birth in a form which no modernist would find acceptable. Thus the conservative finds himself to be an objector to the ecumenical movement for reasons perfectly valid to him but which are not valid nor are they understood and appreciated by the modernist.

There is still another barrier to the ecumenical movement among conservatives, which, if there were common agreement on all other matters, would still make this idea impossible. Just as the conservatives are staunch defenders of certain doctrines like the virgin birth, the physical resurrection, etc. so they are also staunch defenders of those doctrines which differentiate one denomination from another. A true Baptist will never sacrifice his convictions concerning infant baptism or his belief in immersion. Likewise a Presbyterian will not sacrifice his view of the Church and her polity and officers. Likewise the Lutheran who is a true Lutheran is not prone to deny the real presence of Christ in the supper as do the Presbyterian and the Baptist. To sacrifice these elements is to produce uniformity which the Roman Catholic Church champions so vigorously. And unity at this price which means the sacrifice of convictions is not worth it. Nowhere in the Scriptures is organic union taught. Everywhere there is an emphasis on spiritual unity and union of the believer as a member of the body of Christ.

There is a true ecumenicity to which all Christians ought to adhere. This ecumenicity is painfully aware that the Church lives an inbetween life while it waits for its full consummation. It sees that the problem of union here on earth is too big to be solved, nor can we see our way through it. Underlying this is the deep and abiding conviction that God is guiding His true Church with the assurance that ultimately we shall all be members of the one body in an ecumenical sense that is not temporal but transcendental. The kingdom of God in its fullest sense is yet future. But when that time does come all differences will be wiped out and complete union and unity will prevail. Perhaps it is needless to point out that in this eschatological sense the unity and union are preceded by the elimination of the tares as well as by the transformation of the believers who shall "know as they are known", and in the light of this all variations and deviations will be washed away. Then in a real sense as well as in a spiritual sense we can sing: "All one body we. One in hope and doctrine; one in charity." Until then the ecumenical movement will fail.

The Church visible as we have seen is an indestructible organism which draws its life from Christ and the Holy Spirit. It is not organically related to the state nor can it be except where confusion exists as to the nature of the Church or where the Church sacrifices its unique nature. It is not coterminus with society nor ecumenical in nature either and is never to be identified synonymously with the world in its political, social, and economic relationships. If all of this be true then there is a need in our day to clarify the function of the Church as well as its nature. It is possible to know the nature of the Church and not know its function. Then, too, it is possible to know both the nature and the function without carrying out the function at all.

Again we approach the subject from a negative point of view. There are some things which the Church is not supposed to do. There are some things which are not the aim of the Church. Many people have confused the issue and have made ridiculous claims of what the Church ought to do, having no basis for their claims in the revelation. Much of the disrepute gained by the Church in this age has arisen from its failure to accomplish what enthusiasts have claimed to be the function of the Church but which has never really been its job.

The Church is not here to accomplish or bring about the solution of the economic, social, and political problems. Enthusiastic conservatives speak forcefully that if men will permit Christ to govern their lives all of the problems of society will be solved. There are two errors in this widespread assertion. First, men will never all permit Christ to dominate their lives so far as salvation is concerned. Thus the Church will never be able to resolve problems which demand that all people be Christian. Secondly, if it were true that all men were to accept Christ there still remains the problem that will not be solved in this empirical world. Because a man becomes a Christian does not mean nor will it ever mean that all Christians will be governed by the principles of the faith—some through ignorance, some through half-hearted commitment, and some through overt disobedience. The realization of the ideal cultural, social, and political conditions will occur transcendentally not empirically. To confuse the transcendental perfection with this world which is finite, relative, imperfect, and transient produces terrible confusion and substitutes human values for divine standards.

To state that Christianity will not solve the economic, social, and political problems of the world does not mean that Christianity will not influence society in these spheres nor does it mean that Christianity ought not exert its beneficent influence here. Nevertheless the Christian can never forget that the kingdom of God is transcendental and will not be realized on earth apart from the supernatural intervention of Christ. The various spheres of life can be influenced and altered by Christianity but they cannot be Christianized in the sense of that word according to revelation. Human finiteness, the human ego, and the awful reality of sin in a sphere that is relative makes this accomplishment impossible. Parenthetically it ought to be added that the revelation itself does not look for nor expect the Christianization of the social order. Whatever the Church does in this sphere is but an expression of the Church's power and does not constitute a part of its basic nature nor does it stand central in its essential program.

More concretely than it has been expressed before we can state that there are many programs and acts which are perfectly valid and worthy in themselves but which have no vital relation to the real function of the Church. These things are not obligations to which the Church has fallen heir and nowhere do we discover that it is a part of the function of the Church to discharge them. The Church does not function to change or alter governments whether they be democratic or autocratic. The Church is not a social service agency whose duty it is to relieve suffering, starvation, and economic dislocation. It is not even the function of the Church to establish and maintain schools and hospitals, fine as they may be in helping the peoples of the world materially, socially, economically, and physically. The Church is not here to civilize the world (whatever that word may mean. And its meaning varies all over the world) or to add to man's knowledge or to change the habits of man's life. The Church is not even here to convert the world, strange and paradoxical as this may sound to some ears. Continually it must be denied that the function of the Church from the viewpoint of the philosophy of missions is to bring all of the people of the world under the authority of Christ and to bring all social, economic, and political relations under His authority also. Transcendentally this is true, but not empirically in this work of the historical.

It is not to be thought that Christianity ought never concern itself with social uplift, or with hospitals, schools, and labor. But this concern is radically different and far removed from the true function of the Church as the New Testament envisions it. The Church is always enjoined to stand out against injustice, sin, and bigotry wherever it is found. In dealing with the practical affairs of life, the voice of the Church must always be lifted against iniquity without regard to the quarter from which it raises its evil head. To stand against evil and to work for good is an expression of Christian character.

People are everywhere confused and have been led to believe that it is the function of the Church to suppress all of the evils and injustice in the world. Somehow they feel that the churches of America ought to remake India or China or some other nation by the elimination of specific evils. What is overlooked is that pivotal truth that the churches of America cannot do in India what they are doing in America along social lines. What they do in America is not something that is basic to the function of the Church but it is something that rises out of the Church as an outward expression of the new life that has come into the hearts of men. The voice of the Church lifted to speak vocally on the issues of life is a fruit of regeneration. It follows the establishment of the Church, neither preceding it nor being the purpose for which the gospel is spread. Let no man think for an instant that it is the work of the churches of any Christian land to pursue a policy of mitigating evil through social action, pressure groups, etc. for the heathen countries of the world. The work is to save men and to shepherd them into churches from which the social impulse ought to spring.

We repeat that it is not the function of the Church to change the social structure of the world as such. Revelationally the Church is to take the gospel of Christ to all the world. The primary aim is to reach individuals with the gospel of Christ and to bring them together into churches. It is to plant in areas where it is not, the living seed of the gospel of the living God. This is not a social objective or movement, but a radically religious motive and movement.

The Church is a fellowship of believers who are rooted and grounded in God and in His divine redemptive order. This intimate fellowship implies a full commitment of the individual to the program of God which means the commitment of the individual to the service and the salvation of the world. In each generation the people who make up the Church must become conscious of the task of the Church and be willing to identify themselves in the redemptive work that uniquely belongs to the Church. It demands a Church that is acquainted with the world outside of Christ and in which we live. It means a Church free from all entanglements, and worldliness so as to be able to accomplish the job committed to it.

Increasingly it is evident that the Church has gotten its eyes off the main objective and has spent its time and energy in peripheral matters. Schism, internal dissension, doctrinal hobbies, and living for self, have kept the Church busy to the virtual exclusion of the primary objective which is the evangelization of the world, the fulfillment of the divine function of the Church. The evangelization of the world is the function of the Church but the idea must be individualized so that more than intellectual assent be given to it. The members of the body of Christ must actively identify themselves in the task and bend every effort for the completion of that task. This needs to be repeated over and over again and will be dealt with more in detail when we consider the relationship of the individual and the individual's responsibility to this task.

When the Church of Christ realizes that it is supposed to take the gospel to the whole world, and when it commits itself to that task, the job will get done. It is the doing of this job that needs the emphasis. There can be no naive understanding of what is meant by taking the gospel to the whole world. By this is meant that Jesus is proclaimed according to the revelation: that He died vicariously, and was buried, and rose again the third day according to the Scriptures.

Inevitably questions arise as to when the gospel has effectually been taken to the ends of the earth and when it has been presented sufficiently. Surely none can deny that it has not always been presented effectively and we know that it has not gone to the ends of the earth. We will know that the gospel has been taken to all the world and that it has been done effectively for the coming of the Lord will follow. It behooves us to be about God's business, seeking to improve our methods, etcetera, knowing that the task has not been finished else the Lord would come. Further we know that the completion of the task is not a matter of techniques alone, nor is it true that the job will be done when we have sent out our best. All God ever asks is that men be yielded to Him. This surrender plus the work of the Holy Spirit is enough, for after all the Spirit of God is the One who reveals Christ, as well as convicts of sin, and regenerates. Men, with the best they have, must preach Christ.

Preaching Jesus Christ is not enough, however, for there are three facets to the missionary task. We can tell that He has been preached when the second facet of the task becomes a reality. Men are to be saved when the gospel is taken to them. The Church is to look for and expect results. It is true that the results are not to be confused with the aim, and results are not finally decisive. But there must be fruit, providing the aim and the methods are biblical. The aim of missions specifically includes the salvation of individual men and means a new birth from above. Simply to sow the seed is not to complete the task. Any man who sows grain, is most unpleasantly surprised when he does not reap according to what he has sown. We are to expect and obtain results. This is the proof that our aim and methods are biblical.

The third facet of taking the gospel (which includes preaching Christ and winning men to Him) is that of naturalizing the faith in heathen lands. This consists in bringing together those of like faith and establishing indigenous organizations for the edification of the new Christians and for the further propagation of the faith by them. This is not the Europeanization or the Americanization or the western culturization of the natives, for the faith cannot be accented in terms of a single culture. Naturalization cannot mean the impartation of our civilization *per se*. Consequently to indigenize is difficult for it implies outward differences, springing from similar inner experiences, in which the new faith roots itself in a new land.

The indigenization of the Church in pagan lands ought never mean the overlordship of the white man above his black, yellow, or brown brother. To indigenize properly means to see the establishment of a Church that is self-governing, self-supporting, and self-propagating. Less than this is to create a human organization when the Church ought to be a divine organism.

When the faith has been preached, men have been won, and the new faith indigenized, there will be released energies and forces the consequence of which no man can foretell. There will be economic, social, and political effects. These are inevitable, but they are not the aim of missions. They are proper fruits of mission work or accessory results. Throughout the history of the Christian Church results have been accruing because of the Christian faith. Our own generation is profiting from the faith of our fathers of years gone by. Often the binding tie that links men with that faith of their fathers has disappeared and men today fail to see that many of the supreme advantages that have been gained over the years are directly due to the Christian faith as it has operated in the hearts, and minds, and consciences of men, producing economic, political, and social changes of tremendous import. The destruction of the tie between the Christian faith, which produced a social consciousness that made changes, and the actual changes which sprang from the Christian faith has been most unfortunate. Were there no such destruction and did men know what the faith has done in every area of life, it would not in itself change the hearts of men who are antagonistic to the gospel and whose hearts are hardened against God. But it might give them pause.

When the aim of the Church to preach to men, win them, and indigenize the Church is being accomplished, the Christian faith is then subjected to the insidious attacks which include the charge of being a proselyting agency. This charge never arises when missionary activity is limited to altering living conditions, or social conditions, but it gets life from the success of a dynamic mission which changes the hearts of men via the new birth. Both the charge of proselyting and the consequences rising out of that charge bring serious complications for the true missionary endeavor. Unfortunately for the detractors who dislike proselyting and who argue against the invasion of private spiritual fortresses, the truth remains that proselyting is inherent in the faith. Remove it and the faith ceases to be revelationally grounded. It is impossible to deviate from this view even for those who would like to see Christianity only parallel the non-Christian faiths. Essentially Christianity is designed to take men out of their old religions into the new. When this is compromised the faith is ruined so that it remains for the Christian to proclaim his gospel as an offer for men to break off from the old and to enter the new without consideration of the consequences involved. Expediency here is no factor for the nature of the faith is at stake. By its nature the Christian faith is a proselyting faith and must ever be such.

In dwelling on the task of the Church and its obligation to the divine command, the real danger we face is twofold: that of overestimating the actual task we have and that of underestimating it. Either radical position is productive of tremendous harm. To overestimate is to go beyond the obligations placed on the Church by revelation. It is to assume that we are to do more than to evangelize the world, generally leading to some Utopian dream of Christianizing the world. This produces disjunction and leads to disillusionment when people do not see the results they await but which are actually impossible of attainment. As badly wrong as the adherents of this view are, there are others who are equally wrong. The other group underestimates the task of the Church and places limitations on the job which the Word does not condone. A case in point here would be those men who sit at home and claim that God will save the heathen apart from human instrumentalities. William Carey found this point of view prevalent in his day when he tried to become a foreign missionary. Rock-ribbed fundamentalists have been guilty of a perversion of the missionary task in a view they hold which is correct but which is not the whole thing. Thus to believe that we are to snatch the heathen as brands from the burning is correct. But to make this the farthest extension of the missionary aim is to delimit the aim where the revelation does not do so. Surely those sincere fundamentalists who are employed in hanging on grimly and with determination, pulling souls from eternal hell, while they wait for the coming of the Lord are deserving of fullest sympathy. But it is deadly to the full understanding of the Word which is clear that we are not only to pull men from the clutches of the devil and from perdition, but we are also to see that the task goes beyond the rescue of individual men. It includes the full and complete evangelization of the world. And this is far broader than just saving people from hell. It implies a greater task, and embraces a broader vision, and demands a deeper consecration and purpose. We are not to Christianize the world nor are we simply to snatch brands from the burning. We are, however, to get the gospel to every creature while we save individual men and women from eternal darkness. We must have this adequate conception of our task and we need not be worried about charges of proselyting. We have a divine charge to keep that precludes concern about all else but that.

The aim of the Church or its function is to evangelize the world. The methods employed are another matter. Constantly we are faced with the need of making this distinction plain. Frequently the aim is confounded with the means to that end and the method becomes the end in itself. When the method becomes the aim obscuration obtains and the real function of the Church is concealed. Often the Church contents itself with this state of affairs and continues the prosecution of methods rather than original aims. The reasons are legion. If education and medicine become ends in themselves success will attend one's efforts on every hand.

There are plenty of illnesses to be cured and there are millions of people who need to become literate. It is relatively easy to obtain much success this way, for it can be accomplished apart from the power and work of the Holy Spirit since it is anthropocentric in character. It obviates as needless those moments of deep soul-searching and does away with the need for unbroken hours of difficult praying and meditation. To the activistic American soul this sin comes easily and naturally. Rationalizing our conduct occurs and the belief that expediency demands temporization in continuing the employment of such a policy until a more favorable time follows quickly.

Methods of accomplishing the aim are varied. The use of medicine and education is excellent. Any method that can be legitimately sustained is good. One of the highest methods is preaching but preaching itself is not an aim. A man can lose himself as easily in his preaching as he does in medicine and in education. In each case the important factor is that the method does not dominate and become the aim. The method must be subordinated to the aim and be ever subserviant to that aim. It is only a means to accomplishing something and the moment the method ceases to be that, it has usurped the true aim. How far a man can go in the use of certain methods will depend upon many factors. The moment a medical missionary ceases to have for his central goal the spread of the gospel and the conversion of men that soon he has ceased to be a missionary and is only a doctor. He might as well return to the land he left, for disinterested philanthropy or social uplift, no matter how good the intentions, is a deviation from the revelational concept of the function of a missionary. In spite of what men like Professor Soper say, medical missions are a means to an end, offering an opportunity to evangelize. This principle can be extended to cover all the methods in use for spreading the gospel. The solidarity of the missionary enterprise in its multiform activities lies in the truth that there is but one ultimate aim to be achieved through many methods.

The Church needs to be careful in its choice of methods to see that only those biblically legitimate are employed, and that the ones which they do use are not rendered ineffective by becoming the end rather than the means to the end. At the heart of any method stand the people who employ that method, and to divorce men from the method is non-intelligible, for men employ the methods. Only when the most Godly men are employed in the prosecution of the enterprise, and when they are men who remain true to the faith, and close to the Bible, can we be sure that proper methods will prevail.

The primary method for spreading the gospel is through the lives of those who are engaged in the missionary task. It is incarnating the life of Christ through the missionary's life. It is the personal, man to man, contact that is so vital to the progress of the faith. Too often Godly ends have been sought through the employment of less than Godly men. Thus to expect to reproduce in foreign lands what was done in apostolic times, when men who deny the deity of Christ or His atoning work are used, is less than reasonable. The Church needs to learn afresh that only Christians can make Christianity work; only Christians are suitable for missionary personnel. Regardless of a man's learning and ability in any area of missionary work, he is hurtful to the cause of missions unless there are first positive evidences of regeneration in the life of that individual. Above all other means, therefore, stands the supreme means of reflecting the life of Christ through the life of the regenerated heart as it comes into contact with the heathen.

In the use of methods preaching stands next to that incarnation of the life of Christ in the hearts of those who go abroad. This method includes the setting forth of the facts of the Christian religion so that men will be won to a saving knowledge of Jesus Christ. Preaching can take the form of personal witnessing to individuals in the daily walks of life or it can mean street corner evangelism, or radio work, or it may take the form of writing. Always it means getting the message to men in some concrete form that they will understand, and through which they will be enabled to make an intelligent decision for Jesus Christ.

Beyond the incarnating of the life of Christ in the lives of missionaries, and preaching, are other forms or methods. Among them might be included the committing of the message of the cross to faithful men who are able also to teach others. And this includes the training and education of the children of new converts. Then stretching out into an infinite variety of patterns stand those other activities or methods which are philanthropic, medical, or charitable in nature. Charity is not the aim and all philanthropic or other work must be subjected to the same test that all other methods must meet, the test to determine that the method is correct in relation to the primary function of the Church which is the evangelization of the world.

In the execution of the methods or in the use of them to accomplish the divine aim the Church ought not lose sight of Jesus Christ as her Head and as the sole authority of the Christian fellowship. The remembrance of this serves to give balance and perspective and insures the Church that it is operating on revelational lines.

This assurance that Christ is the sole Head breeds a biblical intolerance toward heathendom which is helpful in an increasing measure to the spirituality of the Church. To be tolerant means to let heathen slip down into hell and perish. Tolerance includes fraternization and leads to a reorientation which cuts the nerve of the missionary motive. To be intolerant is not to equate that with lack of love. True love forbids tolerance, for the right kind of Christian intolerance is not harmful but beneficent. It is in the interest of the destiny of each eternal soul that this intolerance is framed, and there can be no substitute for Christ anywhere along the line. Tolerance for anything non-Christian or anti-Christian is treason.

That form of treason which is named tolerance springs from a slushy sentimentality and an adherence to concepts which are foreign to the revelation. Theoretically it sounds noble to talk of sharing religious experiences with others of unlike faith. It can sound equally noble to say that you will permit other men to follow the truth as they see it and permit them to go on as they like. Christian intolerance teaches that they have this as a right if they wish to exercise it, but it is only to be watched; never to be appreciated and enjoyed. It is to be looked upon with heavy heart after every opportunity has been exhausted to bring them to the light of life which is Jesus Christ. And then even in the midst of seeming unchanging refusal to come to Christ, it ought to be the prayer and the subject of effort on the part of the Christian never to relent or to admit that the change ought not occur or that it is impossible to take place. No compromise, no cessation, no tolerance is possible.

In no place in this discussion of tolerance for non-Christian views should there creep in any thought or act involving violation of the rights of men to believe or disbelieve as they will. Persecution of those who are enemies of the cross is not scripturally permissible. The Christian Church has recourse to prayer, lives of sacrifice, the evidence of a good testimony, but never violence. Persistence, patience, and an unswerving purpose serve the hope of eventual submission of men to the person of Jesus Christ. On the surface this grants to the enemy of true faith an open advantage. It means permission for men of non-Christian faiths to preach their faiths and to compete openly with Christianity. Generally this means, in addition, persecution of the Christian faith in numerous instances because the non-Christian faiths are not so careful about that divinely granted freedom to the individual to accept or to reject a given faith. Persecuted, the Church cannot persecute; maligned the Church cannot malign; having been refused by others, the Church cannot refuse access to others, "for the weapons of our warfare are not carnal, but mighty through God to the pulling down of strongholds." The Church is the servant of the world, not its master.

Truly the Church is the servant of the world and not its master. The Church was launched at Pentecost with that view in the mind of God and it has been sustained through the centuries for the same reason. The world in which we live today is no more hospitable to Jesus than was the world into which the Church was originally launched. It would not be correct to say that it is less hospitable either. In serving the world the Church has come to discover that its position has an unchanging quality about it. It began its existence in a world of tension and it continues in a world of tension. Never could it be said that the Church had truly captured the world nor had the world ceased to fight against it. In this sense the Church has always lived in a crisis state from without. Always the enemies of the cross have been engaged in their battle against God.

Today the enemies from without continue to apply their evil pressures relentlessly. But the main problem of the Church, and the area where the greatest battle is taking place, is not without the Church. God has promised that the gates of hell shall not prevail against His Church. Evil from without can never triumph. But the crisis today is largely an internal one rather than external. The greatest enemies of the Church are not necessarily without the Church. Many of them are within the Church today. Catastrophic as this is to contemplate, its consequences are far worse than the wildest imaginings, for the enemies from within have vitiated the testimony of the Church, hindered the forward progress of its work, and brought reproach upon those within the Church who are true members of His mystical body. As a result of this internal catastrophe the Church has been spending its time on internal strife when it should have been spending its time in taking the gospel to all the world.

Everywhere recognition of the sad state of affairs in the Church is known. The best example of this came several years ago when the *Christian Century* published an editorial entitled "Fundamentalism and Modernism." In part this liberal journal said, "Amiable words cannot bind these worlds together. 'Blest be the tie' may be sung until doomsday but it cannot bind these worlds together. The God of the fundamentalist is one God: the God of the modernist is another. The Christ of fundamentalism is one Christ; the Christ of modernism is another. The Bible of fundamentalism is one Bible; the Bible of modernism is another . . . Which God is the Christian God, which Christ is the Christian Christ, which Bible is the Christian Bible . . . The future will tell."

A divided Church means a divided witness, and a divided witness is the best guarantee for an impotent and unavailing Church. So long as the internal struggle goes on the real work of the

Church is not going to be accomplished. Particularly is this true when the struggle is projected to the foreign fields where the opposing internal forces of the Church battle each other for control of the field. It suggests that judgment must first come to the house of the Lord, and precipitates the unhappy thought that God may yet have to go outside the visible organization we call the Church and use men not connected with ecclesiastical structures to complete the work of evangelization. The existing visible organization, the Church, could complete the task if it were purified and could recapture the vision of what God in Christ expected the Church to be. But its continued impotence in the face of refusal to purify itself and to eliminate the ungodly bodes ill for the future and may be corrected perhaps only by schism in which the elect withdraw themselves from the apostate.

The Church has known that it is divided and the world could not help noting it too. Preaching was without power and was there no demonstration of the Spirit. In June of 1940 the secular magazine *Fortune* was strongly critical of the ineffectiveness of the Church and of its teaching and preaching life. The article in this magazine made the claim that the Church was not shaping life, but was being shaped itself by the current social order. At the heart of the criticism was the belief that the Church had lost contact with the timeless and the eternal and had become temporal and timely instead. This was a criticism directed against the Church by external critics, but within the Church there were voices making the same criticisms. In 1928 at Jerusalem the cry was heard that the Church was beset with materialism as well as the world. It was admitted that the trumpet did not always give forth a certain tone, and that the watchmen on the walls were often asleep. It was recognized that there were serious weaknesses in the empirical Church.

After 1928 the criticism was continued. This time men like Professor Kraemer cried for a Church with a sense of direction and with a renewed understanding of the meaning and purpose of the Christian mission. His cry was for this renewal so that the Church could have an unchanging objective and sense of destiny in the world no matter what the condition of the world itself. Again it was a plea for an objective and eternally valid set of values with reference to the Church, a sound and final foundation on which to rest permanently. Behind Kraemer's plea lay the acknowledged conclusion that the Church had sadly compromised its position and had conformed itself to conditions in the world. The Church rationalized the situation by stating that since it could not be perfect this was the best that could be done. Even rationalization could not hide from those who wished to see that the Church was largely irrelevant to the masses of the people; that it had suffered continued and devastating defeats; that it lacked discernment on vital issues of the day; and that the Church itself which was supposed to be the light of the world was groping about in darkness.

Out of this welter of confusing ideas, certain truths emerge for those who cling to the revelational nature and function of the Church. One is that the Church must take a stand today for truth and right against untruth and wrong. It means that the Church is to set its face strongly against the running tide. Always must she militate against wrong whether it is found in high circles or low. The Church cannot afford to favor one side or the other unless the side she favors is standing for the right. Neither wealth nor political power ought ever to swing the Church to its side as against right. Whatever is wrong in itself, no matter how it is supported or who is for it, the Church must lift its voice. And as this is true in economic, political, and social issues, so it is primarily true for missions. If it is wrong to let the world lie in heathen darkness then the Church must lift her voice against it whatever the time of day or night. And if the Church itself is wrong then the Church must confess its own sins, purge its own self, and seek in penitence to do what it had failed to do in generations past. A perfect Church we can never expect; weaknesses and defects within the empirical body no Christian can deny. In the midst of this, however, the Church needs to be cleansed of its own impurities and stand for truth even when it means conviction within as well as without.

Across the years the great failure of the Church has been the lack of action to match its profession. It did not practice what it preached. Soon the message that was preached was lost because of the failure to practice it. The normal process was to water down the message to match the lives of the people rather than to bring the lives of the people up to the message being preached. At first it was just a failure to live up to the message. Then the message was lost and the practice of the people ceased to be related to the eternal message, eventuating in a superstructure which was devoid of a foundation. The result was fatal to the witness of the Church at home and abroad. Thus today we stand in need of men who will summon the Church to a renewed consciousness of what the true faith is, and then direct the lives of men so that they will demonstrate in action what they hold in faith.

Another great truth we derive, as we have previously stated, is that the Church exists in a state of tension in the world. Because it has been overlooked by the Church or because the Church has been unconscious of it, its effect has been nullified. In other words the Church does not experience times of crisis, it always lives in a crisis situation. Never is it biblically possible to speak of the Church at rest until the consummation. Until that occurs the Church is a militant body. The state of tension exists because the Church knows that this world is the scene of the bloodiest spiritual battle between God and the devil; between right and wrong; between heaven and hell; between death and eternal life. In this conflict the Church is called upon to witness against these forces of darkness which dominate this world and which are the objects of divine wrath. While it is true that the world and men are naturally the objects of divine wrath it is also true that they are the objects of God's redemptive grace. It is in the midst of this fierce struggle that the Church is called to witness to the redeeming mercies of God for individual men and also to the sure hope that God will someday deliver His entire physical creation from the blight of sin and rescue it from the hands of the evil one whose machinations and designs will be frustrated, whose power will be ended, and whose own destruction is certain. For as long as there shall be history the Church stands in a world that is finite, empirical, and transitory, knowing that it is rooted and grounded in a new and divine order that is infinite and eternal.

Further the Church today must demonstrate the relevancy of God to this empirical order. On all sides there is the assumption that God is no longer relevant to this world situation. And with this conclusion, the Church, whose own relevancy depends upon the relevancy of God, is struck a mortal blow that wounds it to its very soul. When God is relevant the Church will be relevant; when the Church is relevant God will be relevant. But when either of these is shown to be irrelevant then the framework of the faith in a total philosophy of missions is destroyed. The relevancy of God not only must be demonstrated in America. Over the whole wide world, whether it be India or Japan or China, there is increasing evidence that people believe all religion to be irrelevant. Secularism and sciencism have replaced all forms of religion, and religion's relevancy for all faiths increasingly remains to be demonstrated. Therefore Christianity faces a grave problem in fulfilling the function of the Church by making the gospel known to all the world. Whereas Christianity formerly demonstrated that Christianity was the true religion among many religions, now it must first demonstrate that religion is relevant at all, and then go on to prove that Christianity is the relevant faith.

Finally the Church must harness its total forces and power in this battle against the world and the devil. There has always been a small nucleus in the Church that has remained true to the nature and function of the Church. But around this small nucleus there has been a large fringe of unconcerned people whose sole use for the Church has been as an ark of safety when the storms become too great. Until that transpires they prefer to trust themselves and forsake the Church, coming to it in moments of extreme crisis. For them the faith is relevant only when tribulation becomes their lot. When all goes well they forget the Church. So it is that the Church must harness its manpower and unify its witness in this hour of great stress.

In all that has been said about the function of the Church, reference has been made primarily to the commission of the Church to evangelize the world. In this framework it means to save individuals souls from eternal death and also to finish the task which has been given the Church to perform. Of the other function of the Church nothing has been said since it is assumed that this second function follows logically upon the first. That second function of the Church is to provide nourishment for the saints and to attend to the work of growth in grace which is the norm after regeneration and admittance into the fellowship of the Church. This function is by no means to be slighted, for it is of inestimable moment in carrying out the first function. Only a spiritually nourished and spiritually mature Church can do this.

It is self evident that a Church which is growing in grace is one that will be obedient to the will and wishes of its Head. It will be rooted and grounded in the soteriological experience of the faith, and immersed in the experience of sanctification. Holiness before the Lord is the safest assurance that the Church will be filled with a divine sense of direction and will be endued with divine power rising out of lives totally consecrated to Jesus Christ. Without the attempt on the part of the Church to fulfill its divine commission there cannot be said to be holiness before the Lord. In its essence holiness means not along purity of life and doctrine, important as they are, but also unquestioned obedience to the divine commands. So also consecration in its deepest biblical meaning connotes unquestioned obedience to the divine command, self or the ego being placed upon the altar of sacrifice and with cords bound to that altar.

The second function of the Church, then is the stimulation of its people into a sanctifying experience whereby they voluntarily identify themselves with the other side of the cross of Christ. The one side is His voluntary death for us; the other side is our voluntary identification in that death as expressed in the words, "I am crucified with Him." A missionary philosophy perishes without this sanctifying experience within the body of Christ, the fruit of which is the increase in passion to do the will of

Chapter 6

A FINAL THEOLOGY—THE INDIVIDUAL AND
THE CHURCH

I T IS IMPOSSIBLE to be abstract about the nature and the function
of the Church and still maintain a healthy and biblical Christian faith. In the preceding chapter the final theology of the
Church as to its nature and function has been outlined. This is
only theory, however, and does not become practical until it is
individualized and made applicable to every member of the visible
church. All too frequently Christians will murmur intellectual
assent to similar declarations concerning the Church but will never
see the subjective reference to personal experience. It is simple
to excuse one's self and place the blame for inaction on someone
else. It is simple to agree that the gospel of Christ has a universal
application and it is likewise easy to let others assume the obligations
and responsibilities which this easy assumption involves.

It is apparent for those who wish to look that the average
Christian today is negligent and misinformed or else disobedient
in his relationship to Jesus Christ and the demands which this
discipleship requires. By and large the claims of Christ are not
taken seriously and the radical disjunction normally inherent in
those whose lives have been touched by the gospel is not seen.
Everywhere there is an unconcern for things which are vital to

the faith, and without which there can be no accomplishment of the divine purposes for the world. Behind the thinking of the average Christian lies the idea that the demands of the Christian faith on individual lives can be fulfilled in conjunction with the normal operation of the patterns of life according to individual wishes and ambitions. In short there is lacking in the lives of individual Christians that separation from the finite world; that yieldedness to the Christ of God that characterized the individuals connected with the early Church.

Of necessity the Church is composed of individuals, the sum total of which constitute that visible body. It is impossible to speak of a dynamic and world shaking Church unless the individuals who make up the Church are dynamic themselves and living in such a way as to shake the world. The nature and function of the Church must be outlined and understood by Christians, but more than this, that truth must be incarnated in the souls of the faithful until their lives radiate that truth in transforming power.

A classic expression of the state of apathy existing among believers comes from the Jerusalem Conference of 1928. Here it was succinctly stated that the Galilean road to many is not one that was built for daily travel. It was to be used occasionally, when no other easier road would avail. Less acceptable was the thought that the way of the cross was to be followed by the bulk of the Christians. It was for nobler souls and sacrificial martyrs, perhaps those with a "special calling" from God. Essentially this meant then as it does today that the cross with reference to the individual has been removed to a peripheral position rather than kept in a central place in Christian experience. Just as religion among the people of the world has been banished from its central place in life so Christianity in its real meaning has been banished from the central place in the Christian life. Truly this is paradoxical and amazing to speak of a Christian life with the Christian aspect given incidental place.

Another way of expressing the same dilemma which the Church faces in its membership is to say that loyalties have been altered. In an age when there are competing forces seeking first place in the loyalties of men, the natural expectation is that some people will succumb to the lures of these competing loyalties and renounce their former allegiance where once it was a reality. In other cases there never was adherence to a biblical loyalty at any time. At this point the leadership of the Church has failed and its failure is miserably reflected in the lives of the people the leadership should have helped into a place and position of true discipleship.

Most concretely the decay and decline of the Church from being dynamic to being static has been reflected in that area for which the Church was called into being. Existing IN and FOR the sake of the world it is natural to observe that when spiritual decay hits the Church it is immediately reflected in the failure of the Church to function in the primary area which is the missionary area. That is why Professor Hocking could discern such awful breaches in the walls of our attack upon the non-Christian world, and his recommendation that the foreign mission of the Church be radically altered or given up sprang from his recognition that the Church at home had changed basically. The conflict at home had also extended itself to the foreign mission field and in both areas the Church was beaten, perplexed, retrogressing, and in despair.

In the painful process of defeat, humiliation, and despair the Church came to see that its centre of reference was gone. Man being rooted and grounded in God in the Christian experience cannot remove God as the centre of his life without losing his own balance and suffering the consequences of his sin. Having tried to make of God for the Christian what the Christian himself wished God to be proved a failure. The insipid, sweet-tasting, sentimental God of love Who was removed from His real character became a comfortable idea to palliate dead and dying consciences. In an effort to proclaim the love of this God of love even the meaning of love itself was lost. Love had been made the ground of excuse for man who had taken God from the centre of his Christian experience. All the time the biblical concept of the God of love should have shaken each sentimental Christian from his fearful devastating lethergy. Prophet voices should have been raised to demonstrate that our God of love is a fearful and awe inspiring God, for all that is not consistent with love must be eradicated and removed whatever the cost. Everything opposed to this divine love is doomed to complete and final destruction. But this truth terrified, so the concept of the biblical God of love was altered to please the tastes of dilettantes and appease the fears of the cowardly.

In the final theology of the individual in relation to God, of which we speak here, several truths emerge with clarity. The Christian is rooted and grounded in the redemptive work of God. At the beginning, in the centre, and at the end of everything there stands the immutable and eternal Father. His is the divine initiative which brings the sinner into vital communion with Himself through His son the Lord Jesus Christ. He alone is the real and rightful Sovereign; He is the Absolute One. And in this concept of God who is the true centre of the Christian life we eliminate relative elements and leave only the eternal and unchanging. This redemption of God is organically connected with the production of a new life, the normal accomplishments of which are specific obligations and responsibilities that are impossible to escape. They are concrete and tangible. Deviation is impossible except as it carries with it violation of the divine will or disobedience or transgression.

At the heart of the redemption which has been wrought for us via the merits of Christ in His atoning work on Calvary there is the radical assumption that every believer is a purchased possession whose will, intellect, and emotions belong by creation and by redemption to Almighty God. This includes every consequence implied in this radical assumption. Needless to say the relation which is here meant is one that demands of the individual Christian in his relationship to Jesus Christ the absolute, undivided surrender of self, with all of his hopes, ambitions, and aspirations to the full and complete control and charge of God. And as the Church in its nature is divinely ordained to be theocentric so also is it the will of God that every Christian life be theocentric

with God as the point of reference, the polestar to guide and
to lead. Little does it matter whether men like this arrangement.
Of great importance is the truth that it springs out of the nature
of God Himself and this, rather than what man thinks, is the
all-important aspect. Again for the individual it must be stressed
as it was for other parts of a final missionary theology that this
is a valid and indestructible law which comes from above and
not from within. For that reason it is eternally valid and everlastingly indestructible. Man was unable to create for himself rules
and standards in soteriology without incurring the penalty of
eternal death; so the Christian whose position rests upon standards
and rules created from above, rests on rules and standards in the
Christian life which come from above and not from within himself.

In this orientation at the centre of which we always find God
there is still room for an infinite variety of religious experiences.
In its objective reference there is an unchanging core around
which all experience is oriented. But there is a subjective elas-
ticity in the experimental which allows for the infinite variety.
The Christ the Scriptures proclaim is thus always the same; His
Person and work change not. But to each man the circumstances
and pattern of his experience may differ. This is true also in
the relationship of the individual to God in the post-regenerative
life which is centered in its reference around the will of God.

The ultimate end and the supreme motive for each Christian
is the will of God. Nowhere is God concerned with individual
happiness *per se*. Perhaps it comes to some as a fruit but to no
one as a direct object. There is no abstraction here, no possibility
to haggle over terminology. Concretely each Christian is called
upon to do God's will. In this there can be no compromise and
no section of a life can remain untouched in this demand. Thus
the Psalmist declares: "Delight thyself also in the Lord; and he
shall give thee the desires of thine heart." Here is a superb paradox,
and an essential truth. The man whose will is centered in the
will of God can ask and obtain whatever he wishes. He can
do whatever he wants. And all this only because there is the
identification of self with the will of God. When His will be-

comes my will then there is full liberty for me to will. And therein is His will reflected and His glory enhanced.

The will of God primarily has to do with the eternal purposes of God in Christ Jesus. This has a theocentric bias and removes the center of reference from man to God. Few believers like to accept this because of the implications. It involves the human will in a decision as to whether the life of the believer shall be one of self-control or of God-control. It involves self-sacrifice. It is the other side of the cross of Christ of which the Apostle Paul speaks in Galatians 2:20. "I am crucified with Christ." Christians must and do believe that Christ died for them. This is the one side of the cross. Believers must die with Him. Death to self changes one's views. This is the other side. A new world outlook springs out of this death which is a Weltanschauung from God's point of view. This view is revealed to those who identify themselves with the cross of Christ.

The will of God is a radical departure from accepted notions. In the death of self all selfish motives are purged and in place thereof is an understanding of the will of God for the individual under any circumstances and at all times. Eliminated is the pampering of self whether physically, intellectually, spiritually, or emotionally. Gone are the relatives which used to predominate in the life of the believer and substituted for that is the absolute and unchanging of the Lord God. Conformity to the world in all of its processes and forms as well as in all of its sins dies at the cross, too. This death sees clearly that even the believer who is regenerate cannot master self. Paradoxically the mastery of self comes through death, and in the death of self the believer travels the road to the highest fulfillment of true self in the very denial of self. "Except a corn of wheat fall into the ground and die . . ." is the biblical answer to the problem of the will of God.

Concretely the will of God is the attainment of His own purposes, for the glory of Himself, and the complete destruction of evil and the devil. More specifically, individual believers are the agents through whom God chooses to work in the accomplishment of the divine purpose. This purpose is to take the gospel of

Christ to all men everywhere. Individuals must confront individuals with God's revelation of Himself in Jesus Christ and demand of those whom they reach that there shall be the acknowledgment of God and the acceptance of His salvation. The presentation of His claims and the acceptance of His offer is followed by building up a community of those who are identified with Jesus Christ. This is the real will of God, and it is on this premise and attitude that apostolic missions were made tenable. Apart from this view of the will of God which embraces the world through the efforts of believers there is no lasting and permanent basis for a missionary philosophy. Without such a final and unchanging foundation the missionary enterprise must die in the long run. Incidentally this radical confrontation of men everywhere with the gospel is not a permeative process. It is not designed to bring to men the blessings of civilization or even a free and enlightened spirit. Believers are not called upon to sacrifice limb and life to bring goodwill to men. They are agents who proclaim the divine wrath of God against sinners and present them with the solution in Jesus. Neither is it "sharing religious experience" anymore than it is the social gospel of amelioration. Essentially the will of God is that objective truth shall be conveyed to men everywhere. And this catches every believer in the web of a threefold triad from which we cannot, nor from which do we wish to, escape: evangelism, proselytism, and conversion.

Modernists have not alone been guilty of perversion here. Conservatives have sometimes fallen into sin in this regard. The orthodox have not always tried, and have often failed, to relate their theology to the world in which we live. There has been some degree of introversion involving a self-centeredness and an other-worldly piousness that has been unbiblical. There have been efforts to delimit the sphere in which Christianity operates, to the extent that the faith has been working in a vacuum without relevancy to the world in which the believer must live and for which he does live that the world may receive benefits. For the believer lives IN the world and FOR the world. "Ye are the salt of the earth" according to Jesus, "and if the salt hath lost its savor . . ." Doctrinal purity is not enough; it must be accompanied by the identification of the believer in the will of God for the whole world.

Many conservatives have spurned education and denied its values. Lurking in the minds of too many there is the false thought that education in itself breeds unbelief and apostasy. As a result there has been a tendency to emphasize only that education which centers in the Bible and to disregard or treat lightly anything beyond this. The will of God is that the gospel shall be taken to the world. This commission does not mean that it has no relevancy to training and education. Indeed a grasp of the structure of primitive life, a knowledge of the religion, morals, and customs of the people to be found in serious cultural anthropological study is not to be underrated. Doing the will of God means making a frontal attack and a lasting impact on non-Christian civilizations. To make this attack is to assail beliefs, customs, social structures, and apprehensions of life. The right execution of the divine task demands more than even many conservatives assume to be necessary.

The will of God is, no doubt, more extensive in its practical applications in the execution of the task than is fancied too. The history of Christian missions might well be studied with the view to discovering what kind of men it is that God has used through the ages. It is no surprise to note that so frequently the doing of the will of God in individual lives has been associated with men and women of great gifts and wide knowledge and learning. All lives with the finest in preparation can alone be the will of God for bringing to a triumphant conclusion that task originating in the giving of the Great Commission.

The Church today needs to be awakened to see several things. First the Church must become openly conscious of the truth that it lives and exists in and for the sake of the world. This truth must filter into the rank and file of the membership until each one sees the second truth that every believer is a constituent member of the Church. And if the Church exists in and for the sake of the world then each individual also exists in and for the sake of the world (a radical departure from generally accepted ideas among believers today who wish to do their own will and live according to human, relative standards rather than divine standards). Then each believer has a specific obligation from which there is no escape. All of this is merely recapturing the vision of what God in Christ meant for the Church to be.

The recapturing of the vision includes an apostolic consciousness of certain truths that are as valid as they were in the first century. This consciousness included the belief that men without Christ are lost. To be lost was not simply a matter of a wrong direction, an opposing slant on life. Lostness meant that men were not properly related to God, and that this condition is one that lasts as long as the relation between God and those who are peculiarly His Children shall last—forever. Even professor Hocking had to admit that the motive for missions is a desire to communicate a spiritual value which those who transmitted it regarded as unique and supreme. He also admits that it indicates a sense of the danger of the unsaved along with the tragedy that being unsaved denotes. The consciousness of the estate of the people without Christ breeds a sense of urgency which breathed through the apostolic Church on every side. To them there was a need for haste.

If men were lost apart from Christ and if there was a sense of urgency, there was also an apostolic belief that no other agency, religion, or individual; no other method of works or acts of merit; nothing normally within an individual could change his lost estate. God meant the Church and the individuals within the Church to be unchangingly sure that apart from Jesus Christ there is no hope. The apostolic Church so believed and so preached. No substitutes were offered; the faith was not watered down; men were pointed unhesitatingly to Christ. In an hour of apparent calm as in the hour of crisis it was still the same to the apostolic Church. It was aware that for the Church there is no calm and that outward aspects of the world situation do not change the vital concern of individual men for the souls of men. Christ the only hope! Christ the only message!

The apostolic Church also made the obligations of that Church specific. There was the consciousness that God works through men and that God wants to work through all believers. The apostolic period is saturated with material showing that converts took this seriously and expected to become identified in the work of God through themselves. There was no question about discipleship. It followed automatically. And where there are indications of looseness there are also words of exhortation leading to eventual exclusion for the failure to obey. Life was counted cheap for the cause of Christ and some sought a martyr's death for the glory of God and the sure hope of reunion with Christ. They did this because they believed that the gospel is the answer to the needs of man and that it is true for all and applicable and open to all. Individuals acknowledged their own obligation before God and the responsibility which came as a result of the transformation in their lives. All believers then and now are in debt to the gospel and the discharge of that debt comes through doing the will of God. There is committed to each believer a divine trusteeship, which is really a stewardship, for which each must give an account before God.

No one can deny that the early Christians believed strongly in a judgment for themselves at which time they were to give an account of their stewardship of life. This consciousness was in part responsible for the kind of lives they lived, and certainly constituted a part of the vision they had of what Christ meant each individual Christian to be. To use properly one's stewardship meant more than to accumulate wealth, fame, or power. Always one senses that apostolic feeling for the hereafter as emphasized by Paul who spoke of the Christian citizenship being in heaven from whence we wait for a Saviour.

All of this being true, the apostolic believers also were looking for His coming. To them there was a shortness of time before that second advent in which they were to be busy doing His will. They faced the fact that no one knew either the day or the hour, and to them who lived in close time sequence to His ascension the second advent was nearer than to many in this hour. They were the harvesters whose supreme business was to bring in the sheaves before the Master returned home.

As in the apostolic time there was this consciousness of certain truths, so today we must regain that same consciousness. Especially is that true in connection with the second advent. The passing of the centuries give us reason to believe that perhaps His coming draweth nigh. But whether He returns visibly within the lifetime of each individual or not, it is certain that for those who die He does come. Their works and labors are over at death and nothing can be added or taken away. Thus it is that while we long for His personal, visible coming, and the establishment of His kingdom, some die each day without that having been fulfilled save in the sense that their day is over, their opportunities are gone. Eternity must then be faced in the light of what has been done during the time of this stewardship.

Each believer must catch the vision of what God expects each one to believe and be. The renewal of the apostolic consciousness of the concepts just mentioned is needed. This does not suffice. To it must be added the expression of inward persuasion and belief in the realm of action. To know that men are lost and to do nothing about it is irrational. To know that we must give an account of our stewardship and then do nothing to press our stewardship is to act foolishly. To see the obligation and responsibility of each Christian and then to sit back while someone else acts is not a normal Christian response. In that crucified life in which the believer is identified in the cross of Christ there are three concrete ways the believer can manifest the fruits of the surrendered life.

First of all, men are everywhere called upon to go. This is predicated upon the biblical doctrine that every believer is called to be a missionary. This calling to be a missionary, which is universal for all believers, is not the limited doctrine to the effect that all must go to a foreign field. As never before we must destroy the idea that the world is divided into two parts—the one in which we live which we designate as the "home" field and the rest of the world which we designate as the "foreign" field. So far as God is concerned the WORLD is the field and every believer is called upon to witness in the world. The particular area where one witnesses is not dramatically important by any means. The important element is that each individual be doing the will of God wherever that will of God may lead. Naturally there are factors which normally would militate for an increased attention to the fields away from home which are less touched by the gospel. Of that we shall have more to say later on.

The central place of stress, which must be reiterated over and over again, is that EVERY Christian is called upon to be a witness to the truth of the gospel. No believer is exempted from the obligation and the responsibility of himself taking that good news of salvation to other men. To be a missionary is not a unique calling limited to those who choose vocational Christian service, whether in the home ministry or on the foreign field. To be a missionary rather is a universal calling for all believers. The Scriptures are perfectly plain that the bulk of the forward progress in the apostolic period was accomplished by reason of the simple Christians who went everywhere preaching the Word. It is not to be understood by this seemingly radical assertion that every Christian ought to be in vocational Christian service. All men ought not be ministers of the gospel in the technical sense of that word. All believers ought not be foreign missionaries in the technical sense of that word either. But all men, regardless of place and position, ought to be missionaries to the people round about them. And if those people in whatever area of life they are working are assured that they are in the will of God there is no further question to be raised. In that will, speaking now specifically of life occupations for income producing purposes, the individual is to be a missionary for Christ. Thus the Christian medical man who is called to work in that field must be a witness to people with whom he comes in contact. The Christian dentist must be a witness in his field of endeavor. The business man, assuming first that this is the will of God for him, must be a living and vocal witness to the saving power of Jesus in his business life and contacts.

Here a word of caution must be expressed for those people who rationalize through the meaning of discipleship and the stewardship of a life. It is biblically satisfactory for any man to be a physician or a dentist or a lawyer if that is God's will for his life. But it remains for each individual to account satisfactorily for the calling into which he goes. Ever before him ought to stand the knowledge that some day he shall face the judgment seat of Christ and there give Him an account of the stewardship of that life. No excuses will do then. Only he that doeth the will of God abideth forever. A man, therefore, had better be careful to see that he is really doing the will of God in the choice of a life work and is not rationalizing through to relieve himself of something that he does not wish to do. Commonly the line of argument which men follow is the same. Those who engage in work other than vocational Christian labor often argue that what they do is necessary and important. This is always true but does not answer the real question. They state that they can make money and be able to support others. Perhaps by their skill in the production of this world's goods they argue they can send out more people than had the individual gone out himself. Multiplying a ministry by money is a familiar argument. But this does not answer the real question either. All of the arguments which men advance to rationalize their actions carry no weight when they are couched in terms that demonstrate their relativity. Before God it makes no difference that a man can earn money and support more missionaries in number than the labor of himself. Before God it makes no difference that a man thinks he can serve God just as well in business or in medicine as in the ministry. These are arguments *ad hominem* which fail to take into account the vital truth of the revelation. God is not interested in argument; He is interested that men should do His will. And doing that will means that they shall yield themselves without wish or will to God that He may choose the field of work and the place of service. This is the radical nature of the demand made upon men by the gospel. It has never been a problem with men as to the nature of their service when once they have settled the question of yielding their wills to God who made them and purchased them. Interpreted in terms of a philosophy of missions this book would fail in its purpose unless it pointed out convincingly that the will of God is that the gospel shall be taken to the ends of the earth. THIS IS HIS WILL!

In the light of the biblical assertion that God has willed that
the gospel shall be taken to the ends of the earth; and in the light
of the same revealing truth that God has ordained that this shall
be done through His children who have been redeemed and called
to this high task or calling, a slightly different approach must now
be advanced over the concessions that have been made so far for
individual Christians. It is true that while each Christian is called
to be a missionary, all ought not be foreign missionaries nor ought
all Christians engage in vocational Christian service. The emphasis
has been laid upon doing the will of God. Unfortunately this true
biblical doctrine has been abused by many Christians who delude
themselves into thinking they are doing the will of God outside
of vocational Christian service.

A close study of statistics will demonstrate the truth of what is
said here. In the year 1938 when a survey of the foreign mission
work of the Protestant world was made, including denominational,
interdenominational, and all kinds of Protestant missionary work,
there were around twenty-seven thousand male and female foreign
missionaries. These figures include every Protestant missionary sending nation in the world, although the majority of the missionaries
came from the English speaking world. These twenty-seven thousand
missionaries, including men and women (married and single
women) ministered to a non-Christian constituency numbering one
billion five hundred million people. Translated into the work of a
single missionary it meant that there was one missionary representative for approximately every fifty thousand people. At the same
time in the United States of America alone there were more Baptist
ministers than that, ministering to a much smaller constituency,
which when extended to include all ministers meant there was one
minister for four hundred people or less. And this against one agent
for every fifty thousand people on the foreign field! It must be
remarked that these figures for the United States DO NOT include
the wives of male ministers nor do they take into account the
innumerable female helpers used by the churches as full and part
time vocational Christian workers.

To put it mildly the conclusion must be that if it is the will of God that the gospel shall be taken to the ends of the earth, there is an amazing disparity in the figures quoted above. Something is radically wrong somewhere! One must conclude that either God is not sufficiently interested in the heathen to warrant His calling enough people to do the job out in the regions beyond, or that He has called enough people, but they have not responded the way they should. It is unthinkable to believe that God (and unscriptural too) is more interested in the white man of the United States than He is in the black man of Africa and the yellow man of India and China. It is ONE world and ONE gospel for all the world. The Church has not taken its task seriously enough to do the divine job that it has been assigned to do. And not the abstract Church is to blame but individual men and women who have not identified themselves individually in the task for which they too must give an account individually in the judgment.

Because of the foregoing we must now interpret the will of God relative to individual Christians. Bearing in mind that it is the will of God for all men to have the gospel and that this task of taking it has been assigned to all believers, certain reasonable conclusions stand forth clearly. Since the evangelization of the world is not a permeative process working in an evolving fashion it follows that the evangelization of the world must be accomplished by some generation in its generation. Not being cumulative or evolving, some generation must enlist every individual and with a great push accomplish the task. Each generation has only its generation in which to do it. Manpower is essential for the completion of the task that is the will of God. God wanting that thing done also makes it possible for it to be done, and Himself "calls" enough people to engage in that task so that it can be accomplished. Every Christian, therefore, must be able to give a creditable account of himself. Inasmuch as the primary will of God concerns the spreading of the knowledge of the gospel of Christ to all, each Christian must be able to give a good reason why he is not specifically engaged in that task. The burden of proof rests on the individual to show that God has not called him to go, rather than that the burden of proof rests on God to give each man a cataclysmic experience of some nebulous kind which occurs rarely. God has already spoken. The revelation exists for any Christian who wishes to know the will of God for an individual life. But it must be remembered that the will of God for individual lives is indestructibly related to the eternal purpose of God for the whole world. The purpose is the gospel to the whole wide world. Each individual Christian must fit himself into that divinely revealed plan and each must play his part in it. Ignorance is no excuse. The plans of self for gain, fame, and any other end are no excuse. There is absolutely no plea of any kind that will suffice before God, anymore than that there is a possibility of escaping from the believer's judgment based upon his works after regeneration.

The Church of Christ must veil its face to hide the tragic tears that flow from the truth that the average Christian lives on the fringe of the Church and is usually disinterested and disinclined to do anything. Lethargically and pathetically quiescent church members sit and watch the years roll by as heaven mourns and angels wait to sing their triumphant victory song. Concerned with the things of life and mortality our people rarely rise above the claims of the hour in the material matters of life and seemingly bury themselves forever in those things which do not count except in time, and which will be burned in the fires of eternity. While it is everlastingly true that God is sovereign and that He can do as He wills, it is true also that God can and does impose upon Himself limitations consistent with His sovereignty. Among them is the freely granted privilege that God's children may freely and without force unite themselves in the divine purpose of taking the gospel to the whole world. This will of God is not an arbitrary decision backed up by an arbitrary force which embraces the world of the believer and forces him into action apart from his own will. There is indeed a divine mystery as to why God should patiently wait for His children to enlist themselves in His army and fall into line with His eternal plan. The answer to this we do not know in time but we shall know it in eternity. Meanwhile, God still waits for individuals to grasp the vision of His purpose and to give their lives in seeking the accomplishment of that purpose. It must be done, it shall be done, and some generation will do it. Each generation failing to do it will be judged according to what each individual has contributed to the task. But the greater number of our people still wait on the sidelines and do nothing with the greatest task in the world, requiring the greatest genius, the highest skill, tremendous faith, undying love, unfailing perseverance, and the knowledge that this is the will of God.

Five hundred million people have never once heard the name of Christ. Twice that number lie in darkness and under the shadow of death even though they have heard the name. So long as this condition continues it remains for every Christian to give satisfactory reason why he is not on the firing line in this battle between the forces of good and evil, of light and darkness, of God and the devil. In this struggle there is nothing that can replace lives yielded to God to do His will in taking the gospel to the world. Money is a vital necessity for carrying out the great commission. Prayer is a *sine qua non* for the same operation. But there are things that neither money nor prayer can do. They cannot do what God has ordained shall be done by men themselves. This is not to underestimate the need of both of these other elements or to reduce their importance. But it remains that manpower is essential to the task in view. And until the flood of men has been released in a frontal assault on all of the strongholds of the devil, for that length of time the task will be undone.

Even as the divine task requires manpower for the fulfillment of the job so must there be money which is the second *sine qua non* for the Christian. A man must not only think of himself in terms of a missionary and perhaps devote his full life to that job as a vocation, he must think in terms of the giving of his money and the use of it in finishing the missionary commission. It is not idle speculation that the spiritual level of men is clearly seen by what they do with their money. Spiritual Christians have no problem about the tithe. To them it comes as automatically as breathing. Many are the arguments to the effect that the New Testament is silent about the obligations of tithing. We are told that it is an Old Testament principle operating under law but not under grace. There is not a single argument or combination of arguments which can be advanced successfully against tithing. There is a wider principle operating in relation to money which, if Christians accepted it, would solve every financial problem. Reference here is made to the biblical truth that all of life is a stewardship. In this the stewardship of money is part of the complete picture. One does not need to give an account to God about the ten percent which belongs to God directly as though his task is finished with this accounting. He must give an account of the remaining ninety percent. Stewardship of money involves ALL money and not simply a portion. However, it appears plain that at least ten percent ought to be set aside specifically for the work of the Lord. This does not mean the payment of doctor's bills on the assumption that if God made you sick you ought to use His portion of your money to be made well. Nor does it include gifts made to secular charity like the Red Cross, Community Fund, etc. The tithe means ten percent of your money going into the Lord's work. Not for self, not for friends, not for secular charity, good as it may be, but ten percent for the Lord.

For anyone who wishes to look there are statistics available which prove that the average Christian is dishonest with God in his financial responsibilities as a Christian. Again one is reminded that being a Christian carries with it peculiar responsibilities and obligations. Tithing, or the use of money, is one of them. On the whole, all of the giving of Christians in America to the churches does not amount to more that two percent of their income. This is exactly one fifth of what it ought to be. Needless to say there is no possible excuse which will satisfy divine justice for the failure to be honest with God in financial matters. Rationalization will not help; ignorance will be no excuse. Even under grace there is a decided amount of law which will be injected into the believer's judgment relative to satisfying the demands of God by His people.

The last two ecumenical missionary conferences took cognizance of the sources of income for foreign missionary work. The gifts of money on which the enterprise rests come from a small group of people. This is not to disparage large gifts from people of means, but it does indicate that the membership of the churches by and large had little interest in the missionary endeavor. Contrary to biblical truth the enterprise was resting altogether too much on a human foundation that was not right. Intrinsically the enterprise is the interest of all Christians and not just a few monied individuals. In the nature of the case the foreign missionary enterprise is the interest of the Church as a whole and not any small group of people no matter how devoted they may be. Recent events seem to foretell the sharp decrease in large gifts. If this be true then the money to maintain and enlarge the missionary work must come from a larger number of smaller givers. And if there is to be the kind of expansion of the program so that the task can be completed it will mean the identification of most of the believers to the full extent of their abilities in a financial way.*

In our generation it needs to be said over and over again that it is impossible to obtain adequate and continued support for the missionary enterprise apart from a persistent and undying belief in the objective of missions. Here the return to a biblical theology of missions in which the facets that go to make up the philosophy of missions are understood by the people will constitute the difference, humanly speaking, between success and failure. When believers truly are conscious that men without Christ are lost; when they are assured that it is the will of God for all men to be given the gospel; when they see their personal obligations and responsibilities, then there will result, normally, action in accord with that knowledge. In the long run people will not be led into the support of educational, and other enterprises in themselves. There is good reason to keep money at home and to use it advantageously here in that case. And there is no indestructible and eternally valid reason why we OUGHT to give money for people apart from the revelation

---

* While final reports for 1948 are not available it is evident that many of the denominations have not been able to obtain funds equal to their budgetary needs. As late as one month before the closing of the books, the U. S. A. Presbyterian Church was more than 50% behind in benevolences. The Northern Baptist Convention was appealing for funds to meet its budget, so as to avoid a deficit.

of God in Jesus Christ. For those who believe that there are returns to our own people for this kind of investment it can be replied that giving then ceases to be giving and becomes a business arrangement from which a return to the giver is expected. And this view is utterly foreign to the Word of God.

The only way missions will become the interest of all the people is by missions becoming the interest of believers one by one. That attitude, which includes the shrug of shoulders accompanied by the thought that if the individual does not do it, it will make no difference, is cancerous when extended to many people. Actually such is the case. Many people who together make up the bulk of the Church are inclined to believe that absence of interest on the part of one believer will not hurt the total cause. Unfortunately this occurs too frequently among many people and the cause is hurt financially. Until Christians arrive at that spiritual maturity of identifying themselves in the will of God for tithing there is little hope that the mission will be completed.

In the United States particularly it is not uncommon to note vast expenditures of money for the "advance" of the kingdom at home. (Again we have the relativist and evolutionary bias.) Huge temples of worship with more than adequate facilities for Sunday Schools, recreation, etc. are constantly being erected. The question is not one of deciding whether we ought to worship in big or little buildings. Rather it is wrapped around the revelational argument that where a man's treasure is there will his heart be also. And when the treasure is at home the heart is at home too. Instead the treasure ought to be out in the regions beyond and then will the heart be out there also for those for whom Christ died.

There are several biblical principles to be applied in the use of money for the Lord. Giving ought to be proportionate. We are to give as the Lord has prospered us. The tithe is not enough for those of larger means. Many outstanding Christians of means have found that the use of fifty or more percent of their income is not too much for God. John Wesley and William Carey stand out as men who have had large incomes for their day, but who willingly lived on a fraction of their incomes that the remainder might be dedicated to the work of Christ and the progress of the kingdom. The tithe is a good start for all, but it does not terminate our giving responsibilities when we have done that.

Another biblical principle is that giving should be systematic. Regularly each week or month we are to lay aside, from what God has given, something for Him. The attitude that some Christians who tithe have is bad. They save their tithe money rather than dispensing it regularly. God means for the believer to use the Lord's money REGULARLY—week by week and month by month depending on the individual case as to the time when it comes in. Giving ought to be designed, not careless. Believers are personally responsible for the use of their money and they are to see that it goes through the proper channels. Money is for God's use and no Christian ought to contribute to programs or men where the money will not glorify God and be used in the promotion of God's work.

The Church must be blamed in some cases for the failure of individual believers to give of their substance. Many people become conscious that campaigns to raise money seem to exist solely for the purpose of raising money. This is spiritually deadening and biblically wrong. The raising of money in itself is a questionable procedure. Instead there is a need for emphasis on the spiritual gains which come from giving. Giving is really designed to reflect the gratitude of the believer to God for what He has done. It is further designed to increase the enthusiasm for the true objective which will result in giving. In this case giving is the reflection of a prior enthusiasm of which giving is the outgrowth. Giving should remind the believers that they are pouring themselves, through their gifts, into the divine undertaking of God, the mission of the Church, and its commission. It is not a human, but a divine cause. Missionary propaganda is not primarily designed to raise money but this actually is what it seems to be so often.

Just as there is a need for a new vision of what the relation of each individual is to the will of God for the world and for each individual in connection with the eternal purpose, there is also a need for a new vision of what giving is and what its objectives are.

Without this there can be no hope of completing the commission which a revelational philosophy of missions demands *per se.*

As an individual expresses himself concretely in going and giving, there is the third angle of this divine triangle involving the believer. All are called to be missionaries in some sense. All are compelled to give of their substance. All are to pray. Prayer has purposely been left for discussion to the end, not because it is less important, but because it is more important.

At the outset of a discussion of prayer every believer ought to be reminded that there are many things we do not know about prayer. There are many paradoxes connected with its use. A rigid Calvinist could conceivably assume that since God is sovereign and does what He wants, events will transpire with or without prayer. An Arminian might conclude that since men have free will, prayer can be dispensed with since one cannot admit too easily the operation of divine grace in the lives of men to such an extent that their free will is eliminated. Whatever the view from the angle of systematic theology, it must be stated that from the biblical point of view prayer is stressed, encouraged, said to be answered, and magnified. It is apparent that prayer releases latent forces in the universe through God on behalf of His children. To this extent prayer may be likened to atomic energy of which much is being said today.

Atomic power has always existed inherently in the universe, but it was not employed until our generation. It was latent energy which responded to the touch of scientific knowledge, and when released was so dramatic in its effect and so startling in its magnitude that the users of this energy became frightened at the prospects. In a good sense this may be said of prayer too. Prayer in itself does not have power. Prayer does release the power of the Almighty God creating situations and bringing to bear forces which alter every picture and transform circumstances in every area of life. Prayer is not scientific knowledge nor is it obedient to the will of evil men. It carries with it its own peculiar guarantee against misuse and abuse, for the simple reason that the wrong kind of prayer, or the wrong use of prayer involves automatic limitations which operate to safeguard this power which prayer releases against possible abuse.

Thus an evil man cannot avail himself of the power which prayer releases because he is not able to command these energies through prayer. The man who would employ prayer selfishly for the attainment of personal ends is sadly disappointed when he discovers that it cannot be used in this fashion.

Prayer is a means which God employs in connection with His eternal purposes. It is consistent with His nature and conforms to His standards. True prayer implies several things. One is that the person praying is actually a child of God. There is nothing in revelation which assures any sinner, except the penitent coming for mercy, that prayer will be answered. The believer does have assurances that his prayers have worth and value because he is coming in the name of Jesus Christ, whose work makes it possible for reborn men to have access to the throne of grace. The second truth prayer implies is that the believers who come are surrendered to the will of God and wish to identify themselves in His purposes and plans for individual lives and for the universe. It will be seen from these two aspects that much that is offered by way of prayer is not really prayer at all. It does not come in the name of Jesus, and if it does, it comes in the interests of personal plans, desires, and ambitions. Or it may come to accomplish aims which are in no wise identified with the eternal purposes of God.

Coming to the problem of why it is that God makes prayer so important in His dealings with man we do not always arrive at the answer. There are elements almost imponderable in this problem. Suffice it to say that the Bible reveals that God has ordained that prayer shall be the means by which He is approached and through which gifts may be secured, His work aided, His immutable purposes attained. To be sure God could work out all things by Himself apart from men and apart from prayer. But He has not deigned to work thus. He indicates that prayer is a means by which His divine power is released for men. Just as a dedicated life is needed by God to supply manpower for doing His will, and just as money is necessary as an instrument for the carrying out of the divine will, so also is prayer a prerequisite for the successful completion of the missionary task. This is not to imply that God cannot work apart from prayer, nor to intimate that He never works apart from any prayer. But let it be said as a general rule that God works in accord with prayer. And the exceptions in no wise invalidate the rules laid down.

Why it is that God should permit apparent limitations to exist in connection with His will is not always plain. We know that He looks for the preaching of the gospel to the ends of the earth. We know that God wants all men to be conformed to the image of His Son. Yet it appears that these and other objectives are contingently related to prayer in some aspect or another, and without prayer much is left undone. We are informed by Christ Himself that requests are granted on the basis of faith. Prayer in many cases is the concrete evidence of that faith. On at least one occasion Jesus stated that demon possession could be terminated only by prayer and fasting. James tells us that men have not because they ask not. Jesus repeatedly stated that we are to ask and we shall receive. One of the main functions of prayer is to ask God for things. The absence of prayer can mean that men will not be saved who ought to be saved, and this in spite of the sophistry which claims that if God foreknows something then it must happen, and somehow the individual foreknown to be saved will have the opportunity. We must answer to that that we believe the revelation does teach adequate foreknowledge; that it does teach God's sovereignty; that it does teach that the lack of prayer prevents things from happening. All we can do is withhold judgment along these lines which appear to be contradictory, since we are finite and must bow before the infinite whose ways are above finding out.

Prayer does change things. It does make a difference. In the face of this truth we can assent to it and act in the light of it. To deny it does not alter the truth; to fail to appropriate what we can expect from it because of wilfulness is unreasonable. I do not need to know all of the principles operating in electricity before I can avail myself of its power. Analogies are limited yet sufficient in this case to illustrate the biblical truth that we do not need to know the full mystery of prayer nor do we need to have plumbed its hidden depths before making use of it. The highest intellect as well as the humblest believer have the same privileges with respect to prayer.

In the use of prayer pertaining to our philosophy of missions the need is irreducible. The whole missionary picture is wrecked without prayer to sustain the enterprise, loose the forces to break down barriers, and produce results which defy human accomplishment. There are no hindrances which in themselves will be broken down. And God Himself works through men and men work with God through prayer. It is not our purpose here to deal with devotional prayer where the believer maintains, strengthens, and possibly severs his relation to his Lord. I am thinking of prayer in terms of the missionary enterprise and the use of prayer in its furtherance.

It ought to be the common prayer of God's people to unite their hearts in asking for laborers for the fields of the world. To be a true prayer and not just a hypocritical utterance it ought to be accompanied by heart searching and the surrender of will on the part of the individual, willing to go himself if so be that God commands it. A parent cannot truly pray for laborers unless willing to let God take his son or daughter for the foreign field. This kind of prayer is not in use among many Christians who are either ignorant of their obligations to ASK God to send forth laborers through His Holy Spirit, or who dare not pray that way because their own hearts are not right as to their part or sacrifice in the enterprise. A united front among Christians on this issue would solve the problem of the manpower shortage and bring about the completion of the divine task.

The prayer for laborers should be in conjunction with the prayer for revival among the believers. When believers are revived there is no problem about the will of God. They desire it, seek it, and pray for it with singleness of heart. The prayer for revival of the believer does many things. It brings spirituality to the body of Christ with a deepening insight into the plan of God for the world. It brings a concern for the lost. It stimulates missionary giving and going. It awakens and quickens the tempo of the spiritual life, strengthening the believer, and conforming him more to the image of Christ. It is related to the missionary goal of the Church.

Prayer is designed to have effect in the hearts of sinful men. It results in conviction of sin by the Holy Spirit and it is effective in bringing men to Christ. Countless examples can be found of people who have prayed, some for many years, for the conversion of individuals and those prayers have been answered. It cannot be said that the salvation would have occurred anyhow. Prayer was an integral part of the effect and there is good biblical ground for this conclusion. Sinners are responsive to the prayers of the saints and wonderful results accrue from the use of this potent weapon which looses spiritual forces of great power. In no wise is this a suggestion that prayer for salvation is some kind of indiscriminate weapon to be used vaguely on all men. In its nature it must be specific and not general. God expects prayer to be aimed at definite objects. More things are missed by prayer because the aim has been hazy or misdirected.

In aiding the missionary program it is beneficial for believers to pray that the Lord will open pocketbooks as well as hearts, the offerer of the prayer himself being willing to have his own pocketbook opened to the extent that is possible. Prayer ought to encompass specific mission fields and people as they labor in the regions beyond. Many missionaries who have been well supported financially, have been left stranded spiritually in foreign lands by the failure of believers to hold the ropes in prayer for them out there in the sea of lost humanity. Missionaries have become physical wrecks because men have failed to uphold their physical needs before God. Mission areas have not responded to the gospel as they should have responded because people at home were too busy to pray. The continuance of stations and work is dependent upon prayer for success and for results.

There cannot be an overemphasis placed upon prayer. Nowhere in the history of the Church has there ever been a place or a case where there was too much prayer. Never has prayer been greater than the return. The spiritual truth is that prayer seems to operate upon principles of adequate return. Much prayer means much fruit. Little prayer means little fruit. Thus the returns are always commensurate with the prayers put forth. If there are cases in which the principle does not seem to operate evenly it always operates so that the answer to the prayers of God's people is beyond and above and over what they have put into their requests. To go is not enough. To give is not enough. The enterprise is truly dependent upon prayer. This is an indissoluble link which cannot be broken without the disruption of the missionary enterprise. As in the case of giving the majority of the believers are on the periphery; few are in the inner circle. There is not enough selfless, sacrificial, soul-searching, God-centered prayer. Any philosophy of missions which does not stress the supreme part that prayer plays in the enterprise, and which does not summon men to action in prayer, does not find itself on revelational ground.

The conclusion of the matter at hand is simple. The function of the Church has no significance without individuals who make up the Church. God works through men; through men who have experienced divine grace in salvation and whose lives are dedicated to Him in totality. Concretely this is expressed in the prayers of men as they identify themselves in the program of God; it is expressed in their gifts of money which reflect an initial spiritual relationship acknowledging obligations and responsibilities; it is expressed by men as they yield themselves to the will of God for the world in bringing to as rapid a completion as possible the divine task of taking the gospel to the ends of the earth. Above all there is the need of bringing home to believers the biblical truth of their stewardship of self, substance, and prayer-life; of getting men to act as they ought in the light of what God meant for believers to be in Christ Jesus. The failure so far is man's failure to conform himself to the plan of God, and it lies in his stubborn refusal to go all the way in identifying himself in the will of God.

The Galilean road may not appear to be suitable for modern travel. But the Master trod that very road. Shall not the servant tread it too?

Chapter 7

A FINAL THEOLOGY—THE ESCHATOLOGICAL PICTURE

THE COURSE of Christian missions has been influenced greatly by varied philosophies of history which Christians have embraced through the years. The fortunes of the missionary enterprise have been subjected, in part, to advances and retrogressions depending upon that philosophy. In some cases there has been neither apparent progress nor retrogression, and still the concept of history held by Christians has prevented any forward movement resulting in the final evangelization of the world.

In the Christian mind there has often been an unconscious compromise in which deadly concessions have been made to philosophies of history which are non-biblical or unbiblical. These concessions have done much to defeat the goal of world evangelization because they have run counter to the true biblical philosophy of history which embraces world evangelization in its view. Again there have been Christians who have held to the biblical philosophy of history in theory but have failed to relate it to their day and practice. As a consequence they have done what their own view would exclude, had they related their actions to the view they professed.

Secular philosophies of history are not usually thought of as being speculative. In fact that is one of the major dangers they seek to avoid. For example the real secular historian does not concern himself with questions of origin, however interesting they may be from other points of view. In theory, at least, he contents himself with those evidences which are clear-cut and tangible and susceptible to scientific historical interpretation. While secular philosophies of history do not pretend to go back beyond the area of available evidence, they do have a legitimate sphere for speculation when they try to peer into the future.

The future, so far as secular historians are concerned, revolves around the world as we know it from the earliest evidence until this very hour. On the basis of this knowledge, and in the light of certain interpretations, the historian peers into the future with the view to forecasting what it has in store for the world of men.

The forecasting of the future by the secular historian rises out of his knowledge of the past and the interpretations which can be derived from its examination. Basic to the idea of forecasting the future is the assumption that recorded human history in some discernible measure reveals the key to the future. Also implied is the idea that man is able and competent to observe historical phenomenon, evaluate it correctly, and reasonably and rationally conclude what the future has in store because of what has preceded.

Regardless of the view of history, from a secular viewpoint, that a man may hold, this much is true—that it is a human judgment involving human decisions, and it has behind it the thought that man is competent and able to judge accurately. Were this concept of the ability of human beings to judge removed there would be no logical basis on which any reputable historian could present a view while maintaining his rationality.

These philosophies of history vary from those which are deeply ingrained with pessimism to those which are highly optimistic. The pessimistic view of history sees inexorable forces in operation which are too great for man. These forces may be economic, social, or political, or a combination of any or all, plus others. In any event man is subject to these forces, the operation of which continue without let or hindrance. It is a form of blind determinism that reduces man to utter impotence. All that man can do is lift his fist toward heaven and shout with despair that all is lost. Rarely does this pessimistic view include a personal God who is at the center of the historical process; a God who is ethical and moral, working out human history in a meaningful way. Rather there is a general resort to the mere animality of man who is one step removed from the savage beast who roams the forest. And God is left out of the picture entirely.

Another secular historical theory is that of the cycle. The adherents of this school of thought see in history recurrent cycles. History is repetitious as man goes through one similar cycle after another. It is immaterial whether these cycles be long or short as far as time duration is concerned. The main thought is that history repeats itself, moving endlessly in a circle so to speak. Obviously it does not imply that history is specifically the same, but generally so. Thus the end of one cycle sees the beginning of another cycle which has the same basic factors and which produces the same general trend until the cycle is completed and a new one begins. This view rarely envisions a consummation or end of history as a grand climax. Continuity is endless unless something should cause the recurring cycles to stop operating.

The spiral view of history varies from that of the cycle by insisting that the process is not one of repetition, but one of rises to new levels and new civilizations. It has a cyclical aspect without the constant factor of recurrence. The recurrence is the cycle, but not in the same pattern each time. Rather due allowance is made for progress and growth; for a rise to higher levels of culture and civilizations. As the cyclical theory posits endless continuity in the same kind of pattern, the spiral view posits endless changes from pattern to pattern in an evolving framework.

A variation from the spiral view is that of the ocean tide theory. In this philosophy, history is likened to the tides of the ocean which sweep in endlessly until they reach a summit. The tides of the ocean may differ in that some do not reach the same distance to the shore as previous rushes, but resistlessly the tide moves onward and upward until its purpose is accomplished. This allows for temporary recessions (which some do not allow) in which one wave having reached a higher crest than ever before, the succeeding one may fall back until a new wave reaches still higher ground. Here some view the tide as never-ending while others believe that it will some day reach a peak at which time there will be some kind of a consummation. In some ways the post-millennial view fits into this picture. They see progress continuing until the golden age is ushered in, and they admit a final consummation which, to that extent, identifies it with the biblical view that also embraces a consummation. Many others who hold the ocean tide theory do not expect a consummation.

It may be said of all these views that they have one common factor which differentiates them from the view which will be advanced here. Except for the post-millennial view which does have a partial grounding in the Bible, these other views are purely man-made and non-revelational. They rise out of the reasonings and observations of the natural man. All of them have in common the elimination of God as the central factor and the determining agent. This does not mean that God is not to be found in any of these theories of the meaning of history. It does mean they are inadequate because they disregard the revelation contained in the Word of God, and the place and position accorded to God is at variance with that of the revelation which they disregard. Frequently God is injected because a need for a Supreme Being is felt but the position relegated to His is secondary and peripheral. Never is God to be found as the One who guides history or who is bringing it to its full fruition.

Differentiated from every secular view of history, because its roots lie in revelation rather than in human history, is the Christian view of history. It is unique because it is grounded in God and His Word, and because its idea of the future is not decided on the basis of the history of the past with all of its numerous lessons but on what God has declared. There is no intention here of defending the idea that previous history can teach us no lessons, or that we ought not study past history to avoid the mistakes made by those who have preceded us. The point is that the revelation itself records history, draws lessons from history, indicates the errors of the past, and suggests ways of life for the future. In this area it does all that secular historians could desire, but in a Biblical framework. But it does not stop there.

Inherent in the structure of history from the biblical viewpoint are two additional elements. One is the *a priori* assumption about God in relation to human history. The other concerns the future of mankind which is unfolded by revelation rather than by human analysis of past history.

In no case is it possible for the Christian to escape the conclusion that God and history are related. History is not an afterthought moving in a vacuum apart from God. God Himself is the author of history and the God of history. The eternally existent God began history in creation; God Himself entered history in the person of Jesus Christ in the fulness of time; and God Himself will eventually consummate history in the personal return of Jesus Christ in history. The supra-historical consummation will then follow on that divine event. Thus to leave God out of history is to commit the greatest historical error possible. This error becomes understandable only in terms of a theology which shows that the natural man cannot comprehend nor believe nor understand history or his own destiny apart from the divine power of the Holy Spirit. This we say because every historian has available sufficient information about the entrance of God into human history in Jesus Christ. Every historian has before him the evidence concerning the cross on which Jesus hung. The failure of the natural man historian does not lie in the lack of knowledge but in the lack of a spiritual preception by which he can understand what the events of history mean.

At this point the additional element inherent in the structure of history from the biblical viewpoint comes into clear perspective. The natural man cannot understand history from God's point of view nor can he interpret it either. Thus human analysis of the future falls far short because it does not take God into account. But for the Christian who disagrees, and believes that God is in history and is operating to accomplish a divine purpose there is the further assurance that what history has in store for man is open to understanding, not by reason but by revelation. This is true, not because it is necessary, but because God has graciously revealed it to those who will receive what He wishes to give. The philosophy of history for the Christian is a revelatory philosophy based upon the Word of God.

It must be remembered that the facts of history in no way run contradictory to the revelation as to the future. There are differences of opinion only because of the distinction to be made between the natural man and regenerate man. Differing premises cause them to arrive at different conclusions. This conflict cannot be reconciled nor can a compromise be effected except at the expense of the Christian view. Reconciliation always weakens the Church, dims its vision, and damages its testimony. Thus the difference between the Christian view of history and the secular view of history is not one of incidentals but of fundamentals.

Among Christians there are differences of opinion over important issues, but there is a common core of agreement on at least one item. All Christians agree that there is a single cord running through the Christian concept of history, namely God. All of history moves under God's divine direction (with a great deal about which we are ignorant) toward the accomplishment of that purpose which God has. There is a recognition among all Christians of a consummation. While great differences of vital import exist about the consummation, and while these differences make for tremendously varying attitudes toward foreign missions, it can still be said that there is common agreement concerning a consummation. This consummation is recognized to be outside history by all, with different views as to a possible consummation in the historical process too.

God is in history. God is controlling history. God is purposively bringing to pass His will. There is an end outside history, a consummation apart from this space-time universe of which Paul speaks: "Then cometh the end when he shall deliver up the Kingdom to God, even the Father; when he shall have abolished all rule and all authority and power. For he must reign, till he hath put his enemies under his feet . . . And when all things have been subjected unto him, then shall the Son also be subjected to him that did subject all things unto him, that God may be all in all" (I Cor. 15:24-28).

The Christian view involves a contingent dualism in the space-time universe. He realizes that just as there is good in this world of men so is there evil also. An unending struggle is being waged between the forces of good and evil; between right and wrong; between light and darkness; between God and the devil, both of whom are neither forces nor abstractions but living personalities. In the time-space universe the struggle between God and the devil is waged over God's creation which was originally perfect both as to man, the highest order in that creation, and to the remainder of the creation. The struggle is not alone over man, a purposive agent, but is also being fought out in the entire universe, the devil seeking to dominate and control the world. Man, in this world struggle, is not simply the object over which the devil contends for supremacy against God but a moral agent who is a part of the struggle and whose actions have meaning in the struggle.

Innumerable problems confront the Christian in the view of two opposing forces. Perhaps the most difficult problem is why God permits the devil to pursue his evil way; why God does not put an end to his depredations immediately. We might explain that with God there is no yesterday or today or tomorrow as mortals think of it. To God everything is an eternal present. The answer to the question why God lets Satan go on we do not know, but the reality that God, for reasons best known to Himself, has permitted Satan time as we know it to employ his tactics against his creator is the reality. We can get along without knowing why it is that God permits him to continue, but it is most important that we be acquainted with the knowledge that he is operating and that this will continue to be the case until history as we know it is no more.

Concerning the origin of sin and the problem this creates, there is much we do not know. While it is true that sin for the human race began with Adam and grew apace for thousands of years, we do not find that sin in the universe had its origin in Adam. It is plain that sin existed prior to the fall, coming into God's creation through the efforts of the devil who is spoken of as a fallen angel of light. It was the introduction of sin into the world of man that has precipitated the struggle about which we have knowledge, the culmination of which shall be the divine triumph over the forces of darkness and the end of human history as such. All of this, however, does not answer the question of the origin of sin nor why it is that God permitted the devil to operate against His Paradisaic creation. While this fertile field of inquiry may be stimulating to the philosophic mind, it avails little in the light of the concrete reality, and it behooves us to beware lest we enter into an area where the finite mind loses itself in questions which it has no right to ask.

In the struggle between good and evil it may be said that the forces of good have made progress over the centuries. The use of the term "progress" is not without difficulties, but its employment in connection with evil will clarify the situation easily. The progress of good over the years may be illustrated and demonstrated without difficulty. No one can deny that the Christian conscience has changed the world. Slavery at one time was an accepted institution. Due to the Christian faith it was eliminated. Humanitarianism as expressed in hospitals, orphanages, and the like can be shown to derive its greatest impetus from the Christian faith. Everywhere the influence of good on the world can be seen in which society has been bettered. This condition was so prevalent by the opening of the twentieth century that mankind took courage and accepted the belief that progress was inevitable. Some men also came to believe that the continuation of this progress would produce a golden age when all men would be changed by the process.

One factor was overlooked which made the view of inevitable progress and the coming of a millennium by human means an impossibility. Side by side with the growth of the influence of Christianity there has been a concurrent growth of evil. As the impact of Christianity has been felt and as its influence has been extended, the forces of darkness have not left the field of battle, but have rather intensified their efforts. Germany is a case in point. The Second World War showed the power of the forces of darkness. This nation had been the focal point in the Reformation movement of the sixteenth century. But by the twentieth century it had become the focal point for evil, the like of which so-called civilized man had not seen for a thousand years. History books will never be able to maintain their decency and describe the actual brutalities that were committed by the people of this land. And surely the forces of evil seemed to be in the majority during this regime of Adolph Hitler. If this is not enough one need only look at the land of Russia. We see here the epitome of evil concentrated in a nation whose strength and might is equalled and exceeded only by that of America. And if the fury of that might is ever loosed upon a frightened world no man will doubt then that the forces of evil have grown concurrently with the forces of good.

In our own land a real danger exists in comparing right and wrong in the unending battle. On the one hand much progress is found in America. On the other hand, retrogression and a positive increase of evil can also be seen for those who wish to take a look. Sin has become refined in frequent instances and public conscience dulled by this refinement. Witness a large American city which re-elected as its mayor a man who twice was found guilty of a felony. Witness the marked increase in crime and the flooding of the jails. Observe the increase in gambling, prostitution, and the consumption of alcoholic beverages. Witness a divorce rate that is soon to equal the marriage rate. And all of this is found, not in Nazi Germany or communist Russia—not in a nation without Christianity, but in a nation which has had the benefits of the Christian faith for more than three hundred years and which has had an opportunity to witness the effect and impact of this faith upon multitudes of people. Good has increased to be sure, but there has been a concurrent growth of evil which has equalled if not exceeded the growth of good.

Biblically there is every reason to support the contention that evil is increasing as good is increasing also. If evil is likened to a tree and good to another tree, we can see how each one started as a seed and grew, developing into mature and full grown trees. There is both change and progress in each case, but the two trees remain intrinsically what they were when only the seeds existed. For the seed contained potentially all that the trees were ever to become. Both trees continue to grow together; both seem to make great progress. To look at one without observing both together results in distortion of the picture. Men do wax worse and worse, and they shall wax worse and worse in the end times. But Christian men are spiritually more mature today in many cases as the Holy Spirit has enlightened consciences. And as evil shall wax worse and worse, so good shall increase also. If one only looks at the Christian tree and notes its growth there is the tendency to become too optimistic. If one looks only at the other tree a defeated pessimism is likely to follow. When, however, both trees are observed in true perspective and in relation to each other, it will produce a realism that is biblical.

The increase of evil and of good could occur interminably without giving significance to an idea of the consummation of history. Recent history, however, has been filled with dire forebodings about the future. Scientists, many of whom have never looked to the Word of God for any help, freely predict that man has in his grasp weapons that can produce the collapse of western culture. Those who foresee the use of these weapons also foresee the doom of civilization approaching. Those who have any hope find it in connection with a changed world of men. The Christian, by contrast, finds that the increase of good and evil will reach a peak at which time history will come to an end. Meanwhile he is not unduly perturbed at the prospect of the complete annihilation which scientists present because he knows that civilization will not end in this manner.

The consummation of history is a prediction revelationally. Reasonably the nature of things demand it too. Just as there was a beginning of time it is reasonable to assume an end of time.

A beginning of history would be a curious phenomenon if there were no end of history. The very nature of the universe demands completion—a culmination when all things are brought into order. For the natural man, even apart from revelation, to deny the idea of an end or a culmination or consummation of history is to deny and disregard history in the lessons it teaches. Important for the Christian is the assurance that what the mind of man demands as a necessity is revealed by God to be a certainty. This gives finality to the idea of the future and confirms the suspicions of man. It must be pointed out that the revelation does not become true because it agrees with the thoughts of man, but because it is valid in itself apart from the thoughts of man. Most of the people of the world, however, probably have no idea about a consummation and give it little thought. Those who do, are not all agreed that there is a consummation as we mean it.

Admitting that there is a biblical view of the consummation, certain aspects of that consummation stand out prominently in the eschatology of the Bible. One outstanding biblical concept to which reference is made again and again is that history shall have and end in history. More and more Bible students are coming to see this great truth. Just as history opened in Eden with God in control so human history will end with God in control. The wrong shall be made right and righteousness and justice shall prevail at the end even as it prevailed at the beginning. History demands this to be so and the Bible is perfectly clear that it shall be so. Many portions of the Word of God are devoted to descriptions of the establishment of a rule and reign of righteousness by Jesus Christ on the earth. The sure word of prophecy speaks of Him as reigning literally upon the throne of His father David to order it and establish it forever. No one would wish to remove the eternal element and the supra-historical aspect of this prophecy, but no one should take away the earthly, literal fulfillment of the same prophecy. Isaiah, Luke, Zechariah, Micah, and the Psalmist, not to mention Jesus Himself, bear out this contention.

Even if there is an end of history in history as we claim, it will not be ushered in by man himself. This is the fallacy maintained by the post-millennialist[1] who believes that the golden age will come by the efforts of man at the end of that age Jesus returning. History has further revealed that man is incapable of ushering in any millennium and it will increasingly demonstrate this truth. Man will try spasmodically (but then not all men) until his inherent depravity and the world situations produce opposite reactions. In theory it is perfectly possible for men to bring in a millennium if they will voluntarily subject themselves to Jesus Christ. This we know all men will never do except for a minority. Even the minority, while in the flesh, still walk, not as perfected creatures, but as those who are heirs to the ills of the human flesh. The Bible does make promises of what God will do for men if they react correctly and accept His invitations, but it also proclaims that men will not all react to His demands as they should, for their sinful hearts are darkened and they will have none of Him.

If man is incapable of bringing in a millennium to end history as it began, and if there is to be such a consummation then it follows that it must be produced outside of man. Again the Bible is clear in its recognition that man is unable, but that the God of history who is in history is the One who is able. Divine intervention in the consummation is just as necessary as divine intervention in redemption. Naturally the one event differs from the other, but they operate together to form a pattern for the purposes of God in history. The reason why the intervention of

---

[1]There are varying post-millennial interpretations of the future and some will object to the idea of a man-made millenium. The modern post-millennial view usually refers to a future thousand years of universal peace and prevailing righteousness (before the return of Christ) which is to be entered into through the preaching of the gospel and the triumph of the gospel. The evangelical post-millennialist would object strenuously to the term "man-made" millennium, since he believes that the millennium will come by the working power of the Holy Spirit, and particularly from the conversion of Israel as a nation. The pre-millenarian is accused of discounting the power of the Holy Spirit. Of course the point made here is to contrast a millennium introduced as a result of the efforts of man in preaching the gospel as against a new crisis introduced by the coming of Christ—that is by a new divine intervention. It is impossible to take away the force of the argument that the post-millennialist golden age comes through the use of existing forces, whether they be social human forces, or in the case of the evangelicals, the preaching of the gospel in the power of the Holy Spirit—that these forces are intended by God to introduce the millennium.

God is necessary in bringing to pass the consummation is wrapped up in the problem of evil. Sin in its essence is leaving God out of the picture; removing Him from the center of reference; making Him irrelevant to the situation. Immediately when this is done, disbalance occurs and man cannot create the world for which he longs. The world for which man instinctively longs is a world which cannot exist without God. But man wants that kind of a world without God whom he has eliminated from the picture. Thus man is ever at odds with himself, wishing for that which is actually centered in the God he will not have. Divine intervention in the production of the kind of world that ought to be becomes necessary since there is no other way by which it can be attained.

The second advent of Jesus Christ will usher in the millennium which man himself is not able to inaugurate. Righteousness and truth will prevail. But men will not have righteousness and truth any more than they would have the Son of righteousness when He came with healing in His wings at Calvary. In that millennium in which God in Jesus Christ personally has a time-space part in the operation of the physical world, the knowledge of God shall surely be known all over the world. At the end of the earthly millennium, human history will terminate and the end of history outside of history will begin.

The end of history outside of history we may call the supra-historical. This comes when the kingdom is delivered up to the Father. When this is done the finite, earthly time-process shall become the infinite, timeless, heavenly, eternal, spiritual kingdom above history and outside of history as we know it. It is the divine fulfillment of history—the "end," not in the sense of coming to a stop, but in the sense of merging into the final and permanent and eternal form from which no further change is necessary or desirable. The "end" here means that the forces of darkness shall have been vanquished forever, to an eternity of separation in the outer darkness where there is wailing and gnashing of teeth, where their worm dieth not and the fire is not quenched. The contingent dualism which now exists shall be no more. Only God and the forces of righteousness shall prevail. The devil and the forces of evil shall continue throughout eternity but they shall be chained in the place God has reserved for them.

This doctrine of everlasting punishment which is here injected for the devil and those who follow him, and which is eternal in duration, is repulsive to many. Yet it remains as a distinctive doctrine of the Bible and is prominently mentioned in conjunction with the many promises of eternal life with God in heaven. It is as much a part of the eschatological picture as the second coming of Christ, the judgment of the saints, the end of history and the like. Any eschatology without this doctrine of eternal punishment is vapid, formless, illogical, and, of course, unbiblical. That this doctrine should be an offense to man is understandable since man can find no satisfaction in the thought that his portion should be like this forever. His first line of defense against this doctrine is the denial of it, usually in a context which implies that a God of love could not be like this. Obviously such thoughts will not alter the situation, nor does this misinterpretation of the character of God excuse a man.

There are many who miss the most important aspect of the doctrine of eternal punishment. It does not rest in the idea that punishment is eternal or that there is punishment as such. The importance of the doctrine rises out of its origin. It is a part of the supernatural revelation to which we are tied in any philosophy of missions that is final and from which we cannot escape. It does not matter that men may refuse to see the justice of such punishment or that they may conceive of it as impossible in their understanding of a God of love. It is terrible reality in the Word and Jesus Himself bears eloquent testimony to the belief in such a grim and fearful place. To destroy the reality of hell, eternal in duration, is to destroy the words of Jesus, and thus to render the revelation vapid and void in other areas.

The doctrine of everlasting punishment is also consistent with the nature of God as He reveals Himself in the Word. Only man can make this doctrine inconsistent, and that from his natural desire, and inordinate desire, to escape from the claims of eternal death or because he will not understand God as God has revealed Himself. But to those who accept without question the revelation of God, this doctrine becomes tenable even in its terrible aspects which bring men to a realization that all humanity without Jesus is facing this fearful future.

It is at this point in our discussion we lose the secular historian. He can make historical guesses as to the future on the basis of the past. Conceivably he can conclude that there will be an end of history in the future. But unless he goes outside of himself and history to the revelation of God, the secular historian can find no ground on which to rest any assumptions about the end of history. There has been no previous consummation; and history itself is silent about it. Most religions do have some concept of an end of history, but this longing or hopeful aspiration connotes little to the secular historian. For the biblical historian the situation is far different. He believes in a God who creates, controls, and consummates. Thus the Biblical historian can project his thinking to the end time with the knowledge that he has the revelation of God that supplies that which history in the ordinary sense cannot supply. With that in mind the Christian historian operates with a distinct advantage over the secular historians.

To the Christian the end of history is interrelated with present history. Present and future history cannot be divorced from each other even though they may be separated by years or centuries of time. The one interacts on the other, and the end is the result of the accumulations of the past. Thus our concept of the end of history must be related to missions because we have made the claim consistently that the end cannot occur apart from the completion of the missionary task of the Church. To divorce missions or overlook missions, then, in thinking of the end is to do great violence to the divine structure of history and to fail miserably in an understanding of the day in which we live as well as of the future into which we must move.

We are forced to bring missions into the picture when we speak of a consummation for we have insisted that before the consummation takes place and history ceases to be, the gospel

must be taken to the ends of the earth. But so far we have been
dealing with the end of history, intimating that the consummation
cannot be produced by man but by the supernatural intervention
of God Himself in the person of Jesus Christ. This sounds, on
the surface, as though man is an inactive agent who simply is acted
upon without any part in the drama himself. There is much truth
in this. The consummation is a divine act springing out of the
return of Jesus Christ. However this does not exclude man as
a responsible agent nor does it preclude his having a part in the
drama.

The actual consummation will be carried out by Jesus Christ,
but the production of that consummation so far as time is concerned is vitally related to the acts of Christians. To exclude man
from this drama is to make him an automaton without part, and
makes God somewhat of an arbitrary being. Obviously if the Bible
were to substantiate this there would be no recourse except to
admit the fact and act in the light of it. But the Bible does not
exclude man by any means, and, in truth, gives him a vital role
to play with reference to the end time. The part of man is not
one in which he does any consummating, but it is one in which
the time of the consummation can be dependent upon what man
does.

There is a relationship between the end of history and the
requirements or acts of history, prophetically, which must occur
before that end can take place. Thus the end is not divorced from
present acts of history but is related to them. The end is the supreme climax or logical and normal finish that follows upon the
completion of certain events that must precede that climax or
consummation. Here is the area where the work of men and of
God are irrevocably linked together. God does not enter history
to end history until the divinely forecast events have occurred
through the action of Christians.

Prior to the return of the Lord Jesus to set up the earthly
millennial kingdom certain events will have transpired. The
apostasy of the professing Church, the tribulation, and others are
included in this. The one that stands out pre-eminently above all

others, however, is the evangelization of the world. Before the
setting up of the earthly kingdom the gospel will have gone out
to all the world. Every tribe and nation will have heard.

The beginning of the end of history for the Christian is thus
tied up organically with the completion of the great commission.
Before Christ returns the commission must be completed. This
is prophetically announced in the Word and is specifically commanded to be the supreme task of the Church of Jesus Christ.
Until this is done there can be no visible return of the Lord.
When this is clearly seen by professing Christians and when
it is observed that the end is contingent upon human action in
the completion of the commission, a new day will dawn for the
missionary enterprise. It is a good motive to go to the foreign
field conscious that without Christ men will perish. It is equally
a good motive to be conscious that the completion of the great
commission will bring history to a climax and to an end, knowing
that the individual is helping to bring that end closer. Again there
is here a divine mystery hidden from man as to how God can
control events and yet fit it in and work it out for man to be
an agent in the events, making man a responsible agent for success and failure. Our only answer can be that God has graciously
perfected His plan with the knowledge of man in view.

Immediately that we insist upon the evangelization of the
world prior to the coming of the Lord, a vigorous dissent will
arise among those who differ widely in their beliefs about the order
of end events and some of the details of that end. This very
evident area of disagreement has been one of the causes for the
failure to finish the task given the Church of Jesus Christ, and the
rabid insistence of some upon the acceptance of their views without
consideration for the views of anyone else has done much to hinder
the spirit of love and retard the work at hand. Time spent in
fruitless argument takes away time that could be better spent in
doing the job that lies before us.

The intention of this work is not to create friction, nor to
insist that those who disagree are absolutely wrong in their interpretations. It will plead for a liberty of viewpoint and for the

operation of the spirit of love, since the purpose of the philosophy of missions is not to increase the area of disagreement but to instil in men the desire to do the will of God in the evangelization of the world. Unfortunately it becomes necessary to enter a field where differences of viewpoint are so great and where tensions exist so strongly that Christians have been torn asunder and have broken their fellowship one with another.

Some Christians will insist that the Church is raptured prior to the tribulation with the Jews completing the evangelization of the world between the time of the rapture and the second coming of the Lord. Others will press for a mid-tribulation rapture,[2] and still others will insist that the Church will go through the entire tribulation until the second coming of the Lord. Some will demand a belief that the rapture is secret and at any moment, whatever events which must precede this rapture having already occurred. Still others insist that it will occur when certain other events have transpired. A great deal of difficulty arises out of the parenthesis concept of the Church age and the meaning of the kingdom of heaven and the kingdom of God. All of this disagreement enters into the interpretations of those who are agreed generally and who hold the pre-millennial view of the Lord's return. Rather than using this as a vantage point for common agreement it has become the place where they diverge into numerous camps.

As far as it is possible the areas of conflict will be avoided lest any sensitive souls shrink back and refuse to accept the burden of the book that the Church must get the gospel out to all the world, regardless of the cost, humanly speaking. But we must insist that the Church in the Bible has significance eschatologically and has a determinative role to play in the coming of the Lord.

All pre-millenarians regardless where they put the rapture of Church do agree and must agree that the Great Commission will

---

[2]To call this view the mid-tribulation rapture is not quite accurate. Men like Dr. J. O. Buswell and Dr. Norman B. Harrison who hold this view do not believe that the Church will go through the tribulation. Rather they hold that the Church is raptured in the middle of Daniel's seventieth week, or in the middle of the last seven year period. The real tribulation begins after the middle of the seventieth week when antichrist is revealed in his true character and breaks the covenant with Israel. There are, of course, modifications of the various views, but in general these represent what most people believe who are pre-millennialists.

be finished before the Church is raptured. Some profess to believe that the Great Commission will be completed by the Jewish remnant after the rapture of the Church. The real teaching here, however, when speaking of the 144,000 Jews who shall preach to all the world is that this remnant shall preach the gospel of the kingdom. And these same people distinctly separate the gospel of the kingdom from the gospel that is today being preached. Only the ultra-dispensationalist can deny the fact that Acts 1:8 is for the Church. In other words Scofield, Gaebelein, Pettingill, and Ironside and all the dispensationalists, except the ultra-dispensationalists, must agree that the gospel will go to the uttermost part of the earth before the Church is raptured.

Dispensationalists who see the problem clearly know that if the preaching of the gospel to every creature still remains to be accomplished before the rapture of the Church, the practical difficulty arises how this can be made to gibe with the secret-any-moment rapture which most of them also hold. Several answers are advanced here. One is that the gospel did go in the first century to the uttermost part of the earth, based on the verse of Paul in Colossians which says that the gospel has been preached to the whole creation. Sound exegesis, however, does not agree that this is what Paul meant. Others say that perhaps every tribe that is now unreached has been reached in a past generation. Still others hold that possibly the gospel has gone to every tribe or nation or nearly so in the full meaning of the prophecy. Therefore, any day may be the day that finishes this prophecy. Regardless of the view acceptable to each individual this much is true: whatever happens after the rapture of the Church (assuming a pre-tribulation or mid-tribulation rapture), cannot be counted as carrying out the prophecy of Acts 1:8.

In this philosophy of the Christian mission we must insist upon the claim that the return of Jesus Christ for His Church is linked vitally to the great commission (not yet completed), and that His coming is distinctly related to the completion of that commission. This is not to argue whether His coming is an any-moment coming. We cannot tell when the last tribe shall be reached, although there are signs indicating the nearness of His advent. Humanly speaking there is no way we can tell that the world has been evangelized except as we note it by His return.

In this picture the Church is in the plan of the ages and has a function consistent with its nature. The function of the Church, we insist, is the evangelization of the world, and this evangelization is to be completed before the return of the Lord. When it has been completed there shall be numbered among the elect some from every tribe and kindred and tongue.

At this point concessions can be made to the variety of views concerning the rapture and the revelation. Our insistence upon the completion of the great commission by the Church would mean, for the pre-tribulation rapturist, that this has been done before Christ takes away His Church. It would mean the same thing is true for those who insist that the Church goes through the tribulation. In either case it is the Church which completes the work for which it was founded. So long as we keep our eyes fixed upon this truth, the question of the rapture will be unfolded for us when it occurs and the truth will then be known to all those who love Christ.

It is no accident that many men of this age who have been so prominent in pushing the claims for world evangelization, and who have given themselves without stint to this end, have held to the point of view that the Church is entrusted with the task of finishing the evangelization of the world. The late founder of the Sudan Interior Mission, Dr. Bingham, and the present Director, Dr. Guy Playfair, are two examples. The late Robert Hall Glover of the China Inland Mission is another. Dr. R. C. McQuilkin of Columbia Bible College who has inspired hundreds to give their lives for the uttermost parts of the earth is still another. These men have been challenged by the thought and captivated by what they believed to be the promised return of Christ contingent upon the completion of the commission.

All Christians know that the coming of the Lord is in some sense outside the control of man. But all Christians ought to be conscious that the coming of His Kingdom is in some measure dependent upon men and what they do in the face of the commands of the Lord God. It is an unbiblical and irrational faith which holds that God will accomplish what He pleases totally apart from the world of men, and what they do in response to the divine plea. Perhaps the argument can be furthered by noting that the four statements of the great commission in the Gospels are post-resurrection commandments of the Lord Jesus and are given, not to the Jew, but to the Church. The book of Acts is replete with instances of the same kind. The first chapter of that book is both a commission and a prophecy, and the meaning of the words "ye shall be my witnesses," is decisive. These words were spoken to those in the faith and either applied to the individuals themselves without reference to those who followed after or they were spoken to them and to us through them. In no way can they be construed to mean men outside the Church. Thus, "ye shall be my witnesses" must be fulfilled since it is prophetic as well as a commandment.

Let it be said over and over again that the Church has an interest in the future and the future will be determined, in part, by the response of the Church to the commands of God. This eschatological emphasis can do much to purify and strengthen the Church, and increase its zeal in hastening the coming of the Lord. It will also put the Church to work, giving herself without let or hindrance to the purpose for which she exists. We have claimed that it exists in and for the sake of the world and this realization coupled with the knowledge that its actions will result in hastening the return of the Lord Jesus provides a beneficial effect and strong motivation.

At stake in all of this is the evangelization of the world. In deference to those who hold variant views on the eschatological nature of the Church some alternatives can be suggested. Here we only wish to bring home to urgent plea of the revelation of God for taking the gospel to the uttermost parts of the earth. In no way should this effort to present the claim of the Word for evangelization be considered an attempt to divide Christians over the question of future events. Rather it is intended to consolidate them and cause them to unite in a common effort to finish the task.

For those who hold an eschatology which will not permit them to agree with our thesis, there are still strong reasons for putting the missionary program in the forefront of Christian thinking. These must be reiterated lest any difference of opinion here destroy the main effort of this thesis. Were one to dispute our eschatology, there remains first the unchanged truth that men without Christ are lost and ought to be reached with the gospel through the agency of men. This is the will of God that no man perish without having heard. Secondly there remains the biblical proposition that Christians are to be subject to the will of God for them, and the will of God for His children includes the evangelization of the world. With or without an eschatology in which the coming of the Lord as to the rapture and revelation is made vital to the Church, these other considerations do not lose their validity, and ought to provide motivation to bring about the completion of the GREAT COMMISSION.

Varying views tend to separate groups of Christians and fragmentize their efforts when a common front is essential to the production of the best results. This fragmentation is highly unfortunate among those who hold to the Bible as the final authority and complete revelation of God and who are agreed on the fundamentals of the faith. Differing slightly in certain interpretations, all conservative Christians have a stake in one view they have in common. Men without Christ need the gospel of salvation and the missionary passion is the supreme passion closest to the heart of our blessed Saviour. Around this core there is enough for all to unite, granting Christian liberty to those who differ in sincerity in their understanding of the eschatological theme so prominently mentioned in the pages of the New Testament.

We all look for that blessed hope and the glorious appearing of our great God and Saviour Jesus Christ. Who will deny that while He tarries Christians ought to be seriously engaged in the effort to put to rout the forces of darkness in those lands where the people lie in darkness and under the shadow of death. A day shall come when differences will be reconciled and our understanding enlightened to see clearly what is hidden at the moment.

Whatever the view that we hold, it remains for the Church to purify herself in the light of her hope and in the expectation that this hope shall be realized concretely on this earth as well as eternally in the heavens. Varying views can never eliminate the unchanging truth that we are aliens and pilgrims whose citizenship is in heaven from whence we wait for our Saviour. Let us live in the light of the hope, act in accordance with the promised reward for faithfulness, and keep ourselves spotless in a world that is normally in opposition to the claims we present and which denies the Lord we seek to exalt.

In spite of these differences in viewpoint over the order of events eschatologically, and despite the opprobrium others may attach to any who disagree with them, the Church of Jesus Christ dare not lose its eschatological nature. Its eye must ever be fixed on the goal and that "far off divine event toward which the whole creation moves." The Church can never be at home in the world without having surrendered its peculiar nature and subverted its important task. We know that the kingdom of God shall become a reality in and out of history. It is an expectation, the loss of which brings frustration and impotency to the Church. Human beings strive and labor and never bring to pass that millennium for which they seek. Their only hope springs out of the biblical claim and the heart-hope that they shall witness the consummation for which they long but it shall be through the personal advent of Christ Himself. While we wait there is a task to perform, there are peoples to reach, there are souls to be saved, there is a world that waits for complete evangelization. It is in the light of our blessed hope that we labor, and as long as the hope is ours it will help to produce purity of life and intensification of effort to reach the last tribe—ere He comes.

Chapter 8

A FINAL THEOLOGY—THE HOLY SPIRIT

THE DOCTRINE of the Holy Spirit is the lost dynamic of the Church. The hard times which have fallen on the missionary enterprise *en toto* may be traced to this elimination of the Holy Spirit, without which no missionary work can be successful or endure.

In recent years the evidence has mounted, demonstrating the refusal to appreciate the work of the Holy Spirit in missions until the very mention of that name in connection with missions brings surprised looks to the faces of people. At the Jerusalem Conference in 1928 the delegates talked more about methods, aim, and paganism that they did of the Spirit. Professor Hocking of Harvard, together with the rest of the laymen's committee, made their investigation of the mission fields of the world and wrote their report without even mentioning the name of the Holy Spirit. It is hardly conceivable that such a departure from true missionary principles could occur, and it can be explained only by the assumption that paganism was not only on the foreign fields but also in the committee that investigated the enterprise.

Kenneth Scott Latourette of Yale University has written the most enterprising history of missions that has ever been produced. It is a masterpiece of research and writing in general. But one looks in vain to find any appropriate mention of the Holy Spirit and His work in connection with the advance of the Christian faith. And this in spite of the truth that the history of missions is the history of the work of the Holy Spirit of God!

At Madras there was some mention of the Holy Spirit. But one does not find that this conference was gripped by the power of the Spirit nor was it essentially aware, as a group, of the part He plays in missions. One encouraging sign was the general feeling that something was missing in the missionary picture. The Pentecostal fires were out and men were becoming aware of the tremendous lack although there is no proof that they were able to place their fingers on the exact element that was missing. They knew that the enterprise was bogged down, but could not secure unanimity as to the cause for that stagnation.

The explanation of the failure to appreciate the part played by the Holy Spirit is not hard to find. The departure from the revealed faith is the basic cause. Jesus Christ was dethroned as God; the Bible was declared fallible and subjected to the findings of science; the social gospel was substituted for blood atonement; naturalism replaced a belief in supernaturalism. In an atmosphere of unbelief like this it was impossible for the person and work of the Holy Spirit to fare any better than Christ fared. He, too, was neglected or denied, and being grieved, His presence was removed together with the power that accompanies that presence. Without Him the work of missions fell into a spiritual decline.

Speaking of the decline of missions because of the removal of the Spirit's presence is not to say that there were no outward signs of apparent progress on the mission fields of the world. Until 1929 at least there were enthusiastic reports of marvelous advances on the field. Education grew by leaps and bounds; social uplift was transforming the peoples of the world; progress, as that word is used, was being made on every side. The paradox of apparent progress of an outward nature made the absence of the Holy Spirit's power less noticeable than if there had been a marked slump immediately. Few people realized that the devil had power to stimu-

late the work of the Spirit and that sometimes prosperity externally
meant poverty spiritually.

By the opening of the first World War all of the large countries
had been reached by the gospel to some degree. Much of the progress discernible after World War I came out of the advances that
had been made in the nineteenth century, rather than being a new
thrust in missionary advance toward the completion of the great
commission. A great deal of the forward movement in missions
came, not in bringing new converts into the churches, but through
the changes brought about by the influence and effect and impact
of the Christian faith on the social structures of the lands with
which it had contact. It is perfectly true, then, to speak superficially of the influence of Christianity as greater than ever before.
But this is not true when the nature of the influence is studied
and it is discovered that its nineteenth century theological grounding
had been considerably modified. Much of the fruit of Christianity
in the twentieth century, while springing out of implications contained in the faith, no longer was in organic union with the seed
from which it sprang. This disassociation did not hinder seeming
progress of a kind, so that externally one could claim forward
strides. It was based upon a different foundation, however, and
often sprang out of "another gospel."

The depression of 1929 soon indicated the foundation on
which much of the missionary work had been grounded. Missionaries were recalled; stations were closed; "rice" Christians deserted
their well paying foreign benefactors, leaving with a shell of religion that had no inner meaning for the hour of adversity. Retreat
and retrenchment were common sights. Even when it was a
"strategic" retreat it was still a defeat that was assuaged by the
application of rationalization.

The emphasis during the period when material advance was
being made had been on the non-spiritual. Methods were advanced
to a place of importance beyond prayer. Men and their visions,
deeds, and daring took the place of the Holy Spirit. Education
into salvation replaced soul-saving evangelism with the gospel mes-

sage. Church councils, planning committees, international organizations, and the like became the processes through which the millennium was to come. The missionary enterprise, except in a few cases, was thoroughly secularized. Sincere, earnest, and devout Christian missionaries and leaders were among those who got caught in the web either because of ignorance or because they were swept with the tide. So we cannot say that the change was intentional among all of the proponents of missions, but to some it was, and the victory was easy for many of the watchmen had left the walls to labor for the Master on the fields of the world.

It is no wonder that when Professor Hocking and his cohorts came on the scene after 1929 and saw the wreckage that they were seriously concerned about the future of missions. It is less than strange that their consternation grew apace when they examined the enterprise in the light of the foundation on which they felt it rested. Their conclusion to abandon the whole mission was perfectly consistent and reasonable with their basic point of view. Having forgotten the historic Christ of the revelation and having denied the separate personality of the Holy Spirit they realized that the work was better eliminated entirely than for it to remain in the moribund state in which they found it. They saw clearly that no valid reason existed for the propagation of the faith unless one held to the view that men without Christ were lost, and that "there is none other name under heaven given among men whereby we must be saved." They could see that the missionary enterprise was a questionable and hardly worthwhile undertaking from their point of view, and from the ground on which its proponents were resting their case. Again this is not to say that every missionary or every agency was under the condemnation. The faith missions they largely neglected. And among the denominational missionaries they looked with little favor on those who were trying to propagate the faith once for all delivered to the saints. These people were subjected to a cruel and ruthless whipping at the hands of men who were not in a position to evaluate the work they were trying to do, at a time when opposing modernistic concepts were running rampant throughout the fields of the world.[1]

Thus in 1932 the missionary enterprise, by and large, was in a sad state of decay. The proud structure, man-made, of. the 1920's had crumbled to dust. Councils, education, planning committees, etc., had come to nought. Had the work been Spirit-led and Spirit-inspired it is safe to say that it would never have suffered the reverses which it now experienced. Advance would have been the order of the day even in the face of grave economic disaster. In fact, it is in this very period that the agencies standing firm for the true faith made notable advances, or at least did not suffer great losses. They made an increasing impact against the forces of darkness. The Holy Spirit made the difference!

Truly the business of missions is a spiritual business; its end is a spiritual end; consequently its methods must be spiritual methods. Remove this truth and the work dies. Take away the Spirit of the living God from missions and they no longer exist. What we need is a fresh look at the Holy Spirit in relation to missions, a truth which the Church easily forgets or disregards.

When Jesus prepared His disciples for His departure He told them that another One should come to replace Him. This Paraclete could not come unless Jesus went away. But when the Holy Spirit did come He was to be the executive of the Godhead. Jesus ascribed to Him the attributes of deity and connected Him with the Father and the Son. This third member of the Trinity, whose office and function differs both from the Father and the Son, but who is of the same essence with them, is

---

[1] In this connection it is more than interesting to observe the reactions by those who believed in the continuance of denominational missions. The Northern Baptist Convention, for example, published a volume in answer to the Hocking volume to reassure their constituency that foreign missions ought to continue. This publication is an excellent example of "fence straddling." RETHINKING MISSIONS is "interpreted" in a way that does violence to Hocking's meanings. Wherever possible the criticisms of Hocking, et al, are answered by trying to show that actually Baptist missions were doing what Hocking criticized them for not doing. It was a studied attempt to undo the damage without doing Hocking any damage. This was an impossibility. On the other hand the answer of Robert E. Speer is, by comparison, a gem, for he calls into question the whole Hocking thesis and the right of the group to investigate the enterprise to begin with. And Dr. Speer has the better of the argument.

omnipresent, omnipotent, and omniscient. He is neither less nor more than Jesus but stands together with Him, differing only in function, having a work to do that is neither the work of the Father nor of the Son and which cannot be the work of either Father or Son.

The aim of the Holy Spirit in missions as in all else is to bring glory to the name of Almighty God. It is His aim to exalt the Lord Jesus Christ to whom has been given a name that is above every name. It is the aim of the Holy Spirit to see that the divine purpose of God in the carrying of the gospel to the ends of the earth is completed. It is also the aim of the Holy Spirit to prepare for the Bridegroom, a Bride for His coming.

We ought to stop here and orient ourselves correctly to the place of the Holy Spirit in the Church and to the end that is in view for that Church. It is biblical to claim that the Spirit, sent from the Father and the Son, is the all-controlling Director of the Church, being alone in this capacity, superior to all men. This is the age of the Holy Spirit. Unquestionably the failure to know this truth and to make it a reality in the life of the Church has been the real reason for the impotence of the Church in our day. Men have acted according to their own wishes, and have made decisions in their own power. Neither for guidance, nor for power, nor for results which are dependent upon the Spirit, have they been willing to submit to Him. The organization has been exalted in many cases and the machinery of that organization has impeded and obstructed the work of God's Spirit. The failure of the Church to be conscious of its divine Holy Spirit headship has prevented the Church from realizing its fullest destiny both internally and externally.

The supreme ecclesiastical authority of the Church rests with the Spirit. The control or the power of the keys rightly belongs to Him. This implies that men who outwardly appear to exercise the power of the keys and who outwardly exercise the discipline of the Church are but agents of the Holy Spirit to do His will. But the ecclesiasticism of our day has disregarded this and this has quenched the Spirit with the result that sterility has come in all other areas of Church life. Godly men have been exiled from the visible churches because of their testimony for the truth of the gospel. Persecution of a deadly and dangerous sort has come to those who resist the authority of ecclesiastical leadership devoid of the power of the Holy Spirit. This ecclesiasticism which appears to be gripping the churches of America today is not the cause of the difficulty. The real root of the problem goes back into the History of the Church for a few decades. In America the rise of certain phenomena politically, socially, and economically, changed the basis of our church life with reference to lay leadership.

Men of financial means, or political power, were elevated to positions of ecclesiastical importance out of proportion to their numbers. This in itself was not wrong since the power or money of an individual should not keep him from sharing the burdens of administration in the Church. The evil was that these men were chosen solely on this basis with no reference to their spiritual qualifications so that "secular" men became the officials of the visible organizations in too many cases. And the ministry aided and abetted this trend because success in the pastorate was measured in terms of dollars, a common American custom. Whether the ministry was primarily responsible for the entrance of secularized laymen to positions of influence in the Church or whether the laymen were responsible for a decline of spirituality among the clergymen is a moot question. Probably the net result was due in part to an interaction from both sides and from direct pressure on the part of both sides. The blame can be shifted conveniently to make a case against one or the other but the outcome cannot be denied—the secularization of the Church with the attendant loss of spiritual power.

When unspiritual men gain places of importance in the Church and when their counsels pervade the atmosphere and their decisions determine action, there are in operation tendencies which, when they reach full flower, ruin the testimony of the Church and render its service ineffective. Consent to an administration of the Church that is unspiritual is offensive to the Spirit of God who is sensitive to this violation of spiritual law. The Spirit is easily quenched or grieved and driven away. Since only spiritual men can perceive spiritual truth, the control of the Church is wrested from the Spirit who cannot cooperate with any except those who know Him and who are obedient to Him. When this occurs, whatever witness is maintained is only formal and without power. The extent of the departure from the truth of the Spirit's leadership can be better seen today when the pollution embraces both the ministers of the gospel as well as the laymen. In those areas where this encroachment has been resisted and among those groups where the supremacy of the Holy Spirit has been sustained, we have the examples of what the Spirit can do.

A strange paradox is apparent in the areas where a true wit· ness is maintained and where the Holy Spirit has control. These areas are subjected to intense persecution. When the children of God are stirred anew to fresh vigor, the devil is not content to rest without trying to do despite to the Spirit of grace. Any effort of the Church which continues without persecution can be reckoned as almost devoid of spiritual power, and the greater the impact of spiritual power the more the forces of darkness will bear down to hinder the work of the Holy Spirit. The paradox is that one would normally expect that less persecution and would attend the work of the true witness whereas the opposite is true. Work that is performed under auspices which are not spiritual appears to have less trouble and to secure greater outward results, while work which is done under the control of the Spirit suffers untold hindrances and is subjected to real difficulties. And the Christian who is so engaged in labor can anticipate that his lot for life will be one of persecution, hardship, suffering, and possibly death.

As the Holy Spirit has the power of the keys and discipline so He also is the restraining agent and insures the safety and spiritual life of the Church. However, He is not a dictator nor does He enforce His will on men. So long as men will submit to Him, the safety and the purity of the Church and the restraint of the devil will take place. He also presides over the councils of men so that His will may be manifested to them as they make decisions and establish policies. The New Testament lays down the rule for us in the words of the Apostles, "It seemed good to us and the Holy Spirit." In the councils today men have forgotten that latter portion of the Apostolic rule, "AND the Holy Spirit."

The Holy Spirit also directs workers to fields of service. He keeps some out and puts others in. Paul essayed to go one place by himself but was prevented by the Spirit and sent elsewhere. Adoniram Judson would have gone to India but the Spirit sent him to Burma. Today the councils of men employ almost every conceivable means to determine where a man shall go except resorting to the Holy Spirit for help. Tests of health, age, linguistic attainment, education, and so on, have been exalted to such a degree that little room is left for the Spirit of God. The Apostle Paul would have been rejected by the average modern mission board for many reasons. He was one-sided, his health was poor, his spirit was divisive, and he had peculiarities.

Now the question must be faced what the relation of this discussion so far has to do with missions. Perhaps it may appear that what has been said is irrelevant to the purpose of this work. However, there is a relationship that is so vital that to disregard what has been said would be fatal to a proper understanding of the work of the Spirit in missions. The assertion has been made again and again that the supreme business of the Church is the evangelization of the world. We are not talking of making the world Christian, but of taking Christ to the world. And the importance of what we have said in relation to the missionary enterprise is this: a Spirit dethroned Church will never have the vision of evangelizing the world because a Spirit dethroned Church with a missionary vision is a contradiction in terms. The only way in which the vision of world evangelization can persist is when the Spirit is enthroned. Conversely, when the Spirit is dethroned, the vision of missions will have disappeared. Thus the Church without the Spirit is a Church without missions.

Great care must be exercised so as to prevent any misinterpretation of what has been said with regard to the quenching of the Spirit in the life of the Church and with regard to unspiritual men in control of the Church. We must clearly distinguish here that we are not referring to unregenerate men when speaking of unspiritual men, but are referring to men who are carnal Christians and who still live in the flesh. They are actually members of the body of Christ, being in the invisible as well as in the visible Church. In those places where men are unregenerate there is no question at all about the situation. They can never dethrone the Spirit whom they have never had in their hearts. They can have no vision of missions until they first have been born from above. It is clear that in many places there is confusion because of a mixture representing men who are regenerate and those who are unregenerate. The Laymen's Committee which reported in 1932 had on it men who were truly Christians but who were unspiritual Christians, not being able to perceive the correct situation because of their spiritual condition. But there were also unregenerate men on that committee who openly denied the deity of Christ and His atoning work, and who could not, in any evangelical understanding of the Word of God, be classified as Christians. The Holy Spirit of God withdrew His presence from those who were unspiritual since they had no business to be associated with unregenerate men in an enterprise that was for regenerate spiritual Christians only. And their failure to stand up against the unregenerate in defense of the faith and the function of the Church was a gross betrayal of the cause they were supposed to be serving.

The return of the Holy Spirit to the headship of the Church will be productive of a great missionary revival. The work of the Spirit is to follow out what Christ began and what Christ commanded to be done. Invariably it must follow that when the Spirit is having leadership in the Church the missionary outreach will be primary and men will be reached with the gospel.

So far the work of the Holy Spirit in the Church has been our interest, the Church being the corporate, visible body including those who are not actually regenerate as against the invisible body which comprises only the true believers. As the work of the Church has no meaning until individuals identify themselves as members of the Church, so the abstraction of the work of the Spirit in the Church has no meaning until individuals appropriate that work into their individual lives.

On every hand we observe Christians who are weak and in-
effectual. Included in this group are those who are thoroughly
orthodox yet dead, who are doctrinally correct yet cold. What we
need is a thorough-going orthodoxy that has spiritual vitality
and dynamic. It must be an orthodoxy set on fire by the Spirit of
God, for it is not "by might nor by power, but by my Spirit,
saith the Lord." Here we wish to make the Spirit of God relevant
to the life of each Christian in such a way that it will advance the
cause of missions.

A fresh look at the Pentecost experience will open up principles basic to our appreciation of the work of the Holy Spirit.
Jesus commanded the disciples to tarry in Jerusalem for the Spirit,
to wait for His enduement with power. Before the advent of the
Spirit the followers of Jesus were defeated and silent. They
were helpless in the face of the foe and lacked any boldness to
declare unto men the counsels of God in the resurrection of Jesus
Christ. Before they had boldness or speech they had to be filled,
and when they were filled it was followed by their speaking. They
spoke because they had been filled, and they were filled that they
might speak in the power and unction of the Holy Spirit.

The enduement of men with Holy Spirit power cannot be a
reality in the lives of those who deny the headship of the Spirit
in the Church today. Excluded from this same benefit of this
filling power are those who insist upon doing their own will. The
first necessity is that men shall submit themselves to the Holy
Spirit in surrender, yielding the control of their lives to Jesus
Christ through the Spirit. All other problems resolve themselves
around the answer to the question whether a Christian is self-
controlled or Spirit-controlled. The thing of which we speak here
was exemplified in the life of David Brainerd who said: "Here
am I, Lord, send me; send me to the ends of the earth; send me
to the rough and savage pagans of the wilderness; send me from
all that is called comfort in the earth; send me even to death
itself; if it be but in Thy service, and to promote Thy kingdom."
Now there has been previous mention of the individual and surrender to the will of God, and here the point to be emphasized

is that when men are yielded to the Spirit of God certain events are very likely to transpire. Since it is the God-willed work of the Spirit to reveal Christ and to see that the evangelization of the world is accomplished, when a man is yielded to the Spirit it is more than likely that that man will find himself with some job to do in connection with that work of the Spirit. More so than that it is quite definite that a man will find himself immersed in the plans of the Spirit because the will of the Spirit has become his will.

It is at this point that most difficulty ensues. Men are willing to go so far with the Spirit of God because to go farther will cost more than they desire to pay. So the work of the Spirit is hindered by men who will not pay the price, and the function of the Church to evangelize the world is hindered by men who hold back from the Spirit of God what they ought to surrender. The Spirit desires to infill men with His presence and to endue them with power. He wishes to witness to Christ and His saving work. He desires that the gospel be taken to the ends of the earth, but He is prevented by the stubbornness of men who will not heed His voice as He speaks for the fulfillment of the divine call for the universe. The task cannot be accompanied without the Holy Spirit nor does the Holy Spirit accomplish the task without the cooperation of men. In no way does this limit the power or the effectiveness of the Spirit but simply presents realistically what the Word of God declares to be true for reasons we know not. Why God should permit His work to be limited by making man a cooperative agent in that work is a divine mystery. But it is also a divine miracle because it indicates the position God has freely granted to man in the work that is so close to the heart of God.

It is the work of the Spirit to call men as well as to endue them with power. This call is specific in the sense that it comes to individuals; it is definite in the sense that it directs men to a particular place of service; it is powerful in the sense that it provides the individual with the equipment to accomplish the task to which he has been assigned. In this work the Spirit does not perform His task haphazardly. There is no chance. Philip met the Ethiopian by plan and not by chance; Paul and Barnabas were set apart for missionary work not by men and chance but by the Spirit of God; the apparently untrained, rough fisherman, Peter, was able to speak at Pentecost in power and conviction, not because of his special work in homiletics or public speaking, but because the Spirit gave him the equipment through which three thousand souls were added to the body of Christ. In this age of grace until the body of Christ is completed and the witness has gone out to all the world, it is the work of the Holy Spirit to call, commission, and equip men for the missionary task which is the main function of the Church that the Spirit heads up.

At this point it is not amiss to point out that prayer has much to do with the calling of men and women by the Holy Spirit. Jesus carefully stated this when He beheld the multitudes of people who were as sheep without a shepherd. His heart was moved with compassion and to His disciples were spoken the words, "Pray ye therefore the Lord of the harvest, that he will send forth labourers into his harvest." It does not matter whether one holds the Lord of the harvest to be the Holy Spirit, or God the Father, or Jesus Christ. In any event we are commissioned to be sufficiently interested to pray to the Lord of the harvest for the sending forth of men to shepherd the sheep. It is not going too far, however, to conclude that the Lord of the harvest here means the Holy Spirit who today thrusts forth labourers into all the world. The Spirit of God is waiting to speak to the hearts of men in response to spirit-filled prayer begging for the Lord of the harvest so to speak and to call. In actual life it can be demonstrated again and again that where effectual prayer has been made for the sending forth of labourers the Spirit has worked in mighty power and countless thousands of men and women have heard His voice speak to their hearts and have answered by going to the ends of the earth. Today men simply do not pray to the Lord of the harvest and consequently He is hindered in the work of calling forth servants to suffer for Christ's sake to the ends of the earth.

Men do not pray to the Lord of the harvest oftentimes because they can do so only when they have presented themselves as possible candidates for the answer to their own prayers. And again we are faced with the problem why God should make prayer the means by which the Spirit of God calls out men. The answer is immaterial; the fact that God so ordains it is all that matters, and when the Spirit has not been enjoined to call forth labourers the fault lies not with the Spirit of God nor in His unwillingness to work, but in the failure of men to prevail before Him in prayer. It is, thus, the work of the Holy Spirit to call forth men in response to the exercise of His power which is released in a proportion commensurate with the prayers of God's people that labourers be sent forth.

If it be true that men are called and sent in answer to prayer, it is also true that the material support of the work is provided in answer to prayer as the Holy Spirit is able to move the hearts of men to give. The effectiveness of missionary enterprise languishes and world evangelization is halted when there is a prayerless Church or a Church without faith to believe that God through the Spirit will answer petitions for material needs. There are legitimate differences of interpretation as to the extent of human effort in connection with the supply of material needs. Some missionary agencies feel that God alone should be acquainted with the need, and in answer to prayer will supply the need. Others feel that the need should be made known among God's people without asking them for money save as they are acquainted with the need and are led of the Spirit of God to do something in answer to that need. Still others believe that the need should be made known and Christians urged to give of their substance in answer to that appeal for support. It appears that each of these, in its own sphere, is a legitimate method, assuming that each is based upon the right motivation. Any of the three could be a source for the display of spiritual pride and any can be subject to misuse. The important aspect is that the Holy Spirit moves men in each case to do something about the need and furthers the evangelization of the world through the use of all of them. In all God can be glorified and the spiritual life of the Church enhanced.

That prayer which looses the power of the Holy Spirit and brings about action in the realm of missions need not be a universal prayer by the whole Church. It is not likely to be universal. God, fortunately, does not limit Himself by waiting for the fervant prayers of all His people. Just a handful of men who will pay the price is enough. When we recall what a handful of men did at Antioch as they prayed it is a lesson to us, teaching that a few persevering souls today can turn the tide for missions—but at a price.

When the prayers of God's children become what they ought to be we shall see that event transpire for which the Church was created, namely the evangelization of the world. This may occur in ways foreign to our present expectations. In the course of human history man is prone to judge the future in the light of what he has known up to the present moment. When World War II began is was called a "phony" war. Then the Germans began their "blitzkrieg," employing something that was new to modern warfare. The old and the established methods had to be thrown out by the nations fighting against Germany, and these nations were forced to meet their foe by the use of similar tactics and by the employment of similar weapons. It is safe to say that the whole theory of warfare was altered because weapons like the tank, the airplane, and moving vehicles employed in a novel fashion, not previously exploited, changed the modern scene. And if this was true, the production of the atomic bomb accomplished a like result in a more dramatic and awe-inspiring fashion which has left every nation in fear as to the ultimate consequences when this new weapon is employed in the threatening future.

Here every Christian should revise his own thinking and refuse to place upon the Holy Spirit of God limitations as to the manner in which He shall accomplish the task which has been given Him to do. Methods, percepts, and attitudes in the evangelization of the world have become stereotyped. There is an accepted procedure for missions whether this be for the modernist or the conservative. We have our own ideas how the enterprise should be conducted and by this narrow approach we may have done much to hinder the free working of the Spirit of God. This is not written with the view to being critical of those agencies and methods which have the approval of God's own Word. But it is given with the assurance that even the most orthodox find it hard to change their own thinking, and they offer resistance to the new and untried. And whatever criticism may be leveled at missionary agencies today, the same criticism can be leveled at the early Church in most cases. In the early Church the Christians settled down to an existence quite the opposite of the dynamic, world-witnessing organism the Church was meant to be. And the Spirit of God had to stir up fierce persecution to separate those Christians from their home attachments before they ventured out so that the gospel could be given to Judea and Samaria. The ideas of the early Christians were shattered by the Spirit, but His purposes were accomplished.

Is it not true that the Church, for the most part, is committing the same error in our generation? Is it not the policy of most missionary agencies to settle down and to dig in? This was the very policy that the Holy Spirit repudiated in the early Church, calling those brethren to an all-out evangelism until the task should be accomplished.

The continuance of this condition where the Church settles down and fails to comply with the "gospel for the world" injunction can only mean that unless there is a radical change and reversal of this policy that the Holy Spirit will have to break through by means and in ways that will surprise many godly Christians whose vision is limited by their proneness to insist upon the completion of the task according to their own ideas. It is indeed a hopeful sign that God's Spirit does not need a visible organization nor the ecclesiastical leadership (although rightfully all of these can be effective channels through which God can work if they will look to His Spirit) to bring to fruition the great commission. It may well be that the Holy Spirit will call out directly chosen vessels without the benefit of organizational backing or Church, and endue these saints with that power which will enable them to sweep over the unreached world before Jesus comes.

When the hour comes and the Spirit moves according to His own ideas for the consummation of the divine plan for the Church we can be sure that the agents of God will be men who are filled with the power of the Spirit and they will have great boldness in their witnessing. This holy boldness is a divine prerequisite of God's witnesses. It has been present in the hearts and lives of God's chosen vessels through the ages. And it is more than likely that the men who finish the task will not be thought of as great missionaries by their contemporaries. Few men would mind being missionaries if they could be great missionaries. But the Apostle Paul states that God takes and uses to exalt Himself the foolish, the weak, the base, the despised, and the things which are not. While this is biblical, in our day there has been an unholy inversion of this divine standard when agencies seek out the "qualified" and the "educated" and the "psychologically integrated" whatever these terms may mean, and they neglect the divine standards which so frequently by-pass our human ones. When the hour strikes, grant that none of us may be found against those brethren or agencies through whom the Spirit will finish the work for this age, and may He also grant us vision to recognize the signs of the times!

Thus far we have been talking about the work of the Holy Spirit in missions in relation to the Church and to individuals. As yet we have not mentioned the work of the Holy Spirit on the fields of the world. Not to do so would be imprudent since the success of evangelism depends upon that work of the Spirit in all the world. From a negative point of view nothing can be accomplished on any foreign field without the help of the Holy Spirit. Not one single person can become a member of the true body of Christ unless there is present the operation of the Spirit. And the full working of the Spirit on the fields of the world takes place when certain conditions have been met.

The paucity of results on the foreign field springs from the work of men who substitute some other gospel for the one of which the Scriptures speak. This in no manner implies that the Holy Spirit is completely unable to break through, depending on circumstances, but that there can be no pentecostal power. The Holy Spirit is unable to do much through the work of the unregenerate. It is possible for some to find Christ in spite of the unregenerate (e.g. by giving them the scriptures which the Spirit can use to bring salvation) rather than because of them, but again the Spirit is limited and greatly hindered in His working. Nor can the Spirit work in pentecostal power in the lives of prayerless Christians. Here, too, there is no claim that the Holy Spirit can do NOTHING, but rather the desire is to express the thought that prayerlessness produces limitations, the absence of which would reveal His mighty power, rather than the puny, helpless manifestation that comes for those who will not pay the price and secure the Spirit's best.

On the field the Spirit of God convicts of sin and prepares the hearts of the heathen for the gospel. This preparation oftentimes precedes the coming of any missionary and has so tenderized those consciences that when the missionaries arrive results are immediate and numerous. Adoniram Judson found that the Spirit had prepared the hearts of many people in the land of Burma, and in his lifetime thousands of men were actually converted by the gospel which the natives readily received. On the other hand this preparation of the hearts of the heathen may not have occurred prior to the sending of missionaries but may come about after the Word has been preached and the Spirit uses that Word to bring conviction of sin.

Prayer is intimately connected with conviction of sin. While there can be and has been prevenient grace operating in heathen hearts without prayer of which we have any knowledge, it is generally true that conviction of sin normally springs out of prayer which releases power to bring conviction through the use of the Word. The life of Praying Hyde is a fascinating and inspiring example of what prayer can do to release the power of the Spirit in bringing conviction of sin and also in bringing actual salvation. Hyde's life opens up a picture for us both in the area of conviction of sin and in regeneration of which we shall speak in a moment. Through his intercessory work he was able to claim from God first one soul a day then two souls a day and then three souls a day. In England the same story was true. Wilbur Chapman was holding meetings that were largely unsuccessful. One day he met Hyde in a hotel and he was permitted to engage in holy intercession with this saint of God. From that moment onward his meetings were accompanied by convicting power, and men and women were won to a saving knowledge of the Lord Jesus Christ. The Holy Spirit was doing His legitimate and rightful work because the channel through which He works was unclogged and power could be released.

The convicting power of the Spirit was promised by Jesus in John's Gospel and it has a threefold bias. It was not to be something intangible on which no man could lay a hand. Rather it was to be definite and specific. The Spirit is to convict men of the sin of unbelief in Christ which, when persistent, many believe to be the unpardonable sin. Secondly, He is to convict men of righteousness and then of judgment. And sufficient conviction on any one of these points is enough to bring man to salvation. This work of the Spirit cannot be simulated by man nor is it a product of man's direct actions. Just as the gift of life is a free gift unto justification so also are all of the elements which play a part in the conversion of man. It is the Spirit who convicts; it is the Spirit who makes Christ real; it is the Spirit who is absolutely necessary to the salvation of man. And if there is no presence of the Spirit there cannot be any legitimate or real salvation.

The Holy Spirit also regenerates. Missionaries and men of God everywhere have the human part to play in salvation, but nothing that man can do will result in regeneration. This alone is the work of the Spirit. It is a final work; it is an instantaneous work; it is a supernatural work; it is that birth from above of which Jesus spoke. If this be true it gives no man reason to boast that he has been able to save his fellowmen. No man can have spiritual life without having been born of the Spirit, this being a mystery whose depths we cannot fully plumb, the extent of which belittles our feeble efforts to embrace its circumference. Parts of this divine mystery we can know and comprehend as much as we need to do so, but the remainder is as though we have spent a lifetime chiseling out of a quarry just a few blocks of granite without having begun to exhaust what still remains.

When the work of regeneration has taken place, the Spirit of God still continues His activity. This broadens out into keeping the one-time sinner unto eternal life, sustaining and nourishing that life until the hour of death. This sustaining and quickening power operates both in the lives of individuals and in the life of the Church. No man can keep himself from falling. This is the peculiar work of the Spirit who completes what He has begun, whose sealing is unto the day of redemption.

In retrospect this much is clear. The work of salvation is a process at the heart of which we find the Holy Spirit. He initiates the work of grace in bringing conviction of sin. He pursues that work in conversion and regeneration. He sustains His work until the day of redemption. In no part of the process is it possible to eliminate the Spirit without destroying that which is essential to the situation and without which there can be no salvation. This is why the doctrine of the Holy Spirit is so important in any consideration of the missionary problem. And this is precisely why the missionary problems are so acute in this generation—because the doctrine of the Holy Spirit has been sidetracked in favor of a homocentric missionary enterprise for the most part.

The Holy Spirit has been relegated to a place of lesser importance for several reasons. One is that the wisdom and pride of men have quenched the Spirit of God in much of the work we call missions and until there is a return to the dominance and power of the Spirit this condition will continue. An aggressive and authoritarian ecclesiasticism has narrowed the scope of activity in missions both geographically and in hindering men from following the guidance of the Spirit so that servile subjection to antiquated modes of thought has resulted, and until such time as this arrogant ecclesiasticism has been repented of, and the Spirit of God enabled to lead men according to His will and not according to the will of men in the Church, the terrible lethargy will remain. Furthermore there has been lacking from the foundation of much missions work the belief that this work is truly of God and that it will be done, in the final analysis, by the power of God and in the way that God, rather than man, wants it done. When a return to this apostolic faith occurs the rejuvenation and revitalization and spiritualization of the missionary passion will once more be a living reality.

We must awaken to the truth that missions without the Holy Spirit is like a human body without life. It is the Spirit that giveth life both to the darkened hearts of men and to the missionary enterprise. Whether it be orthodoxy or modernism, there is always a need for the Holy Spirit. In the case of modernism this is unto regeneration, and in the other unto the dynamic impartation of power which will revitalize orthodoxy and bring it to its legitimate heritage in the gospel. Missions and the Holy Spirit are indissolubly linked together in the eternal plan of God. Men and missions must be rightly linked to the Holy Spirit. The work of the Holy Spirit can be finished in any generation for He awaits the moment to release His power when men place themselves under His control in the message, the methods, the outworking, and the completion of the task.

The Christian faith is faced with a new age, the old one having passed away. Only an apostolic faith will be able to meet the challenge of this new age. The Christian faith of the past fifty years has demonstrated itself to be powerless so that it too must have a pentecostal experience and come again to the place where the deeds of the Church shall be attested to by the dramatic results accorded to the apostolic Church. A new baptism of power must come and then shall there be a mighty surge of missionary movement that will bring to fruition the full-orbed commandment of Jesus, "go ye into all the world and preach the gospel."

Chapter 9

A RELEVANT FAITH FOR THE HOUR

SINCE the opening chapter a long distance has been traversed. The biblical faith relevant to missions has been outlined and pertinent questions answered in a way which is believed to be consistent with the revelation of God. Coming to the end of this road it is almost inevitable that we weigh the present world situation and ask ourselves the question what the future has in store for us. Any such forecast has its dangers because factors are always present and operating which human reason may disregard. Whenever this is true the conclusion will differ, albeit slightly, from what was anticipated. But the possibility of erring is less unsatisfactory than not making the effort at all to see what the future has in store for the Christian faith.

The world of tomorrow is going to be determined by what is done today. Peculiarly this is the case in our generation because we stand at a crossroads of history, the turn that we take markedly affecting the course of history for us and for every nation of the world in an age when we live in one world.

That a crisis exists today is not disputed by men. Every man knows that something is wrong. Everyone wishes that the situation would change—to suit the desires of each individual, of course, and to permit that individual the kind of a world in which he would like to live. Unfortunately man is not quite sure what the real enemy is, nor does he know any better how he can cope with the enemy. And where men are convinced that they have diagnosed conditions, most of them are trying, in hit and miss fashion, to solve their problems.

The current impasse in our culture rises out of numerous problems which have been fused together in one stream to form a veritable sword of Damocles hanging over the collective heads of mankind. Of the greatest magnitude are the advances made by science which have placed in the hands of both scrupulous and unscrupulous men implements of tremendous power for good and for evil. Atomic energy, which we are told will soon be exploited by Russia as well as by the United States and her allies, carries with it fearful implications for the survival of western culture if it is released extensively over a sufficiently large area. This threat is greater still when tied up with recent advances made in aviation so that planes can be directed for thousands of miles without employing men in piloting them or in releasing their death-dealing instruments of destruction. When combined with atomic energy, nations can be effectively destroyed without invasion by ship or men, through the use of the airplane and the atomic bomb. This fear which is real constitutes one of the major reasons why men know that there is a crisis today.

The fear of the employment of the weapons of science wrongly would not agitate men were it not for the division of the world into competing ideologies which seek to dominate and control the world to some extent or other. Communism is a vital and threatening force under Russian leadership which is consolidating its hold on the continent of Europe and which is looking for the death of capitalism as practiced by America and her satellites. Under the leadership of the United States and Russia great blocs of nations have come together in cohesive forces to oppose each other. Suspicions have been engendered and the actions of the leaders in the United Nations meetings clearly reveal the basic antagonism that exists. It seems clear that both of these ideologies will not be able to remain side by side without some conflict developing which

will bring either the defeat of one or the collapse of both.
The diplomatic struggle which now rages between Russia and
the United States clearly foretells a resort to armed force of
some kind in the future (how distant we do not know) whenever
one side determines that it can do longer secure what is desired by
diplomacy and turns over the problem to the military forces of the
nation. In this sense there is a third world war already being fought
around the conference tables of the world, and it will surely result
in appeal to atomic and other force unless something happens which
will forestall it. It is far later than most people think, and the
time to seize the initiative and turn the tide is today—not tomorrow.

Ranking with these two colossi is a third force seeking domination in the world. This is Roman Catholicism which seeks to bring
in a papal Pax Romana through the use of non-military power
of a religious sort. This is the influence of an integrated and
channelized religious organization that transcends national boundaries and gives access to other nations because it recognizes no
competing loyalties with the Roman Catholic Church which takes
precedence over all else, public statements of American Cardinals,
etcetera to the contrary notwithstanding. Its theories embrace the
concept that time has no meaning, and its efforts to break down
and undermine for papal purposes is no less obnoxious nor less
dangerous than Communism against which the Roman Church is
also fighting. The incursions which Romanism has made in America
over the years speak for themselves. Its theories and aims are just
as contrary and devastating to our democracy as those of Communism
And both of them are equally dangerous to the true cause of
Christ and for the missionary program of God for the world. An
impartial examination of the situation will show the Roman
Catholic Church to be far stronger in American life than ever[1].

---

[1]No one doubts the threat which Communism presents to the American way of
life, but many question the dangers arising from Catholicism. Some years ago
André Siegfried, a Frenchman, in his penetrating analysis of American life in
the book AMERICA COMES OF AGE, foretold the struggle for the domination
of American life by Catholicism as against Protestantism which has been the
dominating and shaping element in the heritage and destiny of our nation so far.
He saw clearly that the issue was joined, but not settled. The importance of the
outcome relevant to missions staggers the imagination. America happens to be

Both Communism and Catholicism are arch enemies of America and our way of life and of the true faith. Both have insinuated themselves into places of strategic importance where the most damage can be done. In the State Department of the government, in leading editorial and writing posts, in education, and in political pressure groups on Congress we find fitting examples of the exercise of fifth column activities. The activities of Communists and Roman Catholics contribute much to the present impasse, and they affect the choice that is made at the crossroads in our day.

Added to the basic ideological struggle are other factors that make the world of today a virtual powderhouse of destruction. Post-war social conditions, especially among war stricken nations of Europe, are terrible. Moral decay that accompanied the war has reached a new high and everywhere there are signs of degeneracy, profligacy, immorality, and paganism. Secularism, materialism, and just the struggle for physical existence have reduced much of mankind to an impotent and helpless state. Fear and uncertainty grip the hearts of men in every country of the world, even in America where the poverty, and hunger, and destitution of the war has not struck with any force.

Man sees himself on the edge of the abyss with forces and circumstances steadily forcing him over the cliff that will send him crashing to ultimate doom. And in the face of such a crisis; in the midst of such a critical hour; when so much depends on that solution followed by the world—in this high hour of destiny, we must inject the Christian message! And it must be relevant to our age and carry with it a sense of its own destiny which

the source of the major missionary movements of the hour, especially in view of the debilitation of the British, and the prospects of world evangelization were the Romanists to control America (humanly speaking) would be practically nil. One needs only to read the story of Central and South American Romanist persecution of Protestantism to realize that medieval Roman Catholic practices would be employed in the name of God in America and once again gibbets and faggots would be employed to silence opposition and to exalt the whore of Babylon whose mark of purity has been the blood of saints through the ages. In that hour the spirit of toleration which prevails whenever Catholicism happens to be a minority would become intolerance and our children would have to shed their blood for the faith which their fathers did not defend with letters to their Congressmen!

will dominate history as well as transcend it, for we have both a sense of direction in the Christian message and the assurance that it carries with it power that will insure ultimate triumph.

There is a ray of hope, and the Christian has something to offer the world in this dark hour. Ours is not a pessimistic view of history for we do not believe that man will totally destroy himself by the use of the atomic or any other bomb. This instrument may be employed and tremendous damage may be wrought. Millions may be killed and millions more may be forced to suffer in a way unknown to man before in the history of the world. But the world will not be destroyed by man. We know that before any final destruction can occur Christ will step in and order the world and rule it according to the eternal plan of God. True enough the devil would have the world destroyed in a cataclysm rather than to see Christ triumphantly ruling over it, and in this current situation we see the weight of the forces of evil operating against the purpose of God for the world which is its redemption just as God seeks redemption in the world of men.

The Christian remains ever optimistic because he KNOWS that he has in his hands the solution to the problems which irritate and vex our modern world. He knows that in Jesus Christ there is sufficient dynamic and power which will solve any problem and bring victory in any struggle. But he also knows that the world will never accept the solution that is found in Jesus Christ, and yet he is committed to the task of giving this world the opportunity to do what he knows it will never do. Paradoxically this heightens his optimism because it verifies that which is revealed to him in the Word of God and grants him further assurance that its predictions as yet uncompleted will someday come to pass.

At the same time that the Christian knows that the world will never accept what Jesus came to offer, he does know that men and women everywhere as individuals will individually find in Jesus Christ all that they need to pilot them over the rough seas of life whatever life may hold in store for them. While the Christian must endure all of the tribulations which are the common lot of man, and more besides, there is for him in the message of Jesus all that he needs for this life and the life to come. For the message of Jesus is relevant to any hour in which man may live and provides that which will sustain him and keep him in that hour, in addition to a hope for the life to come. To each is imparted a sense of the infinite worth of man beyond the world of animality; to each is granted a sense of security in a world that shall ever be basically insecure; to each is given power to meet the vicissitudes of life and to live above them; and to each is supplied that other worldly consciousness and sense of destiny that lifts man out of self and ennobles his thoughts, enriches his condition, and moves him to high and godly efforts for the benefit of mankind and the growth of his own spiritual life.

In the midst of the personal enrichment which comes to individual lives through the acceptance of Jesus Christ and His message there stands far above all of this the great hope of His personal coming in triumph and great power for the final conquest of evil and the forces of darkness. The natural man can never understand this. He can never realize that this blessed hope means much to the Christian heart for Jesus shall come to set things right. Scornfully have the critics dubbed those who believe this, "apocalyptic literalists," since the critics could never bow before the sure word of prophecy. But scorn and derision have no effect in the light of the hope which only faith can appropriate and only the Holy Spirit reveal to be truth.

The Church of Jesus Christ has the right to proclaim that the acceptance of our message will solve the dilemma of the world, but it needs to be cautious in clarifying this claim with the added statement that the solution will come IF the world will accept Jesus Christ. This places the burden of responsibility where it rightfully belongs and relieves the Church of the blame for failure when men refuse the way of Christ and then vilely accuse the Church that it has failed in its obligation which is to make the world right in the face of the refusal of men to be governed by principles of righteousness. The Church ought also to be conscious of its own nature and be aware of what men actually will do. And from this the Church can preach with assurance that its message has validity for individuals who will accept it just as it has validity for nations and all humanity if they will accept it. Thus to the extent that Christianity is accepted; to that extent it will be the solution to the problems of men, whether individuals, small groups, nations, or groups of nations.

Knowing that the Church of Jesus Christ always lives in a state of tension because of its peculiar nature and purpose we are not surprised that we are faced with problems today connected with the propagation of our faith. Indeed the Church should be totally surprised if the day dawns in which it is not confronted with radical problems and called upon to meet difficult situations and surmount almost insuperable obstacles. The chief difference between one age and the other is not the absence of conflict and tension, but the varying degrees of that tension and conflict depending on external conditions. Our age is characterized by tensions and conflicts such as the Church has not been called upon to face for centuries. In this sense it appears far more acute and dangerous than actually is the case. We readily forget that the Reformation Church and the Apostolic Church lived in ages when the outlook must have been just as dark to them, and when they were inclined to view their day as close to the second advent of the Lord Jesus. We look back and note how easily they were mistaken because we have the advantage of centuries separating us from those periods and we have the benefit of history which records amazing changes which have been wrought since these saints drew their own conclusions about the end of the age. Then our generation falls into the same specious error, assuming that we have reached the end of the age when it is just barely possible that greater changes than we dream of can occur within the next century and so alter the world that at that time people will look back and see how easily we were misled into thinking that the end of the age had come. It is true that we live in desperate times. And it is also true that Christians have legitimate reasons to believe that the end of the age is rapidly drawing to a close. This we must consider as a distinct possibility and draw our final conclusions with this in mind as a realistic hope.

In the opening chapter of this work we asked ourselves certain questions. Among them were the questions, "Is there a final philosophy of missions and in what does it consist? What is its message?" These questions have been weighed and answered. And in conclusion a restatement of what we are to do, how we are to do it, when we are to do it, and what we have to expect will conclude our program for this philosophy of missions.

Lightfoot made the statement that the end of knowledge is conduct and this is particularly true with reference to the missionary enterprise. To know is not enough. Knowledge must be followed by action whereby we indicate our beliefs by translating them into action. And the purpose here is to make known the truth about missions and then move men to act upon that truth.

We conclude, then, that the Church has a job to do. Anything less than the completion of this job is failure. This failure is tied up with the return of the Lord Jesus Christ as we shall see. The answer to the question WHAT ARE WE TO DO is threefold.

In this grave hour the task of the Church remains exactly what it was when Jesus first gave His commandment, "Go ye into all the world and preach the gospel." This is no less and no more than the evangelization of the world. And by this is meant the reaching of every tribe and tongue with the message of eternal life. It does not mean that the Christianization of the world is expected or that society even on the smallest scale will become distinctively Christian. Nor does it mean the use of a social gospel or the predominant preaching of social themes with the view to bettering the world. This has its place in another aspect of the task of the Church in this age of grace. But the primary business is to witness to the whole world the whole truth about Jesus.

The evangelization of the world is tied up with the second advent of the Lord Jesus. We can this day hasten His coming by completing the commission. The return of Jesus to set up His kingdom in the millennial age will not occur prior to the evangelization of the world. And since the evangelization of the world is the given job of the Church we can be sure that He will not come until that commission has been completed. And this does not strike at the imminence of His coming since we know neither the day nor the hour, but rest assured that when He comes we will know that the task has been completed. While He tarries we can know that the task, on the other hand, has not been completed and it behooves every disciple of the Master to put forth his best to complete the work so that He will come. In that sense every wasted minute when Christians are not engaged in the supreme work to which they are called means a delay in the return of the Lord. This thought should energize men and transform them from servants and slaves to ease to do-ers and die-ers for Christ.

As the Church pursues the task of evangelizing the world she must also pursue the task of winning individual men and women to a saving knowledge of the Lord Jesus Christ. The larger task is the evangelization of the world. Within that larger framework there exists a vital and unchanging passion for the souls of individual men and women. We are not only to evangelize but we are to win some of those whom we evangelize. To evangelize without winning individuals is inconceivable and unbiblical. Truly the knowledge that we have adequately evangelized will be found when, from among those evangelized, some are won to Christ. And any evangelization which does not include this is not biblical evangelism. The constraining passion that urges us on in salvation for the individual has roots in the knowledge that without Christ they are doomed to eternal hell. They are without hope in the life to come. This is further accentuated by the love of God and Christ. In the one case God is not willing that any should perish nor does He arbitrarily ordain that this shall happen. And Jesus Christ died for all men that through faith in His work they might receive the gift of everlasting life. This divine love as displayed and exemplified by God the Father and by Jesus Christ the Son ought to inspire men to cover the globe with the message that Christ receiveth sinful men.

Just as we are to evangelize and win individuals so it is the business of the Church to bring the saved saints together into churches for purposes of larger fellowship and in obedience to the divine command. These visible organizations ought to be self-supporting, self-governing, and self-propagating. The saints are to be brought together for deepening in the Christian faith and for instruction according to Jesus' commandment, "teaching them to observe all things whatsoever I have commanded you." And it is right here that the social aspect of the gospel comes to the fore, It is not the chief purpose of the Church to be a political or propagandizing agency for social matters to the detriment of its primary aim, but the impact that the faith makes on society is found in the secondary element which is the fruit that comes forth from conversion. The fruit or the product of conversion is not to be confused with the function of the Church in the winning of men and women to Christ nor is it to precede that function or be equated with it. The instruction of Christians which is a legitimate business of the Church after conversion automatically ought to include teaching in ethics and morality which will be reflected in society in every area where individual Christians operate. But we need to repeat that this flows out of a Christian experience and is the fruit of Christian teaching.

Knowing what the Church is to do must be combined with the knowledge of how it ought to be done. We have seen that education, legitimate though it may be when subjected to specific limitations, is not the answer. We are not to do it by precept and example, valuable as they are in letting men see Christ through us. We are not to do it through medicine although this method opens the door for the use of right means. And we certainly are not to think that the conveyance of western culture and civilization to the "poor benighted heathen" is the solution either.

The "how" of evangelization is a three-pronged fork, each tine playing a role in the accomplishment of the work. Evangelization must be done by the preaching of the Word of God. The use of medicine, etc. which opens doors to make this possible is legitimate so long as none of these becomes an end in itself as often happens. Because men are born again by the Word of God this insistence upon the use of the Word is necessary and sensible. That preaching can take other forms than pulpiteering is self evident. It may be mouth to mouth propagation; it may be via tract distribution; it may be via personal correspondence; it may be any form or method which brings the Word of God to men in a fashion that will enable the Holy Spirit to use it, and through which mediation it will be possible for men to be born again. We are to take the Word of God. That is "how" we are to do the job.

The Word of God must be accompanied by the Spirit of God. This we have already seen. It is the Spirit who quickeneth. It is the Spirit that giveth life. The gospel or the Word of God must be preached and brought to men under the guidance and leadership of the Holy Spirit who leads and directs the evangelization campaign for the whole world. That effort which is performed in the flesh will give fleshly results. And that which is done in the Spirit will be a Spiritual result. This of course, is closely tied up with prayer, which when combined with submission to the Spirit of God forms a dual power that can break down any barrier and surmount any obstacle. To paraphrase what one great missionary leader said years ago: "When we rely upon organization we get what organization can do; when we rely upon education we get what education can do; when we rely upon eloquence we get what eloquence can do . . . But when we rely upon prayer AND THE HOLY SPIRIT *we get what God can do.* (AND THE HOLY SPIRIT is my inclusion.)

The tine of the Word of God and the tine of the Spirit of God is incomplete without man, the third tine in this three-pronged fork. God works through men. They are the channels and as such are indispensable to the operation of the divine plan. This has been repeatedly stated and in our conclusion is said again for emphasis. It is the glory of the divine commandment that man is chosen of God to be entrusted with this precious responsibility. To him has been committed a function so important that the destiny of the souls of men and the return of God's own Son has a contingent relationship to the acceptance of this responsibility by man. Man is not forced to accept nor does God violate man's free agency, but the task is assigned with the plea from God Himself that man cooperate willingly. The supreme wonder of this mystery is how Christians through the ages could neglect this trust which comes to them and spend precious lives in fields and activities not related to the evangelization of the world. As never before the stewardship of God's children, including that of one's life, one's money, one's time, and one's prayers, must be reiterated and proclaimed with power. To believe that Christianity has a solution for this hour of agony and then to fail to carry that solution to the world of men is unthinkable. It represents base treason to the One we serve and renders ineffective all our feeble protestations of discipleship, loyalty, and devotion to Jesus Christ. If the evangelization of the world is to become a reality it will occur only when the world of Christian men take their commission seriously and respond generously and wholeheartedly in sacrificial living and dying until the task is finished. So long as we play at the task and fragmentize our effort in secondary and superfluous matters, that long will the completion wait and meanwhile the world that stumbles on the edge of the abyss may be catapulted into a greater catastrophe than need be if we were to do our parts for Christ.

This emphasis on men and their part in the evangelization of the world depends upon an acceptance of the apostolic "how" of missions that will invert much missionary thinking of our day and transform the present missionary picture to the horror of those who are unable to employ anything outside the "groove" of their own thinking. Instead of an in-evangelism, settled in one place, backed by the concept of a progressive rather than an all out attack on the world, there must be an out-evangelism. The apostolic method of an out-evangelism was not limited to the use of professional missionaries involved but a radical albeit basic truth that all of God's children are called to be missionaries and are constrained by that truth to be messengers and declarers of God's truth to the people beside them. This does not render unnecessary or unneedful professional missionaries but it does mean that the activities and the emphases of these missionaries will change when they catch a glimpse of the vision.

The possibilities of world evangelization in the space of a short time is evident. If every Christian were to speak to one person a day and continue this, seeking out those to whom no word had been spoken it would not be long before the world would be reached. This can conceivably happen within the space of a month or less. When those who become converted are added to the group doing the speaking the number will be far greater and the time required far shorter. It is too true that our ideas of evangelization of the world have been so stereotyped and so stunted by theories that are progressive and evolutionary that the Church has never been moved by the thought that the completion of the great commission could take place in this generation. Except for isolated instances one looks in vain for a common belief in the possibility of quick evangelization or for the effort which will result in that evangelization. The need of the hour is still the evangelization of the world, and this must be tied up to a great faith which believes it possible and the great push that will prove this faith not to have been in vain.

The present impasse in the world has shown the need for immediate action. For two millennia the Church has been playing with the job it was created to do. And for two thousand years the task remains unfinished. In this hour of challenge the world will not wait for Christianity to gird its loins and then do something. The world must have action and have it quickly. And if the Christian cause is not pushed, men, individually and collectively, will choose something else. And what they choose will not be helpful to Christianity. Right now we see men turning in despair to communism, to Roman Catholicism, to Facism again, and to numerous isms which glamorously prophesy utopian hopes that are not true. But like drowning men they clutch at any straw in the vain hope that it will deliver them from the present impasse.

For the Christian there is a twofold reason for ceasing the delay and springing into action. The first is the condition of the world as it is allied to the completion of the great commission. It is possible for the gospel to be taken to the ends of the earth in our generation. It is commanded that we do this. The hour is ripe. The world is waiting. The idea demands that we do something and do it quickly. Christianity has been guilty of doing too little and doing it too late. And if we continue this practice in the present dilemma it is more than just a possibility that the doing of the job later will be more difficult, more costly, and more demanding. A more favorable time we could not ask when we consider that the world stands bewildered and waiting for that kind of leadership which the Church can supply. At our beck and call are every available means for the doing of the job in the shortest time and with the greatest ease physically speaking. Knowing that it must be done some day, we can rest assured that if the cost is counted it will never be cheaper than at this moment.

The Church should do the job now for the second reason that unless it is done men and women will perish without hope and will sink into eternity in a lost condition. The lack of passion among the bulk of the members of the Church is amazing. There seems to be no realization that unless the gospel reaches the lost they are without hope. There seems to be no compassion, as though Christians were unconcerned that those for whom Christ also died have no opportunity to hear and be saved. There seems to be no corporate sense of responsibility for the commandment of Jesus which embraces the world of lost men and women. We need, as never before, the dynamic which arises out of a sense of urgency, that kind of an urgency which causes men to sacrifice every ambition and to crucify every hindering influence that by some means they may attain to the goal of keeping men from hell. The doing of the job depends on this passion and the existence of this passion will insure the doing of the job.

The evangelization of the world is to be done for several reasons. First of all it is the eternal plan of God. From before the foundation of the world this goal was ordained although it was hidden until the time for it to be made plain. On the other hand while the full truth concerning this world-wide spreading of the Word of God awaited the advent of God's Son, the Old Testament expressed again and again the thought of the universality of the revealed religion. In Abraham should all the nations of the earth be blessed; and the heathen peoples even in the Old Testament were accorded a place and were saved by faith. Witness Rahab the harlot whose faith was counted for righteousness and whose name appears in the eleventh chapter of Hebrews. Surely God from the beginning had in mind the world and in this dispensation we shall see that everlasting plan fulfilled.

The plan of God was concretely given to the Church by Jesus Christ. That commission of His apart from all other considerations is enough to break the heart of the Church as it strives to fulfill His wish and will. The importance of this command can be seen from the number of times it is recorded for us in the New Testament. Every Gospel writer includes it, and Luke in the Acts of the Apostles speaks of it a second time. So far as revelation is concerned there is no evidence that any other post-resurrection statement of Jesus was given such a foremost place. And the fact that this was one of two recorded commandments and is so stressed by the Holy Spirit in the writings of the Apostles has overwhelming meaning to the Church. The best expression of love which man has for his redeemer is revealed in obedience to the wishes of the Person who is the object of that love. Devotion and loyalty to that same Person forms a triad that has impulsive and expulsive power in thrusting men forth to witness for Him, about Him.

The nature of the Christian faith demands a similar response in reaction to its effects. Perpetuation, extension, and propagation are expressions or fruits of the new birth. The joy which comes from this experience and the wells of living water which are opened up in it begin to flow forth in life giving streams for the benefit of other people. The desire to "tell someone what great things the Lord hath done" is an automatic response consistent with the birth from above. The absence of it is an anachronism that bears further explanation and a deeper search to determine the validity of the supposed experience.

There is nothing that can be offered by way of excuse for the failure to obey the divine summons. And there is no excuse that can be considered valid or be accepted by our Father. Obedience is the only possibility and obedience the sole basis for a reward. Failure to comply can mean loss of the reward and entails that awful fate that awaits some who make the gates of heaven by the skin of their teeth with the smell of fire upon their garments.

Of this much every one engaged in the work of evangelizing the world can be sure; that constant, persistent, unholy, and powerful opposition will ever attend the work. We can anticipate that the devil will not permit the work to flourish if he can help it. On every hand the forces of darkness will be apparent to those who labor in this cause for the glory of God. The enemy of evangelization is a strong one. This foe is deadly in his hatred for the things of Christ. The malignity of foulness can be measured by the extreme offering that was required for releasing men from his clutches—the awful death of Christ on the cross of Calvary.

The arch deceiver of the world is a wicked and capricious being whose end is sure but whose activity is presently bringing to bear all of his power to prevent that consummation which will result in his judgment and consignment to the lake of fire. This fanatical warfare is waged unceasingly and involved are all of the resources of this awful creature who frequently poses as an angel of light. He appears to men and entices them in ways that may seem to have no bearing on the work of the gospel. He is not named an arch-deceiver for nothing. The ills of the flesh to which even believers are heir are used by him to hinder the on-going work of the gospel. Temptations are put in the pathways of Christians in the form of terrible sins of awful portent, but then he tempts others by ways and means that have no seeming significance. Carelessness, indifference, lukewarmness, omissions rather than commissions, and many others are used of him to crucify the Lord afresh and anew.

We need to be conscious of the work and intentions of the devil; many things clear up when we are. Into a life God may send suffering for purposes of purification. And promptly the devil will come into that life and insinuate that God does not love the sufferer, or that the suffering has come upon him unfairly. He will try to twist and to turn and to use that instrument of good as an instrument against God who brought it into being in the life of the individual for good. Complaining, whining Christians are helpful to the devil. Ungrateful, antagonistic, nominal, unsurrendered Christians are his specialty. By foul means, and by every trick, of which he is ever the past master, the devil works, night and day without ceasing.

Let us never suppose that opposition can be explained by natural reasons. When the gospel is hindered by communism; when Catholicism is used against the true message of the Cross; when those holding the same basic message are broken into innumerable camps and constantly fragmented by remediable things; when evangelicals are split by lack of love and by bickering and contentiousness of spirit; when great nations swing their weights against the onward force of the gospel; when unneedful wars convulse so-called Christian nations—when all of these things characterize Christians and non-Christians we can know that the enemy of Christ, Satan is doing his evil work.

We can expect that when the correct course of action is being pursued, when the right methods are being employed, and when we are doing what we ought to be doing, the devil will see to it that persecution and tribulation follow after us. Only when we are so living and working that we are playing the game of the devil rather than doing the will of God shall there be moments of letup without trouble in the flesh. And this should be a sign to each Christian and a cause for deep searching of heart to discern the error of his ways that correction can follow. The hope of the hour of trouble which comes to those who do the will of God is the unchanging promise from God: "What shall we then say to these things? If God be for us, who can be against us? He that spared not his own Son, but delivered him up for us all, how shall he not with him also freely give us all things? . . . Nay, in all these things we are more than conquerors through him that loved us. For I am persuaded that neither death, nor life, nor angels, nor principalities, nor powers, nor things present, nor things to come, nor height, nor depth, nor any other creature, shall be able to separate us from the love of God, which is in Christ Jesus our Lord."

The hour is filled with perils. The world is not going to catch on fire; it is already on fire. The future in some ways is obscure and dark. Suffering and punishment may be the lot for many in the days to come. But the Christian must answer to all this: "What does this matter to me? For have not I been commissioned by the Lord of Hosts? Do I not know that I live between the times and that I am but a pilgrim journeying to the Celestial City? Although I live in this world, my citizenship is in heaven from whence I wait for my Saviour." Regardless of the day or the hour; whether in seeming good times or bad, the Christian lives in the world for the good of the world and for the sake of the world. The Christian is the salt of the earth and if the salt hath lost its savor wherewith shall it be salted? Whether by life or by death we dare not fail Him, nor will He ever fail us.

Let us then recapture the vision of what Christ expected the Church to be. Let us joyfully, prayerfully, and with perseverance, finish the task of the Church in the world. Let us never forget that we live in the age of the Church militant until the task is done when it shall become the Church at rest. May our eyes continue to behold those half a thousand million souls for whom Christ died lying out in heathen darkness without the Word of light and life; nor may we forget our obligation to twice that number who have heard His name but do not own Him as Saviour and Lord. The gospel still is the power of God unto salvation. But until that gospel is mediated to men by men it has no power and can produce no salvation. In the hands of the Church is all that she needs to accomplish the task and to proclaim the Evangel unto the uttermost parts of the earth.

> The great world's heart is aching, aching fiercely in
>   the night,
> And God alone can heal it, and God alone give light.
> And the men to bear that message, and to speak the
>   living Word,
> Are you and I, my brother, and the millions that
>   have heard.
>
> Can we close our eyes to duty? Can we fold our hands
>   at ease,
> While the gates of night stand open to the pathway
>   of the seas?

Can we shut up our compassions? Can we leave our
   prayers unsaid,
  Till the lands which sin has blasted have been
  quickened from the dead?

We grovel among trifles and our spirits fret and toss,
  While above us burns the vision of the Christ upon
  the cross,
And the blood of God is streaming from His broken
  hands and side,
  And the lips of God are saying, "Tell my brothers
  I have died."

O Voice of God, we hear Thee, above the shocks of
  time,
  Thine echoes roll around us and the message is
  sublime;
No power of man shall thwart us, no stronghold shall
  dismay
  When God commands obedience and love has led the
  way.

                                        (*Unknown*).